CHALLENGING ANZAC

MIA MARTIN HOBBS is an oral historian of war and conflict, with a research focus on the Vietnam War, War on Terror, gender, peace, security and postwar reconciliation. Her first book, *Return to Vietnam: An Oral History of American and Australian Veterans' Journeys*, won the Oral History Australia Book Award in 2022 and was highly commended for the Memory Studies First Book Award in 2023. She has written widely on anti-war veteran activism, war crimes and the impact of the Anzac revival on Australian veterans' war memory. She is presently an ARC DECRA fellow at Deakin University.

CAROLYN HOLBROOK is a historian at Deakin University. Her latest books are *Australia Fair? Democracy, Bureaucracy and the Making of Modern Australia* with James Walter, and *Gold Standard? Remembering the Hawke Government*, co-edited with Frank Bongiorno and Joshua Black. She is the director of the Australian Policy and History network and the Australian Health and History digital archive.

JOAN BEAUMONT is an internationally recognised historian of Australia in the two world wars, the history of prisoners of war, and the memory and heritage of war. Her publications include *Gull Force: Australian POWs on Ambon and Hainan, 1941–45*; *Australia's Great Depression: How a Nation Shattered by the Great War Survived the Worst Economic Crisis It Has Ever Faced*; and the critically acclaimed *Broken Nation: Australians in the Great War*, joint winner of the 2014 Prime Minister's Literary Award (Australian History), and winner of the 2014 NSW Premier's Award (Australian History), the 2014 Queensland Literary Award for History and the Australian Society of Authors' 2015 Asher Award.

CHALLENGING ANZAC

STORIES THAT DON'T FIT THE LEGEND

EDITED BY MIA MARTIN HOBBS, CAROLYN HOLBROOK AND JOAN BEAUMONT

NEWSOUTH

UNSW Press acknowledges the Bidjigal people, the Traditional Owners of the unceded territory on which the Randwick and Kensington campuses of UNSW are situated, and recognises the continuing connection to Country and culture. We pay our respects to Bidjigal Elders past and present.

A NewSouth book

Published by
NewSouth Publishing
University of New South Wales Press Ltd
University of New South Wales
Sydney NSW 2052
AUSTRALIA
https://unsw.press/

Our authorised representative in the EU for product safety
is Mare Nostrum Group B.V., Doelen 72, 4831 GR Breda,
The Netherlands (gpsr@mare-nostrum.co.uk).

A catalogue record for this
book is available from the
National Library of Australia

ISBN   9781761170706 (paperback)
         9781761179471 (ebook)
         9781761178740 (ePDF)

Cover design Peter Long
Internal design Josephine Pajor-Markus
Printer Griffin Press

All reasonable efforts were taken to obtain permission to use copyright material reproduced in this book, but in some cases copyright could not be traced. The editors welcome information in this regard.

This book is printed on paper using fibre supplied from plantation or sustainably managed forests.

Dedication

Joe Russell, who lost his leg before he killed any Germans

Don and Celie Martin, the only communists in the village

Mick and Marie Hobbs, lifelong pacifists

CONTENTS

ABBREVIATIONS

AAPA	Australian Aboriginal Progressive Association
ADF	Australian Defence Force
AIF	Australian Imperial Force
ANU	Australian National University
ANZAC	Australian and New Zealand Army Corps (but used more generally)
AWM	Australian War Memorial
AWOL	Absent without leave
HMAS	His/Her Majesty's Australian Ship
HMAT	His/Her Majesty's Australian Transport
HMSO	His/Her Majesty's Stationery Office
NAA	National Archives of Australia
NCO	non-commissioned officer
POW	prisoner of war
RAAF	Royal Australian Air Force
RAN	Royal Australian Navy
RSA	Returned Soldiers' and Sailors' Association, Western Australia
RSL	Returned and Services League
RSSILA	Returned Sailors' and Soldiers' Imperial League of Australia
RSSILWA	Returned Sailors' and Soldiers' Imperial League of Australia, Western Australia
SASR	Special Air Service Regiment
SS	Steam Ship
UNSW	University of New South Wales

1

CHALLENGING ANZAC: WHY NOW?

MIA MARTIN HOBBS, JOAN BEAUMONT
AND CAROLYN HOLBROOK

> Australians have gone overseas for us. They have gone because there is so much to fight for. And what we have created as Australians, and nurtured over generations, is something we must never take for granted.[1]

So declared Prime Minister Anthony Albanese at his Anzac Day address in April 2023. We might imagine Albanese's speechwriter – perhaps even Albanese himself – yawning as they wrote these words. Such invocations of Anzac are as common as they are banal and vapid. While the word 'Anzac' remains code for a unifying nationalism, 'Australian values' and support for the projection of military force overseas, it conveys little of substance on matters of war or military service. The ubiquity of 'Anzac' requires us to explain how we understand this remarkable acronym, known variously as the Anzac myth, or legend, or simply by the shorthand term of Anzac.

From its origins, Anzac was a celebration of the Australian soldiers of the First World War. The official historian, Charles Bean, and other early exponents of the Anzac legend believed that these volunteers, although civilians, had proved to be exceptional fighters. Their prowess could be explained only with reference to the society from which they came. This was, Bean claimed, an unusually classless and egalitarian society, where the ethos of the bush infused even urban life. Australian soldiers were resourceful, disrespectful of authority, prone to self-deprecation, quick with laconic humour, courageous, able to endure hardship and, above all, willing to risk their lives for the sake of their mates.[2]

This narrative of the Anzac soldier was always part myth. It described ostensibly historical events in order to embody the ideals, values and institutions of Australian society. Seamlessly, Anzac morphed into the foundational narrative of the nation. Anzac Day soon became established as the day on which 'the consciousness of Australian nationhood was born'.[3] Commemorated originally as a day of mourning the dead, community pride and encouragement of others to enlist, Anzac Day and its rituals became a key element in 'the symbolic repertoire available to the nation-state for binding its citizens into a collective national identity'.[4]

In the century and more since the Australian and New Zealand Army Corps was created in early 1915, this acronym of 'Anzac' has come to acquire multiple meanings.[5] Though Anzac Day came under attack in the post-1945 years, and was expected to wither and die as the veterans of the two world wars died, it survived and resurged during the national memory 'boom' from the 1980s on. Gradually, the term 'Anzac' morphed to be a generic signifier of national identity, or simply 'what it means to be Australian'. Police, firefighters and even celebrity sportsmen – anyone who subordinated their individual will to the collective good – could now be called an Anzac. The memorial to police installed on the banks of Lake Burley Griffin in Canberra in 2006 echoed Anzac symbolism, and the deaths of police inspired the language of war. They were the 'slain', the 'fallen' who made 'the ultimate sacrifice' in the 'line of duty'.[6]

Anzac has also served as a myth of Australian manhood – or, more accurately, white manhood – since Indigenous Australians did not figure in Bean's racialised narrative. (As it was, racially discriminatory policy prevented all but about a thousand Aboriginal Australians from enlisting in the First World War).[7] Bean considered the bronzed, tall Australian 'as fine a fighting man as exists', a reinvigorated colonial version of Anglo-Saxon stock, who by reason of 'the open-air life in the new climate, and of greater abundance of food, [had] developed more fully the large frames which seem normal to Anglo-Saxons living under generous conditions'.[8] One of Bean's team of First World War official historians, F.M. Cutlack, described the word 'Anzac as a war cry, pitiless as a hurled spear', which conveyed 'something savagely masculine, ruthless, resolute, clean driven home'.[9] This relentless masculinity evolved over the decades as the gender profile of the defence forces changed and the recognition of post-traumatic stress syndrome in the 1980s brought the psychological effects of war to the fore. Since the 1980s, the Anzac digger has increasingly been depicted as a tragic hero, revered for his suffering.[10] Arguably this evolution made 'Anzac' more gender inclusive, but the archetypical Anzac of national memory remains a man – and an infantry man at that.

The dual threads of Australia as a nation born in the fire of war and the embodiment of traditional Australian masculinity have meant that, perhaps inevitably, Anzac has long been associated with right-wing politics. From 1916 on, conservative elements among the returned soldiers came to dominate veterans' organisations, most notably the Returned Sailors' and Soldiers' Imperial League of Australia (RSSILA, now known as the RSL).

'Anzac' became identified with anti-communism, unquestioning support for the defence forces and, by implication, endorsement of the wars they fought in the name of Australia. This association with the politics of the right ebbed with the end of the Cold War, but as any critic of Anzac knows, it has far from dissipated. Moreover, since the Anzac revival, beginning in the 1980s, politicians of all stripes have laid claim to Anzac, and the exploitation of the legend by Labor and Coalition elites alike has entrenched associations of Australian military service with nationalistic fervour.

Despite the legend being overtly politicised, there remains a substantial community of Australians for whom Anzac has a profound emotional resonance. The Anzac Day dawn services have always had an element of the semi-sacred. The emphasis on the 'sacrifice' of the Anzac resonated with the Christian theology of redemption whereby God gave his innocent son to save the sinful others. The dawn service soon became set in an Anglo-Celtic and Christian template: prayers, hymns, the recitation of Binyon's Ode, 'They shall grow not old', and the playing of the *Last Post* and *Reveille*. The darkness of dawn and the haunting bugles created a powerful aesthetic of awe. These rituals of Anzac Day are fundamental to Anzac's hold on the Australian cultural imagination. Over the 20th century, the crowds became increasingly secular and active participation narrower, but still Anzac continued to function as a form of civil religion, particularly as efforts have been made to make its rituals more inclusive.[11]

CHALLENGES TO ANZAC

Each of these dimensions to Anzac has attracted scholarly critique over the years. For nearly 50 years after the First World War, academic historians showed relatively little interest in a topic that was dominated by the 12-volume *Official History of Australia in the War of 1914–1918*, edited by Bean and published between 1921 and 1942. Anzac's academic 'discovery' came in the 1960s, when Ken Inglis published several articles that drew academic attention to Anzac Day and the significance of Bean's writings.[12] The Vietnam War and conscription were giving a new salience to the events of 1914–18, and the emerging generation of young scholars, like the student hero of Alan Seymour's highly critical play, *The One Day of the Year* (1958), were inclined to treat Anzac and its conservative champions with a critical eye. Thinking they might discredit the legend if they proved it 'wrong', academic historians schooled in the tradition of robust empiricism took aim at the accuracy of Bean's account. In 1970, Lloyd Robson used statistical data to show that the majority of 1st AIF (Australian Imperial Force) recruits hailed from the urban labouring and clerical classes, rather than the rural backgrounds of Bean's legend.[13] Other historians followed with analyses of foundational elements of the Anzac legend about mateship, courage, fighting capacity and egalitarianism.[14] Bill Gammage's classic, *The Broken Years* (1974), a decisive work in the development of Australian historiography of war, did nothing to unsettle Bean's highly sympathetic depiction of the Australian soldier.[15] To some of his colleagues, however, the birth of the Anzac legend was no longer seen as spontaneous but as the conscious creation of Bean, who constructed the ideal of Australian soldiering in his selection of soldiers' writings for *The Anzac Book* (1916).[16] A British journalist, Ellis Ashmead Bartlett, who had been the first to rouse Australian pride in May 1915 with his purple prose, was shown to have become quickly disillusioned with the Gallipoli campaign.[17] A feminist critique of the Anzac legend also emerged from the 1970s, as Carmel Shute's now classic analysis of sexual mythology in the First World War was followed by studies that refused to conflate male martial activity with the birth of the nation.[18] One leading feminist scholar, Marilyn Lake, turned her attention to the way in which the conservative veterans' organisation, the RSSILA, had established itself as 'the official custodian and interpreter of the Anzac tradition'.[19]

Another strand of Anzac historiography became concerned with explaining the role and function that the legend served within Australian society. In 1960, Ken Inglis was one of the first to discern that the Anzac legend functioned as a kind of 'civil religion'.[20] These questions of ritual and commemoration would bear fruit in Inglis's definitive study of Australian war memorials, *Sacred Places* (1998).[21] Inglis, and later scholars such as Inga Clendinnen and Bruce Scates, were more interested in understanding the subjective experience of Anzac commemoration than in identifying the role of the state and influential individuals in informing that experience.[22] In Alistair Thomson's *Anzac Memories* (1994), what began as an effort to reveal the experiences of working-class diggers morphed into a pioneering study of the interaction between personal and public memory.[23] These works influenced a generation of scholars exploring how veterans of modern wars drew on the Anzac legend to understand their personal and political struggles with postwar adjustment.[24]

A further 'challenge' to Anzac from the 1980s was the growing recognition of the traumatic impact of war, the grief of families, the physical damage to soldiers' bodies and the psychic wounds they carried after war. The exposure of the vulnerability of the maimed and disfigured veteran, and the length of time for which many suffered, sat uncomfortably with a celebratory narrative of war.[25] Yet as Christina Twomey shows, the emerging focus on trauma was drawn into the Anzac legend through that key element, the 'sacrifice' of the soldier.[26] From the 1980s, the soldier was increasingly depicted as victim, not killer.

The lead-up to the Anzac centenary in 2015 unleashed a flood of books, journal articles and media commentary. Many authors were boundlessly enthusiastic and gung-ho about the Anzac legend, while others were unnerved by the extraordinary investment of government monies in the 'memory orgy'.[27] Among the critics, Robin Prior 'sought to strip away the weight of mythology that has so hampered the development of a sophisticated historiography of Gallipoli'.[28] Other scholars noted that the memorial diplomacy between Australia and Türkiye (formerly Turkey) obscured the 'dark underbelly' of another centenary anniversary in 2015 – the Armenian genocide.[29] Peter Stanley and Ashley Ekins exposed behaviour of some Australian soldiers that transgressed even the celebrated larrikinism of the Anzac.[30] New studies of venereal disease and sexuality in the military threatened to undermine the more mythologised versions of Anzac warriors who, while virile and fiercely bonded by mateship, were typically depicted as heterosexual or asexual while absent from home.[31]

Throughout the centenary years, the Honest History website supplied a stream of commentary that aimed to separate Anzac myth from reality: 'there is much more to our war history than nostalgia and tales of heroism', it claimed.[32] Begun in 2013 by a former Commonwealth public servant, David Stephens, and supported by activist scholars who were angered at the proposed expansion of the Australian War Memorial, Honest History made the memorable contribution that there is no strong evidence that the Turkish leader Kemal Ataturk ever said, or wrote, the much quoted paean to Australian mothers, inscribed on a memorial at Gallipoli.[33] *The Honest History Book*, which Stephens edited with Alison Broinowski in 2017, also did the community the valuable service of documenting how much Australia had spent on centenary commemoration – around $600 million, with government and corporate expenditure combined, far more than any other nation, including the major combatants.[34]

Even former soldiers joined in the criticism. In 2014, James Brown, who served in Iraq, Afghanistan and the Solomon Islands, argued that the 'national obsession' with Anzac came at the expense of the modern Australian military, which required skills (innovation, understanding, connection and intellectual excellence) that were not captured in the legend.[35] Other historians echoed Brown's critique of the 'selling of remembrance' by exposing the long history of the commodification of war memory, including through the sale of 'Anzackery'.[36] As the Department of Veterans' Affairs poured resources into educational materials and commemorative grants aimed at reinforcing Anzac, Marilyn Lake, Henry Reynolds, Mark McKenna and Joy Damousi decried 'the militarisation of Australian history', and the relative neglect of alternative national stories, such as the early achievement of democracy and advances in social welfare policy.[37]

These critiques of Anzac over the decades typically triggered a vicious counterchallenge from the right. Lloyd Robson's studies of the 1st AIF earned him death threats. David Kent's critique of Bean's editing of *The Anzac Book* inspired accusations of treason (a charge also levied against Marilyn Lake). In 2009, the conservative *Quadrant* magazine pilloried historians for their 'Assault on Anzac', while Mervyn Bendle devoted some of his retirement to exposing, in *Anzac and its Enemies: The History War on Australia's National Identity* (2015), some 20 historians who were leading 'anti-Anzacs'.[38] These attacks were sometimes intimidating, sometimes laughable – some historians prided themselves on being 'Bendled' – but the vehemence of the attacks on critics of Anzac attested to the legend's unassailable status in the Australian political culture. When one of the editors of this volume aired the view in 2015 that Anzac might be the 'last hurrah of the white male', she received a misogynist tirade on email: 'What a low slag you are. With an abortion of a head like yours I can see why you're angry. Just crawl back under the rock you came from slut.'

Anzac, then, has proved to be profoundly difficult to unsettle. Members of the governing elites, be they Labor or conservative, seem unwilling – or unable – to challenge its semi-sacred status as the foundational narrative of national identity. Prime ministerial attendance at a major dawn service is mandatory, and we can only imagine the fury of the conservative media if they chose not to go. Meanwhile, the majority of Australians, even if they do not attend dawn services and know little about Anzac's origins, seem willing to accept its significance for those who continue to commemorate it. Many communities within Australia appear to be indifferent to Anzac but, perhaps aware of the importance it holds for other Australians, they do not overtly challenge it.

Beyond that, in the hands of many memory agents, the legend has proved flexible enough to accommodate new perspectives. The growing sensitivity to gender, racial and sexual diversity in the defence forces might have challenged the archetypal white, male Anzac, but it did not displace the legend. On the contrary, the politics of recognition meant that previously excluded groups often seemed intent on being incorporated into the legend, in a 'we are all Anzacs' fashion.[39] In the lead-up to the centenary, some Aboriginal veterans expressed concern that Anzac Day was 'a party to which they [had] not been invited'.[40] In recent years, official institutions have endeavoured to make Anzac

Day more overtly inclusive: dawn services feature letters by marginalised service personnel communities, and in 2023, a new arrangement of the *Last Post*, recorded with a didgeridoo as well as the traditional bugle, echoed through the cold air from the ramparts of the Australian War Memorial.[41] Yet backlashes against inclusivity – such as hecklers booing the Welcome to Country at the Melbourne Shrine of Remembrance in 2025 – reveal that Anzac is still seen by many as a legend belonging to white, male, frontline soldiers.[42]

Thus, the Anzac legend continues to endure, even as it evolves. It is malleable, but not endlessly so, meaning many stories of the past, and perhaps some in the future, simply cannot 'fit'. Given its resilience, its extraordinary power and its often cynical deployment by political and commercial interests, the central place of the Anzac legend in Australian society must continue to be challenged.

WHY NOW?

A decade after the centenary, in 2025, news leaked that the Australian War Memorial had effectively overruled a decision to award the Les Carlyon prize for military history to a book that documented Australian war crimes. Leaked correspondence indicated that a panel of external judges had selected Chris Masters' *Flawed Hero: Truth, Lies and War Crimes*, about alleged war criminal Ben Roberts-Smith, as the winning book, but that the War Memorial had retrospectively disqualified Masters' book by imposing eligibility criteria that restricted the prize to emerging authors. Following years of debate about how Victoria Cross–winner Roberts-Smith should be portrayed in the exhibits of the War Memorial, the Les Carlyon prize scandal raised questions about what kinds of stories we tell about Australia's military history, and why.

This collection reveals as yet untold stories of Australian service that challenge the hegemony of Anzac in Australia today. Challenges to Anzac take many forms. They can be explicit, in the form of direct protests against war, militarism, patriarchy or capitalism. Challenges to Anzac might also be private or implicit. Individual veterans might act, during or after war, in ways that transgress the mythic narratives of the Anzac warrior. Whether these men were angered by the carnage of war, or traumatised by their military service, they behaved in ways that, for them or others, unsettled the nationalism and masculinity at the heart of the legend.

Challenges to Anzac can also be found in the processes of collective memory formation. Even battles that have been accorded iconic status, as exemplars of the Anzac legend in the national memory of war, contain contradictions. Some elements might affirm the values of the Anzac legend; others challenge them. Similarly, allegations of Australian conduct in war that contradict ideas of the Anzacs' valour and virtue have been massaged to cohere with the familiar narrative.

A more subtle, but nonetheless significant, challenge to Anzac arises from the changing character of military service over the past century. As the conduct of war has changed, service personnel have increasingly fought war at a distance, and have suffered in ways that differ from traditional notions of the 'ultimate sacrifice'. The incidence of veteran suicide, for instance, is highest among those who have been involuntarily discharged from the armed forces, regardless of whether they ever deployed or saw combat.[43] And the Australian soldier of the future is as likely to be in front of a screen as behind a rifle sight. In other words, there is a tension between the mythology of Anzac – which also functions as a key means of recruitment for the Australian military – and the historic and future day-to-day reality of the Australian Defence Forces (ADF).

In exploring these diverse challenges to Anzac, this book contests the stereotypical view of the Australian soldier as inherently conservative, and highlights the stories of service personnel whose experiences denied them ready inclusion within the Anzac legend. It reveals how dissonant narratives about Australian military service have been elided and adapted by veterans' groups, commemorative institutions and the Australian media to fit into the Anzac legend. It also explores how the reality of warfare has always been at odds with mythic representations, and explains how, despite these challenges, the Anzac legend has survived. The case studies that follow are organised roughly chronologically, because although certain elements of the Anzac legend have persisted across the decades, others have changed along with shifting societal expectations and the evolving demands of the defence forces. In turn, the nature of the challenges to Anzac have changed over time.

We begin with Alistair Thomson's contention that the experiences of First World War veterans posed challenges to Bean's legend. Drawing on original oral histories with working-class soldiers, Thomson reveals not so much Anzac resourcefulness, but the soldiers' sense of powerlessness, refusal, and quiet resistance. His radical digger interviewees credited the core Anzac trait of mateship to socialist tendencies among the working-class ranks against military authority. This chapter was originally written in the 1980s by then-history student Thomson, but was rejected for publication by the Australian War Memorial as 'unrepresentative' of the Great War experience.

Kate Ariotti and Martin Crotty then trace the journey of one of the most remarkable, and least distinguished, service records of any Australian soldier in the First World War, Private Nicholas Permakoff. Instructed to enlist by the Russian Imperial government, Permakoff was something of an unhappy conscript in a famously volunteer army. Allegedly crossing to enemy lines on the Western Front, Permakoff was shot by his own side, an army that famously refused to execute deserters. And in a country that devotes much effort to memorialising its dead servicemen and women, Permakoff was the only Australian to die on a 1914–18 battlefield to be omitted from the Australian War Memorial's Roll of Honour.

Permakoff's was a personal act of resistance, but much of the opposition of returning First World War soldiers was more public and explicit, as Bobbie Oliver shows. In the immediate postwar period in Western Australia, a group of returned soldiers who espoused socialist rhetoric and whose sympathies lay with the labour movement accused the RSSILA of siding with the capitalist class. These returned soldiers also directed violence against non-union labour that had taken their place in the workforce. Ultimately, the alternative veterans' organisation did not survive, but its history shows that not all returned men believed that the conservative RSSILA acted in the interests of Anzacs.

A further example of organised protest in the aftermath of war was the agitation by Aboriginal veterans for political rights in the 1920s. Though they were 'Anzacs' by virtue of having served in the First World War, their race ensured that they did not 'fit' into the emerging mythic narrative. Instead, as John Maynard recounts, they suffered from racism, exclusion and resentment on their return to Australia. Some of these men drew on their soldier status to call attention to their demands for political and civil rights in the Australian Aboriginal Progressive Association (AAPA) the first united all-Aboriginal political organisation to form in Australia.

With Nathan Hobby's chapter we turn to the protest of a single soldier, Hugo Throssell, who challenged those who saw him as the quintessential Anzac. Awarded the Victoria Cross at Gallipoli in 1915, Throssell became a 'celebrity Anzac', but after marrying the recently radicalised writer, Katharine Susannah Prichard (1883–1969), he publicly declared in 1919 that the war had been caused by capitalism – and that he was now a socialist. While Throssell did not experience outright rejection after his public confession and continued to be accorded the status of an Anzac 'celebrity', he was denied opportunities to speak publicly. The VC winner, who was plagued with financial difficulties, war-related poor health and perhaps the contradictions of his own public stance, died by suicide in 1933.

Throssell, tragically, was not alone in choosing to take his own life. Many other veterans of the Great War died by suicide. Margaret Hutchinson and Karen Bird use select case studies from the Queensland archives to analyse the experiences of returned men who died by their own hand. By examining service records, repatriation files, coronial inquests and newspaper reports of these men's deaths, they explore how families and communities came to understand veterans' trauma and the enduring cost of war. Suicides were primarily a response to physical injury rather than mental trauma, suggesting that for the maimed and sick, expectations of the prized Anzac trait of endurance caused suffering and harm to soldiers.

In the chapters that follow we consider challenges to Anzac beyond the experiences of the First World War. Joan Beaumont discusses the Second World War, during which the 1941 defence and siege of Tobruk in North Africa positioned the 'Rats of Tobruk' as exemplars of the Anzac tradition. Yet, before the siege ended in December 1941, most of the Australian forces had been evacuated by sea in the face of strong opposition from the British command. The details of this dispute would be aired publicly by the British prime minister, Winston Churchill, in 1950 to the discomfiture of some Australians. In subsequent decades, the Rats of Tobruk continued to be celebrated as quintessential Anzacs but the relief of Tobruk, and Churchill's critique, slipped to the margins of the public memory, presumably because both challenged the traditional depiction of the Anzacs as the acme of endurance and courage.

The eliding of certain episodes from Anzac was also evident, as Max Billington shows, when Australian military personnel were deployed to support five major test series of nuclear weapons built and owned by the British government between 1952 and 1957. Decades later, Australia's 'nuclear veterans' accused the government of exposing them to harmful radiation during their service. But the Australian government was loath to concede that the tasks performed by Australian servicemen at the nuclear tests constituted military service, or that servicemen were ignorant of the dangers of radiation. The invisible harms suffered unknowingly by 'nuclear veterans' proved highly inconvenient for the state, for whom the willing bodily sacrifice of service personnel was core to the Anzac legend.

A different challenge came in the 1970s from second-wave feminism. Christina Twomey relates how feminist protestors began to appear at Anzac Day marches around Australia carrying banners 'In Memory of Women Raped in War' and declaring that 'Rape is War Against Women'. She examines responses to the activism that exposed rape in wartime, including attempts to suppress it, and explores internal feminist debates about whether there should be a specific focus on war or broader male violence against women. By the 1990s, however, Anzac Day was no longer a focus of feminist protest. Despite the dramatic effort to break the silence about female and civilian suffering in war, male veterans ultimately claimed the status of victim for themselves.

Intriguingly, despite this and other challenges to Anzac, Australia did not witness a robust organisation of anti-war veterans opposing war itself, as did the United States. Mia Martin Hobbs explores the stories of the few Australian veterans who attempted to protest against war. Drawing on oral histories, memoirs and online forums, blogs and social media pages, she reveals how veterans of more recent wars have opposed war and militarism, and explores signs of hesitancy and intimidation in their memories of dissent. She further shows how their anti-war activism has been marginalised by veterans' organisations, the Australian government, the media and the public.

Our study of challenges to Anzac concludes, as it must, with the issue of the Anzac legend's status today, and in the future. Mia Martin Hobbs returns to consider the implications of the allegation of war crimes committed by Australian Special Forces in Afghanistan. This controversy did not prove to be the challenge to Anzac that many anticipated. Alleged atrocities show that Special Forces saw themselves as living up to the legend: enacting warrior rituals to embody the formidable Anzacs, framing their transgressions as anti-establishment, and deploying the idea of mateship to enforce a code of silence. Meanwhile, Australian commentators and veterans drew on the Anzac legend to make sense of the allegations, emphasising the honour, courage and professionalism of the Special Forces and the sense of betrayal experienced by perpetrators, witnesses and the wider Australian

Defence Force. Much like the relief of Tobruk, the retelling of Australian atrocities in Afghanistan shows how stories that should contradict the Anzac legend are shaped and moulded to cohere to the familiar narrative.

A second issue of contemporary relevance is the growing automation of warfare. Bianca Baggiarini and Joan Beaumont consider whether drones and other robotic weapons will make the 'autonomous warrior' a contradiction in terms, given that defence personnel can now inflict violence at a great distance from their enemy. Yet, the situation is ambiguous. Even when drone operators do not place their own lives at risk, they can suffer 'moral injury' rather than physical damage. Furthermore, the war between Russia and Ukraine shows that swarming drones have made soldiers on the ground more vulnerable than ever before. It seems that the dominance on the battlefield of ever more precise weaponry will not exclude the requirement of 'sacrifice' during warfare. Australian defence personnel of the future might be called upon to manifest the traditional Anzac values of endurance, courage and even sacrifice – albeit in different ways from soldiers of the past.

While these stories do not readily 'fit' the Anzac legend, it is highly unlikely to lose its central place in the Australian political culture and society. Seeking to progress the debate on the complex question of why, Carolyn Holbrook asks: what lies behind the enduring power of group mythologies, such as the Anzac legend? Drawing on sociology, anthropology and evolutionary psychology, she argues that the fundamental purpose of religion – and Anzac is arguably such – is group cohesion, including that of the national community. The power of Anzac's group-binding rituals helps us to understand its abiding presence across the generations as a primary signifier of Australian characteristics and values. A more psychologically informed explanation of the nature of Anzac helps us understand why, despite over a century of challenges, the legend endures.

2

THE FORGOTTEN ANZACS
RADICAL DIGGERS CHALLENGE
AN AUSTRALIAN LEGEND

ALISTAIR THOMSON

As Australia's official correspondent accompanying the Australian Imperial Force (AIF) in the Great War, C.E.W. Bean listed the distinctive Anzac characteristics as reckless valour, resourcefulness, endurance, fidelity, comradeship, or 'mateship', and a democratic spirit.[1] These Anzac qualities are used to explain Australian military success, and to explain away the tactical failure of Gallipoli as an individual and national triumph. But it is simplistic and misleading to explain that success in terms of the character of Australian manhood. If we look at each of Bean's Anzac attributes through the eyes of working-class diggers,

Editor's note: This chapter was originally produced as part of a book manuscript exploring the experiences of Australian working-class veterans of the Great War. Written in the 1980s by then-history student Alistair Thomson, the chapter followed the transcripts of interviews with four radical diggers, and offered an alternative reading of Australia's First World War experience and the Anzac legend. Pitched for publication in 1987, Thomson's manuscript was rejected by the Australian War Memorial (which had funded the research) as 'unrepresentative' of the Great War experience. The chapter and interviews went on to inform Thomson's PhD and groundbreaking first book, *Anzac Memories: Living with the Legend* (Oxford University Press, 1994). However, the original manuscript was never published. This chapter is an abridged version of the final chapter of the original manuscript, unaltered by the author but interwoven with quotes drawn from the interviews.

the experience and identity of Australian soldiers become more contradictory.

This chapter draws upon the testimony of four radical diggers of the Great War. Stan D'Altera enlisted in 1915 and fought with the 23rd Infantry Battalion in Egypt and then the 7th Battalion in France.[2] Fred Farrall enlisted in December 1915 and served with the 55th Battalion. Between 1983 and 1985 I spent many hours with Fred in his South Yarra home, and on Anzac Day 1985, we walked beside the official Melbourne parade and he recalled unofficial memories of army jokes and deserters and discontent.[3] Ern Morton served as a frontline soldier through the whole of the war. He enlisted for patriotic reasons in 1914, but by 1916 he was organising the soldiers in France to vote against conscription, and by 1918 avoided any military duty that he could: he had had enough of war.[4] Sid Norris enlisted in 1916 and fought with the 19th Battalion. After the war he decided to have nothing more to do with his soldiering past, and when I first met him in 1983, he showed me his box of First World War service medals, unopened.[5]

The testimony of these four interviews challenges many of the stereotypes about the Great War and Australian soldiers, and this chapter analyses some of the themes of the interviews. In addition, it draws upon my interviews with another 20 Melbourne working-class veterans of the war.[6] They reveal that the view from the ranks was not the same as the view of officers and staff (or war correspondents and military historians), and that Australian soldiers were not so different from the combatants of other armies.

RECKLESS VALOUR

The typical Anzac story commences with innocent, patriotic heroes cramming into city recruiting depots or galloping to enlist at outback police stations. The declaration of war did generate an extraordinary, naive enthusiasm. Ern remembers: 'We were told that it was a "war to end wars" and I felt it a duty that everyone go to the war. I soon changed my mind though [laughs].'[7] Young Australians were schooled in military deeds that made the British Empire 'Great', and many people were delighted that Australian soldiers would at last be able to prove themselves, and the nation, in battle. 'Oh, I was patriotic', Stan remembers, 'you know, the stuff we learned at school. Britons never shall be slaves.'[8]

Yet this legend of August 1914 neglects the prewar life that many Australian men so urgently wanted to leave behind, and conceals less patriotic incentives for enlistment. Working-class Australians grew up in battling families with an uncertain future. Sid explains that 'there was very little education amongst our lot' and that he enlisted because 'there was no work. I had no money'.[9] The rural and urban poverty recalled by my interviewees starkly contrasts with depictions of rustic wellbeing in prewar Australia.[10] An Anzac legend that assumes that Australia was a land of opportunity for enterprising men forgets that the frontiers of opportunity had closed for most working-class Australians by the turn of the century. The enticing adventure of war was an escape from the tough and dissatisfying working lives of many Australian men. Ern, working on a farm in New South Wales, felt that 'it was just working on a farm with no future. And on a farm you're more restricted to one idea of life'.[11] For some men it was also an easy escape from domestic responsibilities into an exhilarating male world. Fred describes growing up 'rough and tough. There was no school. There was not much of anything.' He worked on the family farm 'every morning to late at night and seven days a week. With not much time for amusement or sport or anything else that might be interesting'.[12]

Once at war, Australia's legend focuses on the fighting qualities of the AIF. Yet old working-class diggers are not always proud of their reputation as fearless and fierce fighting men. Ern ironically concludes that the reputation sent the Anzacs into the front line of every major battle of the war, and killed one in five Australian soldiers. He condemns the ugly extremes of military prowess. Men of other armies who admired the bravery of the Anzacs also complained that the Australians could be especially brutal fighters, merciless in their treatment of the wounded or captured enemy.[13] Fred reflects that rather than courage, the AIF's reputation stemmed from a 'cult of hatred' embedded among its men:

> The only good Germans were dead ones, and that's your
> job to see that they're dead, to see that they're good ones.
> And furthermore, we were to always remember that it was
> a case of kill or be killed, and you don't want to be killed
> do you? So you kill the other bloke. Unless you could hate
> really well you wasn't going to be all that good as a soldier,
> and possibly this is why I wasn't much good. Some of our
> chaps would be really enthusiastic about it. The killing
> of Germans wouldn't be any different to them than the
> killing of rabbits.[14]

Fred recognises that the ability to defeat and kill other men is an appalling quality that should be revered by no individual or nation. He also asserts that such fighting qualities are irrelevant in modern nuclear war. Soldier heroes won't save us from the bomb.

Australia's legend of courageous Anzacs contrasts with European memories of the war, which express the individual powerlessness and human waste with grim irony.[15] Ern remembers Kitchener's Army as

> young teenagers that came onto Gallipoli and I saw many of them crying … That frightened that they couldn't stop shedding tears. And I remember that I was a veteran by then, and I was assisting these fellows to try and help them overcome their fear of war.[16]

Yet many Australian veterans have a similar memory of the war. Fred remembers of the Australian contingent: 'I suppose most of them were like me, although we didn't show it and I didn't either I don't suppose, as far as I know I didn't, nevertheless, honestly we were scared.'[17] Similarly, Ern reflects that he empathised with the young British soldiers: 'I think probably the fear that I felt helped me to convey some sort of relief to others.'[18]

Australian war correspondents and historians, determined to celebrate the Australian soldier, have concealed this ugly face of battle. The difference between C.E.W. Bean's Gallipoli diary and the public story of his newspaper articles and historical writing reveals this selective history-making. In the diary, Bean attacks 'the nonsense about wounded soldiers wanting to get back from the hospital to the front', yet in the *Official History* the wounded Anzacs are 'genuinely eager to get back to the front for another blow at the bastards'. His diary mirrors the memories of radical diggers: Sid recalls that many soldiers were only eager to get to into combat because 'you wanted to get it over. As far as I seen, most of them blokes, they were quite anxious to get it over. All the people I was with.'[19] In his diary, Bean admits that soldiers very often run away – 'soldiers, even Australian soldiers, have sometimes to be threatened with a revolver to make them go on' – that self-inflicted wounds are 'not uncommon, even among Australians', and that he has heard Australians boasting of killing Turkish wounded and prisoners. These pitiful facts of war do not appear in Bean's correspondence and are rare in his *Official History*. As he frankly admits in his diary:

> There is a terror and beastliness and cowardice and treachery over all of which the writer, anxious to please the public, has to throw his cloak – but the man who does his job is a hero.[20]

Bean's admission that the national heroes are just ordinary men with the typical responses to battle is one vital key to unlock the Anzac legend. For it is the conditions of war and of military life, far more than any spurious national characteristics, which shape the behaviour of soldiers. Stan, for instance, remembers the Anzacs as 'tall, active, young … I think they were superior', but also admits that his perception of superiority was without evidence: 'at Anzac [Cove] we didn't meet any British. But we've since come to realise that the British done as much as we did at Gallipoli'.[21] Fear and brutality are not the exclusive property of one race or nation, any more than courage or comradeship. The common experience of frontline soldiers in the Great War was more significant than any national distinction. As Fred realised when he met wounded German soldiers, the front-soldiery of both sides suffered and survived the war in very similar ways. Australian veterans of the ranks recall that, contrary to the

Anzacs' warlike reputation, most diggers adopted a 'live and let live' approach to the enemy.

RESOURCEFULNESS

The reality that wartime conditions affect soldiers' behaviour more than national character is true for the other Anzac stereotypes. For example, there is ample evidence of the diggers' 'resourcefulness', but it is usually not compared with the resourcefulness of other armies. All soldiers had to make the most of limited resources and awful conditions. They stole, scavenged, and tinkered to survive and make life in the trenches bearable.

The digger was also reputed to be especially 'resourceful' in battle, able to adapt plans in unexpected situations, or to fight on after officers were killed or wounded. Individual initiative could be a decisive factor in the confusing, close quarters of trench raids. Sid remembers at Villers-Bretonneux:

> Things were in a hell of a mess. Horses dead everywhere and a few men of course. When we eventually got into the line it was just coming daylight and raining all the time. I had a waterproof sheet over the machine gun. Taking more care of that than myself.[22]

Yet the Australian reputation exaggerates the opportunities for this initiative in the massed armies of the Great War. Soldiers were often pawns in battle plans drawn up far behind the lines, and personal heroics were limited by the awesome destructive power of modern weapons. Cunning and heroics could not repel clouds of mustard gas or artillery bombardments. The writer Bill Harney was a cattle drover before he enlisted in the AIF, and in his memoir he contrasts life in the trenches with 'the old days of the cattle station where a man rounded up the cattle and used his own initiative – that's all gone. You're just a big cog in the machine.'[23] Most soldiers proudly remember the ways in which they survived the war, but they also admit the powerlessness and frustration of life in the line. Fred recalls a moment when 'I'd lost my rifle, as a matter of fact I'd nearly lost my sense, and I'd lost [the Lieutenant], so I just started off across no man's land in a sort of haze.'[24]

ENDURANCE

'Endurance' is another quality that Bean ascribes to the Australian soldiers. Most men did stick to the task. 'How we put up with it I'll never know, never been able to know since. We were half starved, particularly when the stores couldn't be landed in stormy weather', Stan remembers. 'We suffered from dysentery and weakness. But yet we stick it out, because … will power.'[25] Even today, Fred cannot explain why he knocked back an opportunity to leave the front line and join his brother in the Veterinary Corps.

A man's reputation in the eyes of his mates was one pressure against giving up. However, there were also stern punishments to discourage men from breaking ranks. Fred remembers a friend of his challenging authorities at the Somme. 'They had tied a digger to a cartwheel. The wheel of an artillery piece. They called it being "spread-eagled". It was bitterly cold.' Fred's friend, Bill, asked the officer of the Guard to take the digger down. The Guard complied but then ordered the Sergeant, '"take him out there and let him see what it's like". So they tied Bill to the wheel.'[26] Out of the line, the order to return to the trenches was an effective deterrent; in battle most men were afraid, but knew that it was usually safer to go forward in numbers than to run away.[27] Fred recalls a 'young chap' in

> one of our gaols, and he said to me, 'much and all as I
> hate going back to France, I'd rather do that than do any
> more time in the clink'. Because they were treated so
> brutally in there that it was preferable that he go back to
> the Battalion.[28]

Despite these sanctions, many diggers described how they would do anything to get out of the line at Gallipoli, and especially on the Western Front. Each man hoped to cop a 'blighty', a minor wound, which guaranteed a trip to England, or even back to Australia. They tell stories of friends inflicting wounds upon themselves, or placing condensed milk upon their penises so they would be hospitalised with venereal disease. 'They'd stoop to anything at all to get off Gallipoli', Ern remembers.

> It wasn't unusual to find men that had rammed a pick into
> their legs or in their shin. The night I was wounded one
> of my cobbers mentioned some sum of money, 'if you'll
> exchange your wound'. There was no desire to stay there.[29]

Sid even suggests that men put themselves in unnecessary danger in order to get out of the trenches: 'One bloke said to me, "well", he said, "I've had enough of this. I want to go get hit and get out of it."'[30]

Desertion was relatively uncommon in the AIF (unlike European soldiers, Australians could not easily escape to home), but the number of Australian offenders increased towards the end of the war. Others went absent without leave. 'I went round having a good time, to what they call the pub, the *estaminet*, and having some good feeds and that', Stan remembers of his time in France. 'It took them three weeks to find me [laughs].'[31] Ern 'turned against the war' after meeting a stricken German officer, and subsequently avoided military duties. His private rebellion was part of a sullen opposition to the war that is not recorded in official statistics. Sid remembers, 'We used to go out every night, you know, on patrols, patrolling every night. I remember I used to be dragging my shoes, getting along [laughs].' There was a widespread but quiet resistance; 'they was all getting bloody sick of what was going on'.[32]

FIDELITY

Anzac 'fidelity', to the battalion and to Australia, is an explanation of the endurance and success of the diggers. In strange countries, far away from loved ones, the diggers inevitably formed close bonds with each other, and became attached to the battalion, which was their family and their home. They still proudly remember that the AIF was the only fully volunteer army of the war, and that because of this the men did not accept the strict discipline and customs of regular or conscripted armies. They also respected the government's refusal to let its volunteer soldiers suffer the death penalty for military offences. The war years undoubtedly forged a powerful Anzac loyalty. It's not surprising that the AIF did not have the massive mutinies of other armies, and that one of the major Australian mutinies was an attempt to stop a proposed merger of depleted battalions: the diggers wanted to keep each family intact.

Yet the Australian soldiers also gained a formidable reputation for their anti-authoritarian behaviour. Working-class diggers recall countless incidents of rebellion against unfair rulings on drill, leave or rations, and even in battle. There were also innumerable contemporary complaints of Anzac misconduct. Haig, the British commander, condemned the Australians for the 'excessive indiscipline' and 'inordinate vanity'.[33] Sid remembers, 'We did have a bit of a strike one time, you know. Oh, that was in Plugge Street because we were getting nothing to eat.' After various excuses from the officer class, the soldiers 'wouldn't go out for parade'. However, Sid remembers that the army strikes 'never had the bite', because soldiers 'wouldn't revolt in the line', believing they would have to win the war to finish it.[34] Nonetheless, Australian soldiers were prominent in unrest at the British army base camps, most notoriously at Étaples, where the Anzacs led a 1917 uprising against the harsh regime enforced by training staff and camp police.[35] After the Armistice, the Australian soldiers were even more difficult to restrain, as they ran riot while waiting to be repatriated to Australia.

Other diggers do recall more direct protests against returning to the front line. By 1918 the frontline soldiers of the AIF were increasingly restless. They were suffering terrific casualties and believed that they were being used as shock troops. In September of that year, Fred was surprised to find a large group of 1st Battalion soldiers 'in the clink'. These men had been ordered to return to the front line immediately after they had been relieved; they refused to obey the order and were jailed. Fred also recalls the exhausted men of his own battalion hurling dirt at the inspecting general, Talbot Hobbs, who had warned them that they would be sent back into the line if peace was not declared. 'Well, that's as far as he got. It was easy to get clods of dirt which were aimed at his horse, if not at him.' Hobbs removed himself. 'That was the frame of mind that the soldiers had got into, generally speaking. They didn't want any more front line.'[36] These protests are reminders that Anzac fidelity could only be stretched so far before it would snap. Like the frontline soldiers of every army in Europe, they had had enough.

MATESHIP

Mateship is the most celebrated quality of the Anzacs. It is a quality that the diggers themselves revered. On Gallipoli, Stan developed the 'spirit of mateship', 'to help your mate and stick it out'. In France, the soldiers of Sid's battalion were sick of the trenches but they determined to keep on and stay with their mates. A man who took more than his fair share of food, or who left another soldier in danger, was despised. Mateship was an emotional bond of selfless friendship, which helped men to cope in appalling conditions. Stan evoked that bond in a story he wrote in 1931 for *Smith's Weekly*. Jim and Ted are tired and hungry after four German attacks, and crave a cigarette. Jim finds a butt and declares 'we're cobbers and we share alike'.[37] Mateship also improved the physical comfort and safety of the soldiers. Mates could share equipment and skills, or sleep together for extra warmth and security. In the line, a good mate could save your life if you were wounded or in trouble. Of course, some men preferred to look after 'number one', but most soldiers believed they had a better chance of survival if they helped each other.

The evidence of wartime comradeship is undeniable. The trouble is that mateship is assumed to be yet another distinctively Australian habit. War, like other isolated, stressful situations, out in the bush or on the goldfields, encourages men to form close and supportive relationships (women don't need a war to form intimate friendships and support networks – yet our national myths only celebrate the mateship of men). A few days after the landing at Gallipoli, Bean remarked in his diary that it was

> extraordinary how our men have come to lean on one another. When they started out they wouldn't share a tin of bully beef, but now they have come to lean on one another, and their officers, almost like a family.[38]

Bean, who was one of the first historians of war to write about ordinary soldiers, believed the camaraderie was uniquely Australian, when he was simply describing the characteristic behaviour of most men, in all armies, at war. For example, in the war memoirs of British private soldiers 'the daily comradeship of my pals' is the most valued memory of the war, and the usual explanation of survival.[39] Comradeship is the sacred memory of the Anzacs, but it is also revered by veterans' groups around the world.

Mateship is the most politically ambiguous and controversial theme of the Anzac legend. Some historians claim that mateship in the AIF derived from a male, working-class ethic with an anti-authoritarian, socialist tendency.[40] Fred attributes the origins of mateship to Henry Lawson's bush stories and the influence of trade union men in the AIF. His own experience and ideal of mateship is the solidarity in the ranks against the twin oppressions of military conditions and authority, and he cites unionist soldiers who wanted the creed of the diggers to be a radical inspiration in peacetime Australia. In fact, several diggers recall that mateship was extended across national boundaries in war. Ern remembers a 24-hour armistice on Gallipoli:

not a shot was fired and we went out in no man's land. The
Turks came out and we went out, to bury the dead. They
couldn't stand the conditions. To see all these corpses
lying out in no man's land. We went out and I was the one
that assisted. We exchanged cigarettes and spoke as much
as we could to the enemy … if during the war we could
have an armistice, a twenty-four-hour peace, meet on
no man's land and decide to settle the war with no more
fighting … it can be done in actual war, why can't it be
done in peace time. And I still think it can too.[41]

Anzac Day orators stretched the concept of mateship in the
opposite political direction, to portray the officers and men
of the AIF as one big national family, the classless army of a
classless society (despite the bitter divisions of the 1890s strikes,
Bean depicted a rustic class harmony in prewar Australia, and
transposed that legacy into the AIF). They assumed that the fierce
loyalty of the diggers was an identification with nation instead of
class and that this loyal digger was the 'true' Australian. In the
postwar years, Australian conservatives fought for the dominance
of this version of mateship.

EGALITARIANISM

The relationship between AIF officers and other ranks was a key
issue in this fight. When asked about that relationship, the first,
instinctive response of most working-class diggers is to praise
the AIF as a relatively democratic army. As citizen soldiers in a
volunteer army, they did not feel bound by formal military custom
and were pleased that many Australian officers accepted their
relaxed attitude to drilling and saluting. Pay differentials between

AIF officers and other ranks were less marked than in other Allied armies, and Australian officers' messes tended to be less luxurious than their British counterparts. Working-class soldiers remember that they usually got on well with battalion officers; Ern explains that this reflected the egalitarian Australian practice of treating each man as a cobber, whatever his rank. The diggers hated any unjust use of authority, but these abuses are usually identified with the English officer class. The democratic AIF is contrasted with the 'feudal' British army in which subservient Tommies kowtowed to officious, aristocratic officers. This comparison was often made during the war, and is a familiar part of the Anzac legend.

The Australian stereotype of the British army is misleading. One theme of the British memory of the war is the close and even affectionate bond between frontline officers and other ranks.[42] British veterans of the ranks do recall the class distinction of their officers, but significantly, their anger is primarily directed at staff officers, base shirkers and the military police. These were the enemies of the frontline soldiers of every army, including the Anzacs. But because the AIF was part of the British army and suffered the authority of British generals, training camps and military police, diggers often identified that enemy as British, and not Australian. Tensions between soldiers and authority were experienced and remembered as a national class rivalry (diggers against upper-class English officers), which let Australian officers and government off the hook.

Furthermore, there was still a gulf between officers and other ranks in the AIF, as there is in every army. Officers enjoyed privileges that men in the ranks often envied or resented, such as the services of a batman, higher quality equipment, or a ready supply of whisky or rum. Out of the line the distinction was greater, and officers were exempted from physical work, had fewer leave restrictions, and did not suffer the close surveillance of the military police. Officers were also distinguished by their disciplinary power, and stories of military punishments and prisons, authoritarian officers and indignant, angry men tarnish the democratic image. The Australian volunteers usually accepted the orders of the men who proved themselves to be reliable and careful leaders, and who disregarded strict military status and discipline out of the line. But they hated officers who put on airs or abused their power. Ern remembers that 'a little bit of power goes to anyone's head' and that the AIF officers 'felt they were beyond the ordinary man', so that later in the war 'officers were officers and men were men'.[43] Diggers like Ern sullenly or loudly resented the abuse, and played cruel and humorous pranks at the expense of the offenders. In extreme cases, officers were killed by their own men under the cover of battle.[44] The myth of the diggers points the finger of injustice at English officers; working-class diggers remember that some of their own officers could be just as bad.

More importantly, Australian officers and men usually came from quite different class backgrounds. One of the most powerful themes of the Anzac legend asserts that any capable soldier could rise from the ranks of the AIF, and that officers and other ranks came from the same social and economic background. According to AIF policy, officers were selected from the ranks on the basis of personal merit. Fred cites the *Official History* to confirm his memory that carpenters, plumbers and labourers became officers, contrasted with British army officers, who 'had to have a certain social background'. Yet Stan counters that working-class soldiers could only be promoted to a certain rank. Statistical evidence of the origin and character of the AIF proves that Bean exaggerated the working-class opportunities for promotion.[45] Most Australian soldiers were workers from primary and secondary industry, but the majority of officers came from the commercial and professional classes. The informal workings of the AIF make sense of this disparity. Recruits who were deemed officer material were sent to officer training school. Many of those selected were middle- and upper-class men who had been born and groomed to lead in private school cadet forces. When senior officers promoted soldiers from the ranks, they often applied the same criteria; it was easier to work alongside men with similar accents, customs and beliefs.

Working-class diggers did not necessarily want to become officers. Some, like Ern, did not want the additional responsibility. Others thought that promotion was a betrayal of mates. Railway worker Robert Roper was an Australian soldier in Palestine during the Great War. He recalls that he was told that he would never be promoted:

> Because I was not the right type ... you see as a chap
> [an officer] told me ... he said, 'you know you would never
> take discipline', he said, 'I've got your pedigree. You'd
> never leave your mates.'

> And I said, 'No, and I wouldn't leave them now.' You
> had to be ruthless and leave your mates. There were
> some fellows and they thought the same as me – we were
> mates and we just got the wrong end of the stick. And we
> learned to hate.[46]

Not all diggers hated their officers, but most agreed with Bill Harney, who distinguished the 'common working men' who were his mates in the ranks from the 'heads' who ruled over them.[47] In this memory of the war, officers are not mates and mates cannot be officers; mateship was the solidarity of working men in the ranks. Their egalitarian beliefs told them that they were the equal of their officers, but they also knew that did not make the AIF a democratic army, and they resisted the rule of officers at every opportunity.

CHALLENGING ANZAC

The memories of working-class soldiers debunk the legend of Australians at war. They show how the common experience of all frontline soldiers are more significant than any distinctive national characteristics. Veterans from every army – Turks, Tommies and Diggers – tell stories of resilience and comradeship, of fear and brutality. Old soldiers deserve our sympathy and respect, but selective praise for the Anzacs too easily becomes a patriotic celebration of warriors, war and nation.

Furthermore, while the Anzac legend positions the First World War as a baptism of fire for Australia, after the war these soldiers expressed disillusionment with the entire war effort. 'I had an idea that war and everything connected to it was wrong', explained Fred Farrall.[48] Ern Morton suggested that this view was widespread among soldiers: 'I know that the majority, yes I could say the majority, were opposed to the war.'[49] The four radical diggers discussed went on to read widely about politics and became involved in radical politics in Australia, which consolidated and helped them articulate their anti-war views. Stan D'Altera explained that the war 'broadened my mind', encouraging him to read more widely:

I lost all this idea about a wonderful British Empire.
I studied up a bit and I'd come to the conclusion that it
was an unjust war. It was just for trade. It was to divide
the world between the great powers.[50]

Similarly, Ern explained that after the war he read about its origins, and 'when I read the books I was in that state of mind that I immediately grasped it. It was really a climax to what I was thinking about the war.'[51] They also disagree with the elevation of soldiers to a heroic status in Australia. 'I don't trade on being a soldier. In any way, shape or form', explained Sid Norris. 'I seen afterwards that I should never have been there.'[52] While these radical diggers initially joined returned servicemen's organisations upon return to Australia, they struggled with the increasing conservatism of the movement and opposed the privileging of soldiers above other working-class Australians.[53] As a result, the concept of the radical digger became a contradiction, and many left-wing veterans eventually shed their identity as returned servicemen.[54]

3

A MAN OF DISTINCTION?
THE STRANGE CASE OF PRIVATE NICHOLAS PERMAKOFF

KATE ARIOTTI AND MARTIN CROTTY

The final resting place of Private Nicholas Permakoff, 4th Battalion Australian Imperial Force (AIF), who died on 14 June 1918, is notable only for its ordinariness. His headstone is inscribed with bare details: his name, service number, rank, unit and date of death. There is no epitaph. The cemetery in which his grave lies, Esquelbecq Military Cemetery, is rather unexceptional, on the outskirts of the attractive but similarly unremarkable French town of the same name, with a population now of a little over two thousand. Only two of the 636 graves in the cemetery are AIF burials, so it is not a place of Australian battlefield pilgrimage.[1] The bland headstone and modest setting bear poor witness to one of the AIF's most confounding and distinctive stories.

While no individual soldier completely contradicts the ideals of Anzac, Permakoff surely comes closer than anyone else accepted for service in the AIF. The 27-year-old Russian was working as a miner when he enlisted in Sydney in early May 1916. Two years later he was disgraced, dishonoured and dead: shot by his own unit for allegedly deserting to the enemy. This chapter traces Permakoff's journey, from his enlistment to his ultimate 'forgetting' by the nation, revealing how, at almost every step in his military career, Permakoff represented a departure from Anzac ideals, stereotypes and norms.

ENLISTMENT

Unlike most men of the AIF, Permakoff was neither Australian-born, nor of British heritage. He was born in Russia and thus belonged to one of the ethnic minorities – German, Jewish, Chinese, Russian and Indigenous – within the Australian forces of the First World War that have drawn the attention of historians in recent decades.[2] Little is known of Permakoff's life before enlistment. His attestation papers reveal only that he was born in Archangel in 1889, was single, and that he claimed to have two years of service in the Russian Army as an artilleryman between 1909 and 1911.[3]

Permakoff was one of a relatively substantial contingent of Russians in the AIF. There were 3413 men of Russian nationality in Australia at the time of the 1911 census, the last undertaken before the declaration of war in 1914; of these 969 enlisted in the AIF and 762 saw active service overseas.[4] Elena Govor, author of *Russian Anzacs*, quotes men at the time claiming that 'there is hardly a single Australian unit without a few Russian volunteers in it'.[5]

The Russians' status as volunteers is, however, questionable. As part of the Russian imperial government's mobilisation of its forces, Russian men of military age living abroad were directed to either return to Russia and enlist, or join the armies of one of the Allied nations.[6] From late 1915, the Melbourne-based Russian Consul-General in Australia, Alexander Abaza, was in constant contact with the Ministry of Defence, providing circulars to recruitment depots asking for lists of Russians who had enlisted, or attempted to enlist, in the AIF.[7] Abaza's deputies in Adelaide and Sydney placed notices in state newspapers publicising their government's insistence that Russian subjects enlist so that 'after the war it may not be said that the Russian residents outside of their own country did not take part in the fighting line'.[8] Some industries – including, importantly for Permakoff's story, the mining sector – effectively told their Russian employees to enlist or provide evidence they had attempted to. In what Govor argues was an attempt to compel their enlistment, Russians in Australia between the ages of 18 and 50 were temporarily denied naturalisation.[9] This also rendered them ineligible for several basic citizenship rights and, as Govor states, 'foster[ed] increased suspicion of them as non-naturalised aliens'.[10] Indeed, from 1916, official government agencies were monitoring the correspondence of Russians in Australia.[11] The combined effect of Russian diplomatic directives and Australian government and industry actions was, as Raymond Evans writes, the virtual imposition of military service on Russians in Australia.[12]

Permakoff duly presented at a recruitment centre in the Sydney Showgrounds in May 1916. He carried with him a Consular Consent form proving his nationality and intention to enlist. This form, bearing the official stamp of the Russian Consulate and stating 'the bearer … a Russian subject, is a Reservist of the Russian Imperial Army and has to join the Australian Expeditionary Forces owing to his inability to return to Russia', is still in his service record held in the National Archives of Australia. It appears that Permakoff enlisted on the understanding that he would eventually join the Russian forces. This seems to have been an inducement that Abaza proffered to other Russian recruits, as several who later requested a transfer or discharge from the AIF cited in their claims Abaza's assurances they would end up among their countrymen.[13] In some cases transfers were approved; several Russian 'specialists' were released from the AIF to work on the purchase of war materiel for the Russian government in London, and in May 1917 one soldier in France was permitted to transfer from the AIF to the Russian forces (though he ultimately remained with the Australians).[14] Permakoff's efforts to escape the AIF were much more drastic, and proved much less fruitful.

DISCIPLINARY RECORD

Permakoff commenced his service in Dubbo in a Depot Battalion before being transferred in June 1916 to the Liverpool-based 2nd Battalion. Only two months later he was sent to Milson Island on the Hawkesbury River, an isolated location used as a treatment hospital for servicemen afflicted with venereal disease (VD). After a two-month stint in the hospital, Permakoff was transferred back to Liverpool and the 2nd Battalion. He was then briefly posted to a Field Artillery Regiment, but was soon transferred back to an infantry battalion, this time the 36th. In November, Permakoff was charged with twice disobeying orders and was punished with two days of confinement to barracks. In December 1916, once again suffering from VD, Permakoff returned to Milson Island. The papers outlining his transfer from Darlinghurst Detention Barracks to the island were addended with a message from the officer in charge at Darlinghurst: 'this man will probably ask to be paraded to the Russian Consul. The Consul however refuses to see him. It would be advisable to keep a good watch on him.'[15] There was no further elaboration of this intriguing statement, but it would suggest that Permakoff had attempted to see the Consul regarding his service and that the Sydney military authorities were already dubious about his suitability for the AIF.

Permakoff remained on Milson Island until 14 February 1917. In May he boarded a troopship bound for England as part of a draft of reinforcement troops for the 4th Battalion. After some time in the UK, Permakoff proceeded to France, where he immediately fell foul of the military authorities. Upon arriving in Le Havre in mid-November, Permakoff was told by a non-commissioned officer (NCO) to pick up his pack in preparation for a march to another camp. He replied: 'I don't want any fucking pack.' When the order was repeated by an officer, Lieutenant Gordon, Permakoff stated: 'Fuck you, I don't want any fucking pack' (another soldier later claimed he had said 'Fuck you and the pack too'). Permakoff was then arrested and charged with disobeying a lawful command and using insubordinate language towards a superior officer.[16]

A few days later, a Field General Court Martial assembled to try Permakoff's case. Witnesses recalled Permakoff's colourful reaction to the command to shoulder his pack. He declined to cross-examine anyone, simply stating that he did not speak English very well – despite revealing in his profane responses to Lieutenant Gordon's orders that he had picked up at least some of the vernacular of the Australian mining towns he had inhabited – and reiterating the claim of other Russian soldiers that he had been told he would be transferred to the Russian forces when he arrived in England. Permakoff was found guilty of the first charge but not guilty of the second, and was sentenced to six months imprisonment with hard labour at the British-run Number 3 Military Prison in Le Havre.[17] He left the prison in late May 1918 at the end of his sentence, and several days later was taken onto the strength of the 4th Battalion. Just over two years after his enlistment, Permakoff was finally in the trenches of the Western Front. It had been a long journey on the part of the military authorities to get Permakoff where they wanted him. His stay was to prove short-lived.

DESERTION AND DEATH

As part of the 1st Australian Division, the 4th Battalion started to participate in actions in the Somme Valley to blunt the German 'Spring Offensive' of March 1918. But in April it returned to Flanders to contain another German attack, towards Hazebrouck. By June, when Permakoff arrived, the division controlled the front line to the west of Hazebrouck in the Ypres sector. The 4th Battalion was along this line in an area known as Rouge Croix, and was occupied with so-called 'peaceful penetration', the stealthy patrolling of no man's land and raiding of enemy trenches to capture prisoners and supplies.[18]

The battalion's B Company 8th Platoon soldiers were likely wary of their new comrade. Aside from the fact that he arrived straight from military prison, anti-Russian sentiment in the AIF had increased after the 1917 October Revolution and the subsequent withdrawal of Russian forces from the war. By the time Russia and Germany signed the separate peace treaty, the Treaty of Brest-Litovsk in March 1918, Russian Anzacs were, according to Govor, 'in a particularly vulnerable position'.[19] Those who requested discharge on the grounds that Russia was no longer a belligerent were accused of disloyalty, and some of being spies.[20] Several reported mistreatment and aggression at the hands of their Australian comrades. One Russian soldier, Peter Chervin, took his own life on a troopship returning to Australia in 1919; just prior to his death, he told superior officers that he had long been subjected to 'a lot of ragging about his Russian parentage' and that he had been constantly referred to as 'Bolshie'.[21]

Permakoff thus joined his unit already an outsider, a friendless man in a force he never intended being part of, fighting at the behest of a tsarist regime that no longer existed. The details of his brief and unhappy time with the 4th Battalion are evident from the court of enquiry held following his death. He made an early and unfavourable impression by refusing to take ammunition from Sergeant Alfred Osmond, telling him, 'I will not shoot'. On that occasion, Osmond forced Permakoff to put 170 rounds in his pouches. A few nights later, on 12 June, Osmond warned Permakoff to be ready to move forward to the front line. Once more, Permakoff replied, 'I won't shoot, I won't do anything.'[22] This behaviour, as well as reportedly asking about troop dispositions and the location of the German lines, aroused the suspicions of his fellow soldiers. Osmond reported his misgivings about Permakoff to his platoon commander, Lieutenant Norman Grant. In turn, Grant spoke to Permakoff, who allegedly told him that he would not shoot at any Germans as his father was German. Grant told his platoon NCOs to keep a close watch on Permakoff and, after his troops had moved into the front line, he reported the incident to his commanding officer, Captain William Estall. In an instruction that left little room for ambiguity, Estall told Grant to 'shoot him [Permakoff] if he showed any sign of treachery'.[23]

About 3pm on 13 June, sentries manning No. 5 Post saw a man on their left start to walk towards the enemy lines. Private Bruce asked his comrade, Private Dunlop, if the man was Permakoff. Dunlop recognised him and shouted for him to stop but Permakoff, who was about 20 yards (18 metres) beyond the 4th Battalion lines and who was not holding a rifle or any equipment, reportedly 'increased his pace'. Lieutenant Grant then ordered Bruce to fire on Permakoff; and when Bruce missed, ordered a sentry at another post, Lance Corporal Norman, to shoot. Norman hit Permakoff in the right hip and Permakoff fell to the ground, though Grant stated that he kept crawling towards enemy lines. Grant and a Corporal Warren went out of their lines to retrieve Permakoff. He had travelled, according to Grant, some 100 yards (91 metres).[24]

Permakoff was escorted to the 3rd Australian Casualty Clearing Station, at Esquelbecq, where he was admitted with a gunshot wound to the right hip, which had penetrated his abdomen. He died the next day.[25] A 'Report on accidental or self-inflicted injuries' signed by the Commanding Officer of the 4th Battalion, Lieutenant Colonel Cecil Sasse, and Commander of the 1st Australian Brigade, Brigadier General Iven Mackay, was completed in the days after Permakoff's death. Mackay wrote, 'My opinion is that the man who shot Pte Permakoff should be commended for doing his duty.'[26] The Court of Enquiry ultimately declared that 'having cast aside his arms, and in the act of deserting to the enemy, [Permakoff] was deliberately shot by … L/Cpl Norman W. 4th Battalion AIF being in the execution of his duty'.[27]

The use of the term 'execution' is ironic. Under the provisions of the *British Army Act* of 1881, British soldiers could be executed for a number of offences, including desertion. Desertion was defined as leaving the front lines without permission, refusing to enter the front lines when ordered to do so, or being otherwise absent for such a period, or undertaking such activities while absent, that indicated an intention of not returning.[28] It was for such desertion that the great majority of the British soldiers executed in the First World War were condemned. According to War Office figures published in 1922, the British Army as a whole (including overseas contingents and colonial troops) sentenced 3080 men to death for various crimes and carried out 346 of those sentences. Of those, 266 were for desertion, and many of the remainder were for similar offences, such as cowardice and quitting one's post.[29] Colonial troops were not exempt: five New Zealanders and 25 Canadians were among those executed.[30]

However, Australian soldiers could not be executed for desertion under the terms of the 1903/1909 *Defence Act*, which restricted the application of the death penalty to instances of mutiny, desertion to the enemy, or traitorous conduct in, for example, delivering up a post or supplying information to the enemy.[31] In not carrying out death sentences for desertion, Australia was an outlier. Despite the entreaties of Field Marshal Douglas Haig, Commander of the British Expeditionary Force on the Western Front, and various senior AIF commanders, the Australian government stood firm in insisting that Australian deserters could not be executed.[32] Over 100 Australian soldiers were court-martialled and sentenced to death for desertion, but all sentences were commuted, usually to a substantial term of imprisonment, which was then often suspended in part or whole. It is yet another oddity in Permakoff's story, then, that while some Australian deserters were sentenced to death but not executed, Permakoff was neither court-martialled nor sentenced, but was executed. In a force that did not, distinctively among British Empire armies, shoot and kill its own, Permakoff was shot and killed by his own.

ATTEMPTS TO CONTACT NEXT OF KIN

In 1919, the Public Trust Office wrote to AIF Base Records in Melbourne asking for copies of Permakoff's death certificate and details of his next of kin. This information was required to authorise the Public Trustee to pass on Permakoff's estate, a sum of nearly £59, or approximately $5700 in today's money.[33] His estate would not include any medals, war gratuity or pension for family members because his disciplinary record, particularly his period of detention after the November 1917 Court of Enquiry, rendered him ineligible for these tangible markers of war service.[34] Permakoff had left only vague details for his next of kin: his mother, 'Mrs Permakoff', care of the Imperial Russian Consul in Sydney. Such limited information about next of kin was common among foreign-born soldiers in the AIF and caused significant issues – and heartache – for many families after the war.[35]

In February 1921, the Officer in Charge of Base Records, Major James Lean, sent the standard three photographs of Permakoff's grave to his mother, duly if rather hopefully addressed to 'Mrs Permakoff, Archangel, Russia'. This letter was returned to Base Records several months later by the Dead Letter Office, stamped 'service suspended'. It is not surprising that postal service to Archangel had been suspended, and that the letter and photographs of Permakoff's grave never reached his mother. From 1918 to 1920, the north Russian port city of Archangel – at which a large amount of Allied war materiel was located – was the site of serious fighting between Allied forces and the new Soviet Army. After being ground down by a series of Bolshevik attacks, White Russian troop mutinies and challenging climatic conditions, the last Allied troops left the city in September 1919. A Bolshevik offensive launched in December of that year defeated the White Russians who remained, and the city was left in disarray. White Russian refugees tried to flee, transport stopped running, food was scarce and looting broke out.[36] Nevertheless, the Public Trustee's Office did not give up trying to locate Mrs Permakoff. They sent another letter in June 1926, but the lack of further correspondence in Permakoff's records indicates they never heard back.

COMMEMORATION

Eligibility for commemoration on war memorials and rolls of honour has always been, perhaps counterintuitively, difficult and contentious. What of those who did not see active service, even though they had volunteered? What of those who died of non-war related causes while on active service? Or those who died afterwards, with the connection between their service and their demise being distant or difficult to prove? And what, most pertinently in Permakoff's case, of those who died in dishonourable circumstances?

The Australian approach has usually been to adopt an inclusive attitude, but different parties have drawn their own demarcation lines between those who are worthy of commemoration and those who are not. Many war memorial committees in Australia chose to include the names of all who served rather than only those who died, as distinct from the usual British and New Zealand practices, because in a country that did not have conscription for overseas service, the act of enlisting deserved to be acknowledged, even without the sacrifice of life. Some war memorials even listed the names of rejected volunteers. They had, at least, tried to serve and were considered to belong with the men who had volunteered, rather than with the 'slackers and shirkers' who had not.[37] The Returned Sailors' and Soldiers' Imperial League of Australia allowed all who had embarked for service overseas to become members, but not those men of the military forces who were denied the opportunity to serve overseas because they were needed in Australia. Even then, there were informal distinctions among members, with occasional barbs at 'Horseferry Road Anzacs' or 'Auckland Anzacs', referring to those who served in administrative positions in the United Kingdom or who did not even complete the journey to Europe.[38] The Department of Repatriation, later Veterans' Affairs, has also had its own shifting definitions and thresholds for eligibility for various benefits.[39] Distinctions between service and non-service have thus always been blurry and contested.

Death on service did not necessarily clarify matters and presented different authorities with dilemmas to which they devised varying solutions. The British War Office traditionally adopted a 'maximal' attitude, focusing not on how a person died, but only on when. Administratively convenient though this might have been, it meant that state memorialisation could be accorded to men with ignominious records, and even those who were executed for military or civil crimes. This occasionally caused controversy later as some felt the honourable were sullied by the presence of the dishonourable.[40] American authorities after the Second World War, for example, keen to distinguish the honourable fallen from those they regarded as suspect, adopted the expedient of establishing a 'dishonoured' plot, known as 'Plot E', at the Oise-Aisne American Cemetery in France. This plot included those who were executed for the crimes of rape and murder, and the sole US servicemen, Eddie Slovik, executed for desertion during the Second World War. The great majority of the soldiers buried there are Black, and they are spatially and symbolically separated from their purportedly more honourable – and mainly white – counterparts.[41]

Permakoff was, as we have seen, given a standard Imperial War Graves Commission grave and headstone in Esquelbecq Military Cemetery, close to the casualty clearing station where he died. However, he was not included on perhaps the most 'sacred' of Australian commemorative records, the Australian War Memorial's Roll of Honour. He is one of just four Australian dead of the First World War to be excluded. In memorialisation and commemoration, therefore, he is again an outlier – *in* but not *of.*

The decision to establish a Roll of Honour at the Australian War Memorial (AWM) dates to July 1919, although it was not commenced until 1927. The project was then delayed until the 1950s by the need for Cabinet approval, the slow construction of the memorial, difficulties in sorting out records, and the need to incorporate the dead of the Second World War, albeit in a separate roll.[42] Deciding on eligibility for the Roll was no easy task. There was, for example, the matter of dates of death. The cessation of hostilities in 1918 might seem an obvious end point but it excluded those who died shortly thereafter from war-related causes, or from events such as the Spanish influenza pandemic. Ultimately, in November 1955, the AWM Board of Management decided that the Roll should include all who died before discharge up to 1 April 1921 (and 30 June 1947 for the Second World War).[43] Practical considerations meant that earlier intentions to include members of the Mercantile Marine and those who died in other British Empire forces, and an original intention to list the dead according to the towns and cities they came from rather than the unit to which they belonged, had to be abandoned.[44] In the end, therefore, pragmatism decided much about the Roll of Honour. While the British War Office had a comprehensive list of British war dead from the armed services, including Australians, there were no equivalent lists for members of the Merchant Marine, or those who died after discharge as a result of war wounds.[45] Death between enlistment and discharge during the period of the conflict and its immediate aftermath became the principal criterion for inclusion.

It was the circumstances of a serviceman's death that provoked most debate, and which saw Permakoff excluded.

When the Roll of Honour was first discussed in detail and tentatively designed in the mid- to late 1920s, the criteria for inclusion had a significant behavioural element. On 15 March 1928, the AWM Board decided that the Roll would include all whose deaths resulted from any occurrence during their period of service, as long as those deaths did not result from intentionally self-inflicted injuries and did not arise from or occur during the commission of a breach of discipline.[46] By the mid-1950s, the Board appears to have been more liberal in its attitudes, and in 1955 it appointed a committee to consider the inclusion of those whose deaths were connected to or resulted from self-inflicted injuries or breaches of discipline, as well as a further five doubtful cases: three men who had been hanged for murder after civil trials, one who was an honorary member of the AIF, and Permakoff.[47]

The list of categories supplied to the committee shows the Board understood that many Australian soldiers' deaths in wartime could be considered less than honourable or had occurred before they had rendered any substantial service. They included 94 men who died by suicide and self-inflicted wounds, ten who died in prison while serving sentences for desertion, six who died of illness while absent without leave, eight who died attempting to escape legal custody, eight shot by guards during riots in camp, three hanged for committing murder, eight killed in murders or manslaughter incidents, one who was shot while deserting to the enemy, and one who was given honorary rank in the forces that occupied Rabaul. The committee adopted an inclusive position and recommended that all be included in the Roll of Honour, with the exception of the honorary appointment as he was never a properly attested member of the armed forces, and 'the one who was shot while attempting to desert to the enemy after having cast aside his arms and equipment'.[48] They thus removed most of the exclusions of the earlier 1928 policy.

The committee's recommendations were accepted by the Board, although General Sir Edmund Herring questioned the inclusion of the three men hanged for murder. The committee argued that these three men had committed civil crimes, not military ones, and that they might have had exemplary military careers up to that point. As a rule, then, executed murderers, fraudsters, deserters, brawlers, self-harmers and others who lost their lives were accepted as eligible, but Permakoff was not.[49] The three executed murderers were eventually excluded on the basis that their deaths had nothing to do with their war service but were the result of civil crimes.[50] Before the final decision was made, a committee of the Board had investigated whether the next of kin had been notified about the circumstances of each man's death, and the quality of their services rendered prior to their deaths.[51] No such inquiries appear to have been made in Permakoff's case.

That the committee was initially inclined to include murderers on the Roll of Honour but not Permakoff, that they displayed an interest in their prior service records and their next of kin that they did not extend to Permakoff, and that they allowed many men to remain on the Roll of Honour despite lamentable service records and dishonourable deaths, can be explained on two principal grounds, neither of which necessarily reflect natural justice or equity to modern sensibilities. The first is that Permakoff was not just a deserter but, uniquely in the British Army of the First World War, was deserting to the enemy, a significantly worse military crime – akin to treason – than mere desertion. As mentioned, the *Defence Act* allowed execution for desertion to the enemy.[52] The second more speculative possibility is that as an 'alien', Permakoff attracted less sympathy. Indeed, in the mid-1950s the Cold War was at a peak of intensity; Permakoff hailed from what was then effectively an enemy nation.

Permakoff's omission from the Roll of Honour at the AWM is consistent with the New Zealand decision to omit soldiers executed for military crimes from its Roll of Honour, printed in book form in 1924. It also accords with the Canadian decision to exclude such soldiers from its *First World War Book of Remembrance*, dedicated in 1942.[53] The United Kingdom, the other obvious comparator, does not have a national Roll of Honour. Yet, in some regards, the exclusion does Permakoff an injustice, and it is hard not to feel at least some sympathy for him. It appears that he did not wish to fight with the AIF and only enlisted when instructed by Russian authorities. Through his own misdeeds, he was on the receiving end of extensive disciplinary sanctions. He was most likely regarded as something of an outsider by his comrades and his superiors on account of his nationality and his foreign-sounding name. He was forced into the front lines when there would have been ample opportunity to keep him occupied in the rear. And although he was excluded because of having committed a 'dishonourable military action', the list of 'doubtful cases' supplied to the committee that considered eligibility for commemoration on the Roll of Honour make it clear that he was in good company. And yet Permakoff alone was denied a listing. Although this can be justified on the grounds of the treasonous nature of attempting to desert to the enemy, had the men responsible for his exclusion enquired more closely into his experiences (there is no evidence that they did) or had they not been considering his case at a time of considerable anti-Russian and anti-Soviet feeling given the Cold War environment, they might just have seen him as a victim deserving of the same consideration and commemoration given to men who deserted to the rear areas, feigned illness or inflicted wounds upon themselves in similar quests to avoid fighting. When Permakoff left the Australian trenches and started towards the enemy's, it was only one in a chain of decisions that left him dead, disgraced and dishonoured.

A final irony is that if Australia had routinely executed deserters in the First World War, Permakoff may have had his reputation restored. After lengthy campaigns led by descendants of the five executed New Zealand soldiers, the *Pardon for Soldiers of the Great War Act*, which specifically sought to 'remove … the dishonour that the execution … brought to those soldiers and their families' passed New Zealand's parliament in 2000.[54] In Britain, Ireland and Canada there have also been large-scale public campaigns to appropriately (re)remember those sentenced to death for crimes such as desertion and cowardice. In 2001 the Shot at Dawn memorial was dedicated in the National Memorial Arboretum in Staffordshire, England. The evocative memorial features an 8-foot-tall sculpture of a blindfolded soldier, hands tied behind his back, wearing an aiming disc around his neck. Six conifers, representing the firing squad, were planted in front of the sculpture and 306 stakes, symbolising each British Empire soldier executed for military crimes, were placed behind. The memorial was unveiled by the 87-year-old daughter of one of those sentenced to death. In the same year, the Canadian government approved the addition of the names of Canadian soldiers shot for desertion to their national *Book of Remembrance* as one of the outcomes from the campaign to have them pardoned.[55] In 2004, after petitioning by the Shot at Dawn (Ireland) Campaign, the Irish government submitted a formal request to the British government to re-evaluate the death sentences handed down to

26 Irish soldiers.[56] Despite some protest, section 359 of the United Kingdom's 2006 *Armed Forces Act* symbolically pardoned over 300 soldiers of the British Empire forces who had been executed for various military offences during the war.[57] Permakoff, having been shot in the field rather than executed through the military justice system, was yet again the exception.

ANZAC EXCEPTIONALISM

Permakoff was not the only Russian in the AIF. He was not the only foreigner who found it difficult to fit in. He was one of many to contract venereal disease, one of thousands who were court-martialled, and one of a great many who developed long records of poor discipline.[58] He is one of over 60 000 AIF dead from the First World War, one of approximately 40 000 buried in an overseas military cemetery, and one of many whose next of kin could not be contacted for notification of his death, return of his effects and distribution of his assets. In none of these features of his war service is Permakoff particularly distinctive. In their combination, however, Permakoff challenges both the norms and the stereotypes of Anzac. He was forced to enlist and, before he even made it to the Western Front, had made it clear through his words and actions that he did not wish to remain in the AIF, let alone serve in the front lines. Mateship, courage, valour and discipline in the lines (if not out of them) are seen as hallmarks of the Anzac. There is little evidence of any of these qualities in Permakoff's service. But what really sets Permakoff apart, and makes him distinctive rather than merely unusual, are the circumstances of his death. Australian deserters were typically court-martialled but, even if sentenced to death, not executed. Because Permakoff deserted towards the enemy he was not arrested and tried, but was effectively executed on the battlefield. Such was the disgrace and dishonour attached to his actions, and unease about the circumstances of his death, that Permakoff was omitted from the Australian War Memorial's Roll of Honour. He is the only member of the AIF who died on the battlefield to be excluded. The institution devoted to remembering and honouring Australia's war dead has decided that Permakoff is best forgotten. It is this very exceptionalism, however, that draws the eye of the historian.

4

'THAT ABORTIVE ORGANISATION KNOWN AS THE IMPERIAL LEAGUE'

DIVISION AMONG RETURNED SOLDIER ORGANISATIONS IN WESTERN AUSTRALIA AFTER THE FIRST WORLD WAR

BOBBIE OLIVER

For much of the 20th century the word 'Anzac' was intimately associated with the Returned and Services League (RSL). This organisation, created in 1916 under the name Returned Sailors' and Soldiers' Imperial League of Australia (RSSILA), emerged from the First World War as the dominant organisation representing returned soldiers. It claimed, at least in its early days, to be apolitical, but it progressively became more conservative and deeply anti-communist. It also championed a representation of the Australian soldier that accorded with the celebratory Anzac legend. The publication of anti-war novels in the late 1920s, such the German Eric Maria Remarque's *All Quiet on the Western Front* and the British Robert Graves' *Goodbye to All That*, provoked the federal

An earlier version of portions of this chapter appeared in the *Journal of the Australian War Memorial*, no. 23, 1993. I thank the Australian War Memorial for permission to republish this material. I also thank Joan Beaumont and Martin Crotty for their helpful comments in the drafting of this chapter.

executive of RSSILA to pass a resolution that the Minister of Customs should 'prohibit war books which defamed the soldiers of the Empire'.[1] The organisation's numbers swelled with the Second World War, but by the 1960s its leadership came under attack for its martial nationalist ideology and opposition to feminists, communists, homosexuals and non-white immigrants.[2] In the decades that followed, the RSL's influence declined as Australia became a more diverse and multicultural society and memory of the world wars faded. But the RSL remained 'a fixture in the Australian military and civilian landscape' with sub-branches in most towns and suburbs.[3]

However, it was not always assumed that the RSSILA spoke for all returned servicemen. During and immediately after the First World War, a plethora of organisations fought to represent the interests of the returned soldiers, and the RSSILA itself was fractured.[4] While it soon emerged as the dominant lobby group, and during the Great Depression successfully championed the rights of returned soldiers to maintain preferential access to government employment and their pensions at full value, informal radical groupings of returned soldiers also sprang up to lobby local councils on behalf of the unemployed and those evicted from their homes.[5] The landscape of early returned soldiers' politics was thus more turbulent and unsettled than the later history of the RSL would suggest.

In the period immediately following the First World War, a group of Western Australian returned soldiers, who espoused socialist rhetoric and whose sympathies lay with the labour movement, objected to the conservative politics of the RSSILA. They accused the association of siding with the capitalist class and directed violence against non-union labour that had taken their places in the workforce while they were serving overseas.

Ultimately, the alternative veteran organisations did not survive. But the radical voices of Anzacs who challenged an emerging conservative dominance should not be lost a century later. These events in Western Australia require us to qualify Martin Crotty's assertion that the RSSILA 'was never seriously challenged as the legitimate voice of the veteran community'.[6]

A VIOLENT HOMECOMING

On the morning of Sunday, 4 May 1919, all was quiet in Fremantle Harbour. On the troopship SS *Khyber*, moored opposite F Shed, 1465 men of the Australian Imperial Force (AIF), including 214 Western Australians, waited impatiently to land.[7] Then all hell broke loose on the wharf. The 'Bloody Sunday' wharf riot, when the Fremantle Lumpers Union (later known as the Waterside Workers Federation) fought and defeated rival 'scab' unionists for control of the wharf, had begun. Soldiers on board the *Khyber* signalled to the shore, and Mick Donnes, the president of the South Fremantle branch of the Returned Soldiers' and Sailors' Association, Western Australia (RSA), rowed out to the ship. According to his later account, the soldiers told him, 'If you want us, we will get out the boats and come'. However, Donnes told the soldiers not to come ashore as the ship was flying a yellow quarantine flag, and they might endanger the population by spreading influenza.[8]

There are many accounts of violence by returned soldiers, including breaking up anti-conscription meetings on the Perth Esplanade in 1916 and 1917; acting as special constables to quell labour strikes in the Eastern Goldfields of Western Australia; and attacking groups in Queensland who were perceived to be 'Bolsheviks'.[9] This violence revealed what John Horne has called, in relation to France, the problems of 'cultural demobilisation' or 'demobilisation of the mind' after the violence of war, but the returning men also had practical grievances.[10] Federal and state governments were confronting huge challenges in dealing with the enormous influx of temporarily or permanently disabled men. It was hoped that disabled ex-servicemen could be cared for either by their families or by charities such as the Ugly Men's Association, a group of Perth businessmen who raised money, established an employment bureau and distributed relief funds. But the need was so great that government intervention on an unprecedented scale was clearly required. Inevitably, in some cases, the response of the Commonwealth Department of Repatriation was thought to be inadequate, even inhumane.[11]

Meanwhile, returning soldiers struggled to find employment, since the Nationalist Prime Minister W.M. 'Billy' Hughes had responded to a wave of strikes in 1917 by creating so-called 'nationalist unions' to work in competition with wharfies and miners. These 'unions', whose members the labour movement regarded as 'scabs', still existed at the end of the war.

WHO SHOULD SPEAK FOR THE RETURNED SOLDIERS?

The controversy over who had the right to represent returned soldiers in Western Australia arose in this turbulent context. For a period in 1919 and 1920, some returned men seriously challenged the RSSILA's right to speak on their behalf. Notably, two returned soldiers, Edwin 'Ted' Corboy and Joseph Napoleon O'Neill, opposed the direction of the national soldiers' organisation. Victorian-born Corboy arrived in Western Australia and worked as a clerk until he joined the AIF in 1915. He served with the

28th Battalion at Gallipoli and then with the 70th Battalion at Pozières and Flers in France. Twice wounded, he was invalided back to Australia. In 1918, aged only 22 years, he was elected in a by-election as Labor member for the seat of Swan. Defeated in the 1919 federal election, Corby entered state politics as the member for Yilgarn in 1921, and served until 1933.[12]

O'Neill, also originally from Victoria, was working in a Bunbury timber mill in the state's south-west when the First World War began. He enlisted in 1915, aged nearly 40, and served with the 44th Infantry Battalion on the Western Front in 1916 and 1917.[13] Perhaps his war service radicalised O'Neill, for by May 1919 he was espousing socialist views about soldiers being used as 'the tools of Capitalism' and 'the nasty Tory'.[14]

The battle over representation of returned soldiers began during the war. In May 1916, some disgruntled Western Australian veterans from a number of military units formed the Returned Soldiers' and Sailors' Association (RSA). This was only a month before the RSSILA was founded as a national organisation in Sydney. Both organisations aimed to protect and advance the interests of returned men, but Western Australia was the last state to affiliate with the national league. The path to a consolidated RSSILA, however, was hardly smooth. In March 1918, another Western Australian returned soldiers' organisation formed, calling itself the Western Australian branch of the RSSILA (RSSILWA). The reason for the split appears to have been dissatisfaction with the RSA's reluctance to affiliate with the national association, and a disagreement over allocation of land to returned soldiers in an area known as the Riverton Estate.[15]

The new body quickly applied to affiliate with the RSSILA and was accepted at the congress in Hobart. It then proceeded to form branches in Fremantle, the country town of Tambellup in

Western Australia's south-west and elsewhere. Meanwhile, the RSA, attempting to start a branch in Collie in Western Australia, was rebuffed and told that the local returned men had formed their own association. They preferred to wait until it was decided whether the RSA and the RSSILWA would amalgamate before linking up with either organisation.[16]

However, Corboy, who was a Western Australian delegate to the next national congress in Adelaide in 1919, insisted that the RSSILWA was not the state's 'senior Association' representing ex-service personnel. The RSA, known colloquially as the 'Digger's Association', had that status, he claimed. The RSSILA president, Gilbert Dyett, then overturned the Hobart congress's decision and refused to grant affiliation to Western Australia until the RSA and the RSSILWA amalgamated, which they did in September 1919, taking the title of the latter, although there was an unsuccessful motion to drop the word 'Imperial' from the title.[17] Others favoured a completely separate body, affiliated with the Australian Labor Party (ALP).

Meanwhile on 5 January 1919, some RSA members had formed a Heresy Committee, which Joseph O'Neill chaired. This committee resolved to hold a mass meeting, after the RSA president refused to call one. It claimed that 'it was for members to choose between the officers of the [RSA] and a few "dinkum diggers" who were working to get a fair deal for their comrades'. Alex Panton, later a Labor member of the Legislative Council, chaired the meeting. He said that it was useless to pass resolutions. The members should decide whether 'they were content with the association which was an organisation for the assistance of returned soldiers in name only' or whether they should form 'an organisation which would do real work for members'. Panton claimed that no proper repatriation system had been established, and that the returned soldier's position was little better than it had been after the Crimean (1853–56) or South African (1899–1901) wars. This, he asserted, was either because of incompetence or because the government wanted to flood the labour market with returned men and drive down wages. ALP Senator Edward Needham said that returned soldiers wanted jobs, not charity; they should march on Parliament House and demand their rights. He moved that: 'This meeting of returned soldiers emphatically protests against the non-fulfillment of the promise made to the soldiers by the federal and state governments'. O'Neill seconded the motion. An amendment that 'returned soldiers should march to Parliament House and demand that their representatives be heard at the Bar of the House' was passed unanimously. A resolution demanding that state and federal governments work with employers to place all unemployed returned soldiers was also passed unanimously.[18]

O'Neill moved a further motion that 'all official positions should be held by men who have not held commissioned rank' (that is, those who were not officers). After much discussion, the motion was carried by a large majority – but, significantly, not unanimously. This indicates a strong belief within the association that officers who were elected to executive positions did not serve the needs of the rank-and-file soldiers. A further motion declaring that the federal Minister for Defence, Senator George Pearce, was 'totally unfit to deal with demobilisation matters and calling on the federal government to recall him' was passed unanimously.[19]

The Heresy Committee blamed the federal and state governments, the RSSILA's executive council and the RSA's state committee for the lack of employment for returned soldiers. At a further meeting on 8 January 1919, members accused the state government of having 'failed palpably, especially in providing land for our returned soldiers' and employers had also failed to 'make good promises that were made to departing troops'. They accused employers of exploiting soldiers' wives and children and asserted that the current situation could have been avoided if the executive of the RSSILA and the various state executives had acted to bring governments and employers together to fulfill their responsibilities toward returned soldiers. Not everyone agreed with the anti-officer sentiment. W.J. Henderson asked if the branch was to be run by 'mob rule'. Mr Gadson said that if the branch didn't want officers in the executive, they should bring a motion to the conference and, if it were passed, return the officers' membership subscriptions.[20] The Heresy Committee did not succeed in banning officers from the executive; it seems to have ceased functioning soon after.

In April 1919, Senator Edward Millen, the Nationalist Minister for Repatriation, addressed a meeting of returned soldiers in Perth, where some of the audience reportedly 'caused a disturbance'. Afterwards, the president of the RSA's East Perth branch, T. Gorman, and O'Neill were summoned to appear before the RSA executive and 'show cause why they should not be expelled from the association on a charge of having conducted themselves in a manner unbecoming to gentlemen and subversive to the objects of the association'. O'Neill was accused of using 'threatening and abusive language' and of saying that he would set up a rival returned soldiers' organisation. The executive referred the matter to a tribunal consisting of two of its members and two appointed by Gorman and O'Neill, with 'a prominent legal advocate as chair'.[21] The tribunal met on 17 April and decided that the charges were 'unfounded', but the East Perth branch resented interference from the executive.[22]

O'Neill wrote to Alex McCallum, the ALP state secretary, complaining of the 'damnably unsatisfactory' situation that existed for returned soldiers in Western Australia, and stating that they bore 'many grievances' that they wanted to make public:

> The Soldier must no longer be used as the tools of Capitalism & the nasty Tory who has so long bled him together with the toiler to his heart's content. There is no doubt that the Capitalists are still striving by devious means & deceitful practices to hold tight to the Army for obvious reasons, & the democratic section of the people through its leaders would act wisely if they took time by the forelock & got in first. The Soldiers are waiting for a lead. They are waiting for a guide. They are in No Man's Land & it would be calamitous to the democratic movement to abandon them to the enemy. It would be heinous; it would be a monsterous [sic] crime. Let us get together & strafe the common foe. Our interests are identical although our enemies would have the Boys believe otherwise, but you of the democracy must move in another direction, & counteract the evil dope so skilfully administered to the men of the AIF by the piratical crowd who used them so long & who would now abandon them to any old fate pending further necessity of their services.[23]

The language is unambiguous. O'Neill was calling for the ALP to lead a soldiers' revolt to overthrow the conservative state government.

To progress his agenda, O'Neill called a returned soldiers' meeting for 4 May on the Perth Esplanade, where a series of resolutions would be put and a committee formed to carry them out. But events took a dramatic turn. The returned soldiers' meeting was scheduled for the day that the wharf riot, described earlier, occurred. Consequently, it did not take place, although the *West Australian* reported a returned soldiers' meeting in Fremantle the following day. When McCallum answered O'Neill's letter almost three weeks later, he wrote cautiously that the ALP state executive appreciated O'Neill's sentiments and was 'willing to assist you to the best of our ability consistent with our rules'.[24]

ALP state executive members negotiated with the RSA's East Perth branch representatives, including at a conference in August 1919, attended by Messrs O'Neill, Gorman, Rogers and W.J. MacGilvray. Gorman advocated forming a soldiers' and sailors' organisation that would affiliate with the ALP. Rogers suggested that it should be named the Returned Soldiers' and Sailors' Political Labor League, possibly inspired by the Returned Soldiers' and Sailors' Labor League of Queensland, also formed in 1919, which claimed a membership of 1500 in its first two months of operation.[25] The meeting decided that the RSA East Perth branch should take the initiative in forming an organisation of a political character.[26] Reading between the lines, it seems that the ALP was reluctant to be involved.

The turbulence in the rival servicemen's associations was more than matched by political events. On 5 May 1919, the day after Bloody Sunday, a meeting of 400 returned soldiers at Fremantle Trades Hall resolved to condemn the Western Australian government's use of armed police to put down the disturbance on the wharf. They pledged themselves to 'resist any such future action of the government'.[27] The RSA convened another returned soldiers' meeting on the same evening. Two factions emerged, one consisting mostly of members of the East Perth and Fremantle branches, and the other headed by the association's executive. Although newspaper accounts do not state this, the two 'factions' may well have been the members of the two rival organisations, the RSSILWA and the RSA, which had yet to merge. Despite disagreements among those attending, this meeting also passed a resolution condemning Premier Hal Colebatch's action in travelling to Fremantle wharf the previous Sunday with a boatload of scab unionists to unload the SS *Dimboola* while it was in quarantine.[28]

On the Eastern Goldfields, a rival union was set up in competition with the mining section of the Australian Workers' Union (AWU). Divisions ran deep, not just between former mates and fellow battalion members who supported different political solutions, but between family members. In November 1919, when the AWU miners – among them Tom Axford, who had won the Victoria Cross at the Battle of Hamel on 4 July 1918 – refused to work with the scab unionists, they were faced by a contingent of returned soldiers whom the state government had signed up as special constables to assist police. Tom Axford's brother, Harry, who was president of the RSA in Kalgoorlie, was among them.[29]

SECESSION

The RSA's absorption into the RSSILWA did not recreate a unified body. O'Neill maintained his threat that East Perth would secede. By November 1919, there were two major issues creating division among returned soldiers in Western Australia. Firstly, there was the industrial strife in the Eastern Goldfields, where numerous violent incidents occurred between the AWU strikers on one side, and the 'scabs' and the soldiers sent to protect them. Returned soldiers were on both sides and several heated meetings occurred among members of the Kalgoorlie and Boulder RSSILWA.[30]

Second was the payment of war gratuity bonds. Prime Minister Hughes promised that soldiers would be able to cash in their bonds at branches of the Commonwealth Bank, but then altered some of the conditions for claiming balances, including enabling soldiers to exchange bonds for goods and services. This was a particularly inflammatory issue in the East Perth and Fremantle sub-branches, where angry meetings of several hundred soldiers denounced the RSSILWA executive and the federal body. O'Neill and East Perth sub-branch president J. Maloney (who had replaced Gorman) cabled federal president Gilbert Dyett, saying 'eight hundred diggers denounced you last night. We are prepared to secede.' Dyett passed the telegram to the RSSILWA General Secretary, W.J. Henderson, who stated that the men who sent such a message should be expelled immediately. If the East Perth sub-branch had authorised the telegram, the entire branch should be expelled. It was decided to place the matter with the No. 2 District Council of the RSSILWA.[31]

Meanwhile, a mass meeting of soldiers from several Western Australian sub-branches appointed a Vigilance Committee to address the dissatisfaction with war gratuity payments. At the Shaftesbury Theatre on 23 November 1919, W.J. MacGilvray stated that the committee recognised 'no particular branch, but the soldiers generally'. J. Maloney complained that the RSSILWA executive had thwarted the Vigilance Committee's efforts to get the war gratuity paid to returned soldiers. Although a motion of no confidence in the RSSILWA executive was withdrawn, resolutions were passed expressing confidence in the Vigilance Committee; asking Senator Pearce to explain his statement that the gratuity would be paid only for the period between embarkation and discharge; and calling upon the prime minister to submit a written statement promising payment of the gratuity.[32]

The formation of the Heresy Committee and then the Vigilance Committee indicate that dissidents attempted to reform the RSA and then the RSSILWA before deciding to secede. In December, the RSSILWA expelled Maloney and O'Neill. On 10 December, the East Perth sub-branch convened a special meeting, attended by 300 members, and resolved to secede from the League and re-form as the Returned Sailors' and Soldiers' Association of Australia (RSA).[33] Why they opted to revert to this title rather than adopt the proposed Political Labor League is unknown, but perhaps some members were not keen on a close association with the ALP, whose response to their counterparts had been tepid.

The re-formed RSA adopted a new coat of arms without either imperial or military symbols. Instead, it depicted an emu and a kangaroo with an Australian flag. The motto 'Australia first and forever best' powerfully indicated the RSA's nationalistic stance. O'Neill's name appeared on the new organisation's letterhead as RSA secretary. The address, 35 Barrack Street, Perth, was that of the former East Perth sub-branch, indicating that the entire sub-branch membership, or a substantial majority, had decided to join the RSA. O'Neill wrote to McCallum, asking that the ALP recognise the new organisation, which challenged 'the existence of that abortive organisation known as the Imperial League of Australia'. He accused the RSSILWA of neglecting the interests of the 'rank & file', and of being sectarian and political, despite its constitution. Hence, in O'Neill's opinion, the League was guilty of dishonesty and hypocrisy. McCallum sent copies of O'Neill's letter to the ALP District Councils, but affiliation did not occur.[34]

In further correspondence with McCallum in April 1920, O'Neill emphasised that the RSA was founded by 'the Diggers' section of the returnees, who had been fighting unsuccessfully for the past two and a half years to gain a voice in the RSSILWA. He accused the League of setting out to weaken or destroy trade unionism, 'the latest glaring instance being the arming of the specials scabs on the Goldfields'. O'Neill advocated setting up a 'Diggers' Association' everywhere that there was an RSSILWA sub-branch, for 'it is up to the dinkum worker to fully support the Diggers in their fight against militaristic tyranny in Australia today'.[35]

The ALP state executive received a 'Diggers' delegation consisting of O'Neill and a Mr Appleyard but was divided over the amount of assistance that the labour movement should give the RSA. They finally decided that a three-member delegation should wait on the RSA and 'explain the Party's attitude towards them'. Unfortunately, the minutes do not elaborate on what the party's 'attitude' was. Nor is there any record of the meeting, which was originally set for 10 May 1920, and then postponed by O'Neill.[36] All further correspondence held in the ALP state executive's 'RSL' file is with the RSSILWA, not the RSA.

Western Australia's returned servicemen disagreed over political matters, and this was reflected in the upheavals in the RSA and its successor, the RSSILWA, regarding attitudes to unions and industrial action. Many branch members were unionists. Indeed, the South Fremantle branch required its members to be full financial union members. Following the Fremantle wharf riot on 4 May 1919, Edwin Corboy angered members of the RSA Kalgoorlie branch by stating publicly that he would 'rather have fought on the Wharf than for the capitalists in the Big War'. Shocked, the RSSILA president, Senator William Bolton (Dyett's predecessor) asserted in a telegram to all state branches that 'all genuine returned soldiers … will support constitutional authority in maintaining law and order'. Corboy believed that Bolton's position did not reflect the majority opinion among returned soldiers in Western Australia: soldiers who supported the lumpers at Fremantle outnumbered their opponents by three to one.[37]

Corboy also challenged the federal executive's right to make policies on state branch matters. For Bolton, this threatened the federal character of the RSSILA, for 'each state would be justified in taking any action it liked in any great crisis that may arise'.[38] The Western Australian League had agreed to become a branch of the federal body on the basis that the former would retain control over local matters. This difference of opinion might have marked the end of Corboy's association with the RSSILA. Although he had served as a state representative on the federal executive after Western Australia's affiliation, his name did not appear in the records of the 1920 federal congress in Perth.[39] Corboy's departure was despite Bolton losing the presidency at the federal congress in June 1919 to Gilbert Dyett.[40]

INCREASING CONSERVATISM IN THE RSSILWA

Conservative political views became increasingly evident in the RSSILWA. At the Western Australian State Congress, held just after the merger, four politically conservative men – John Cornell, T.A.L. Davy, Hal Colebatch and Peter Wedd – were among the 15 representatives elected to the RSSILWA state executive. At the same conference, a motion was passed supporting the RSSILA's policy of law and order, reflecting Bolton's claim that 'all genuine returned servicemen' would 'support constitutional authority in maintaining law and order'.[41]

The RSSILWA's move to the right had influenced O'Neill's decision to form a rival organisation. He believed the RSSILWA did not represent the interests of the 'rank and file' serviceman; its leaders had become 'friends of the capitalistic class' and had taken the bosses' part in several industrial disputes, including at Fremantle wharf. The RSSILWA stood 'condemned by its own constitution', which claimed that the organisation was non-sectarian and non-political, whereas its Kalgoorlie sub-branch played an important strike-breaking role on the Goldfields in 1919. Yet it seems that the sentiments of the conservative leadership were shared by a majority of the membership. Several hundred returned servicemen signed on as special constables to protect scab union members working on the Kalgoorlie mines in November 1919. Large numbers of returned men joined the bogus 'national' union – regarded as 'scabs' by the AWU and the wider union movement. These men were singled out for attack and were at the centre of all reported incidents of violence involving AWU members on the Goldfields.[42]

Despite their assertions that they were apolitical, both the Western Australian and the federal executives supported conservative political candidates, arguing that Nationalists' policies were beneficial to serving soldiers and ex-service personnel. As early as 1917, the Western Australian executive had held a special meeting to discuss whether to nominate RSA candidates to contest Senate seats. A motion to support candidates in Billy Hughes' Nationalist Party was passed unanimously and became the RSA's general policy throughout the war. Postwar moves by the RSSILA to form a non-political soldiers' party failed, and the 1919 constitution reiterated the League's role as a national, non-sectarian and 'politically neutral' body.[43] Shortly afterwards, the RSSILWA amended its policy to support any candidates who were interested in ex-servicemen's affairs. The South Fremantle sub-branch campaigned for Alex Panton, a

Labor candidate for the Western Australian Legislative Council, in the June 1919 by-election.[44]

All reference to the RSA disappeared from the media or the ALP's or RSSILWA's existing records by mid-1920. No firm conclusions about the impact of the split on the returned soldiers' movement can be drawn, given the lack of archival material. It is clear, however, that the RSSILA was keen to downplay the existence of division and uphold claims that the organisation benefitted all members equally. In his speech to the Annual Congress at Perth in 1920, Dyett smoothed over the divisions, saying:

> You will recollect that as a result of a decision of the Federal Executive, I visited Western Australia last September [1919]. Certain undesirable conditions were reported to exist there. I came in the hope of bringing about a better understanding and a compromise. I found that the trouble that was supposed to exist was not in existence, and of all the conferences I have attended none exceeded that one in fair mindedness and tolerance … Western Australia is in one of the best positions in the Commonwealth today, in view of the position it occupied at the last Congress.[45]

Incredibly, these words were uttered about a period when the dissidents in East Perth were organising their breakaway, and Corboy was challenging the right of the federal body to dictate policy to branches, and they were delivered after the split had occurred and Corboy had left the executive.

In March 1920, news of the 'troubles' among the returned soldiers in Perth reached General Sir William Birdwood, the British commander of the Anzac forces for the greater part of the war. Birdwood expressed his regret to Western Australia's governor, Sir Francis Newdegate. He wrote that he knew trouble had been 'brewing' but Sir J.J. Talbot Hobbs, the former commander of the 5th AIF Division, Western Australia's highest-ranking soldier and a prominent figure in the RSSILWA, had informed him that his (Birdwood's) visit to Perth and his 'talking to the men' had improved matters 'and, I had hoped, settled any internal difficulties'.[46] It seems unlikely that Birdwood's audience included the breakaway branch members.

What became of Joseph Napoleon O'Neill? In April 1920, he appeared in court, accused of stealing £800 – the profits from a lottery run by the RSA's East Perth branch prior to the merger.[47] The case was adjourned, and the outcome is unknown. In December 1921, O'Neill gave evidence before the soldiers' bond committee, complaining that he had been cheated when he cashed in his gratuity bonds.[48] There is no further mention of him, including the outcome of his complaint. Even Western Australian cemetery records do not reveal O'Neill's fate.

Incomplete as it is, the story of division in the early years of the Western Australian Branch indicates that the RSSILA was not a monolithic body that spoke with one voice and had one purpose, or that all returned soldiers were attracted to the conservative side of politics. Had the dissidents prevailed and changed the culture, the Western Australian branch might have become a radical, militant, left-leaning body, rather than a conservative, militant, right-leaning body. The years 1919 and 1920 marked a significant turning point for the association. There was a struggle, and a split which left the conservative majority in control of the RSSILWA and doubtless strengthened the position of the federal body, with considerable ramifications for the history and politics of Australia.

5

FIGHTING ON THE WESTERN FRONT AND RETURNING HOME TO FIGHT AGAIN
DIGGERS IN THE AUSTRALIAN ABORIGINAL PROGRESSIVE ASSOCIATION

JOHN MAYNARD

Aboriginal experiences of the First World War played a crucial role in the rise of organised Aboriginal political activism during the 1920s. The Australian Aboriginal Progressive Association (AAPA) is today recognised as the first united all-Aboriginal political organisation to form in Australia. During its years of operation, the AAPA fought a bitter five-year public campaign on behalf of the Aboriginal community with the New South Wales government's Aborigines Protection Board. Two key organisers of the AAPA, Dick Johnson and Edward Walker, served in the First World War, while another significant member, Tom Lacey, was the father of two soldiers who served. After the war, Aboriginal soldiers faced racism and discrimination and, unlike white soldiers, they were not feted as heroes. This injustice was a motivating force for the organisers of the AAPA, and their exposure to international conflict helped them connect racism in Australia with an international struggle for black liberation.

VOLUNTEERING TO SERVE

Until May 1917 Aboriginal Australians were prohibited from volunteering for the Australian Imperial Force (AIF). The *Defence Act* of 1909 precluded from service men who were 'not substantially of European descent', and instructions for enlisting officers at approved military recruiting depots issued in 1916 stated that 'Aboriginals, half-castes, or men with Asiatic blood are not to be enlisted – This applies to all coloured men'.[1] While official barriers to Aboriginal enlistment were relaxed in the latter years of war as the need for volunteers became acute, discretion remained in the hands of the authorities, and overt racism prevented some Aboriginal men from serving. In 1917, 16 Aboriginal volunteers were suddenly discharged from a training camp in Queensland because 'white men have an objection to a "blackfella" being associated with them at the camp'.[2] Yet despite this racist legislation and attitudes within the military, many Aboriginal men still tried to volunteer, and historians estimate that over a thousand served in the First World War.[3] Why did Aboriginal soldiers join to fight for a country that discriminated against them? While they shared some of the same reasons as white soldiers – such as the opportunity for pay and the excitement of adventure – Aboriginal soldiers may also have been motivated by the hope for 'equal rights during and after the war', with some expressing that they were 'willing to fight to a man if they were accepted by the military authorities'.[4] In some cases, 'joining the military was one of the few acts Aboriginal men living under the Protection Acts could undertake' without asking permission from the authorities.[5] Some managed to convince the medical authorities, who vetted recruitment, to allow them to join, their Aboriginal appearance notwithstanding.

Dick Johnson was one. A Yuin Aboriginal man, born at Batemans Bay, New South Wales, in 1886, he married Mabel Stewart from Wallaga Lake Mission in 1914. Dick worked at the Bawley Point and Kioloa saw mills. Tragedy was to follow as Mabel died after delivering their stillborn son at the Nurse Claydon Private Hospital at Milton. The devastated and grieving Dick Johnson enlisted in the First World War in June 1916, presumably to escape the trauma and heartache of his loss.[6] Dick was one of 20 Aboriginal men from the Ulladulla region who served in the war. On his enlistment form he was noted as being of dark complexion with dark brown eyes and black hair – a common descriptor used by military authorities for Aboriginal volunteers.[7]

Some Aboriginal men who were accepted at their initial point of recruitment were discharged when they had a medical examination at a later point. Another Aboriginal volunteer, Ernest Lacey, initially enlisted in March 1916 but was medically discharged with the comment: 'unlikely to become an efficient soldier not due to misconduct'.[8] This may have been due to racial discrimination, although Ernest was listed as having deformed little toes on both feet. (About 5 per cent of men trying to enlist for the AIF were found unfit because of deformity of their feet.)[9] Ernest enlisted again, this time successfully, at Wollongong in September 1916. He was recorded as a hatter and set sail on the *Ascanius* and docked in Devonport in England on 28 December 1916. However, Ernest did not see active service in a 'prescribed' theatre of war. He returned to Australia as medically unfit onboard HMAT *Runic* on 6 July 1917 and was discharged on 12 August 1917. He tried to enlist for a third time, but was refused.[10]

Ernest Lacey's brother, Louis, also enlisted, on 15 August 1916 at Sydney. He was recorded as a glassworker and noted as a 'coloured lad', with a 'dark complexion, brown eyes and black hair'. Since Louis was just 18 years of age, his mother, Emily, wrote a letter of consent from Redfern to the military authorities saying she was 'willing to let her son Louis go to the front with his brother Ernest'.[11] The Lacey brothers' father, Tom Lacey, carried strong convictions over Aboriginal rights and would later play a significant role in the AAPA.

Edward Walker was one of another set of Aboriginal brothers who enlisted or attempted to enlist in the Great War. A Yuin man from the south coast of New South Wales, Edward had been born in Kiama in 1893.[12] At the time of enlisting, he was working as a horse breaker at Casino. His brother, Tom Walker, was the first to join up in 1916 and served on the Western Front. Robert Walker enlisted in mid-1917, but was discharged as 'medically unfit' on the same day.[13] Edward then enlisted and was shipped to England onboard the *Medic* alongside several Aboriginal men from Queensland. He joined the 25th Battalion in January 1918 at Neuve Eglise in Belgium. Tom Walker was in the same battalion but in a different company.

EXPERIENCE OF WAR

Phillipa Scarlett has argued that the popular memory of 'mateship' overshadows the extent of racism in the AIF. 'The AIF was dominated by the overarching philosophy of White Australia and believed it was fighting to keep Australia white', she reports, citing evidence of white soldiers refusing to eat with Aboriginal men in the ranks and disproportionate punishment of Aboriginal soldiers for offences.[14]

It seems likely that this context shaped the stories of the Lacey brothers, who set sail from Sydney on HMAT *Ascanius* and disembarked at Devonport. Both had come under the notice of military officers. Before their departure in May 1916, Ernest had been charged as absent without leave and had to forfeit three days' pay, and on the voyage to England, he was awarded a further 72 hours detention. Similarly, Louis was recorded as absent without leave on the voyage to England and given 96 hours detention, despite being confined to the ship. He was found to have contracted venereal disease on shore leave at Sierra Leone. While Ernest was found medically unfit in England and sent back to Australia, Louis continued to draw the ire of military officers. While in England, Louis was disciplined on another two occasions; the second, in September 1917, was for drunkenness and behaviour conducive to the 'prejudice of good order and military discipline', in that while he was at Fargo Hospital he behaved 'in a disorderly manner'.[15] As Scarlett notes, Aboriginal soldiers were subject to excessive discipline in relation to alcohol use, with some military police attempting to enforce Australian legislation prohibiting Aboriginal men from drinking.[16] While many Australian soldiers displayed insubordination in the military, for Aboriginal soldiers, repeated records of military discipline may indicate racism among the ranks.

In November 1917 Louis was finally shipped to France to join the 17th Battalion, and was again in trouble, using insulting language to his superior officer, and taking another 14 days absence without leave. Louis was clearly one severely irritated soldier and evidently not coping with the military discipline of the AIF. In June 1918, he was charged with desertion: it was claimed that 'when the Battalion was in the forward area [on 17 May], he absented himself without leave and remained so absent until arrested'. He was sent back to England under escort.[17] The *17th Battalion War Diary* shows that at the time that Louis Lacey deserted his battalion, it was in the front line near Sailly-le-sec on the Somme. It also records that just prior to his desertion, the battalion had been involved in heavy fighting and repelled an attack, which resulted in the capture of thousands of German prisoners. The battalion itself suffered 17 killed and another 36 wounded. On 16 May 1918, the battalion was relieved from the front line and sent back to a reserve position near Vaux-sur-Somme. That night the reserve area came under heavy cannon fire, and another member of the battalion was killed, and 11 wounded.[18] It appears, then, that Louis was traumatised from his experiences. He was arrested at Oisemont, over 60 kilometres from Sailly-le-sec on the Somme, a distance that suggests he was desperate to get away from the front line. Louis was sentenced to five years in jail at H.M. Prison Gloucester.

Dick Johnson left Australia onboard HMAT *Ceramic* on 7 October 1916 and arrived in Plymouth on 21 November. On 15 February 1917, he was shipped to France and arrived in Étaples to witness 'immense concentrations of Commonwealth reinforcement camps and hospitals':

> [Étaples] served as a training and retraining ground for forces about to enter battle; a depot for supplies; a detention centre for prisoners, both allied and enemy; and, administered nearly 20 general hospitals that served the wounded from the Somme battlefields. By 1917, there were 100,000 troops camped there.[19]

Johnson joined the 13th Battalion, which was soon involved in some of the heaviest fighting on the Western Front at Bullecourt. One survivor recalled this terrible and futile battle:

A tornado of thunder and flame fell upon us, beyond anything I had known or imagined. Close as trees in a forest were the trees of flame. The blast of one heel would send me reeling forward, while another would halt with a wave of driven air, A headless man fell at my feet … A score of men just in front melted in bloody fragments as a big-calibre shell landed. The air was dense with crackling billets … The plain was carpeted with bodies, most lying still, but some crawling laggingly for cover … But there was no sound of human voice in all the storm.[20]

In early June 1917, Johnson was admitted to hospital with an injury to his right heel. He rejoined his unit on 14 July. For the remainder of 1917, the battalion was in Belgium advancing on the Hindenburg Line.[21] In June 1918, Johnson was wounded again, and he was eventually invalided back to Plymouth with a knee injury. While convalescing in the United Kingdom, he met a Scottish woman, Thomasina Douglas, and they were married on 4 January 1919 in Edinburgh. The couple returned to Australia on SS *City of Exeter* eight days later.[22] Thomasina clearly helped Johnson heal from the pain of the loss of his first wife. They would be together for the rest of their lives, later living in Belmore in Sydney.

Meanwhile, Edward Walker, seven months after arriving in France, was wounded in action in July 1918 and then shipped to England for treatment at the Southern General Hospital in Plymouth. From there, he wrote a concerned letter to the Red Cross seeking information on his brother Tom. He had heard that Tom had been killed in action but had not received any official notification. Sadly, it was confirmed that Tom had been killed on 11 August 1918 at Bayonvillers. A low-flying German plane had dropped a bomb directly onto the trench, killing Tom instantly.

He left behind his wife, Lily, and two young children who were living on the Aboriginal reserve at Ulgundahi Island on the Clarence River. Months after the loss of his brother, Edward was released from hospital – only to contract Spanish influenza. The impact of the Spanish influenza, which the returning soldiers brought back to Australia, was devastating, with an estimated 15 000 people dying during the pandemic. Walker survived the illness but 'was deemed no longer fit for active service'.[23] Just after the Armistice was signed in November 1918, he sailed back to Australia onboard HMAT *Bakara*. Walker returned to Ulgundahi Island and lived with his family there.

BATTLES AT HOME

At war's end, men of the AIF suffered physical and psychological wounds, but Aboriginal soldiers did not have the same level of support that many returned soldiers enjoyed. For instance, only a handful of Indigenous soldiers were successful in their applications under the soldier resettlement scheme and even then, they faced blatant racism. One Aboriginal man was granted a block near Forbes in western New South Wales, but his application for a loan to develop the land was rejected by an inspector: 'This case is unsatisfactory … the holder is a blackman … altogether the wrong sort of man.' At least three other Aboriginal men faced overt discrimination that blocked their claims.[24] While Aboriginal soldiers were entitled to repatriation benefits, the policy was likely not 'applied equally across the board': 'there were sporadic complaints about discrimination against Aboriginal war veterans during the 1920s and 1930s'.[25] Moreover, Aboriginal soldiers had the additional burden of facing continued racism and prejudice in broader society when they returned home.

Edward Walker's postwar experiences provide stark evidence of the disadvantage endured by Aboriginal returned soldiers. In 1919, he was forced to appear in court when a publican was charged with serving liquor to him and two friends in the Federal Hotel in Casino, New South Wales. Edward was summoned to the trial of the publican, where the defence argued that the publican ought to be let off because Edward was a returned soldier and it was unclear whether he was Aboriginal.[26] No white soldier was hauled to court for partaking of a beer in a pub. Four years later, Edward was back in court, this time as the defendant. 'Edward Walker, a well-educated half-caste Aboriginal, was charged with using insulting words to Allan Cameron, manager of the Aborigines settlement on Ulgundahi Island.' Cameron alleged that Edward had assaulted him on River Street, Maclean. He stated that he had known Edward for about four years and given permission for him to live on the island, but when Edward requested that his mother be allowed to also live there, Cameron refused: 'If you go over, I will get the police to remove you.'[27] Cameron claimed that Edward became very aggressive, although he did not

> give him any provocation to use language, nor did I
> assault him. We had a scuffle, and he tore my coat. He
> kicked me in the stomach, and I called for somebody to
> call the police. I let him go and he caught me by the throat
> and scratched my face.[28]

Yet, it would appear from the evidence that the one under assault was, in fact, Edward Walker. He claimed, for his part, that he had only said to Cameron, 'I do not think that you can object to me taking my mother to the island to nurse my wife', when he

> struck at me and I stepped back … He caught my coat
> and said that I was bludgeoning on the returned soldiers'
> badge. He again hit at me, and I pushed him off. He
> rushed at me and caught me by the throat, threw me on
> the ground and placed his two knees on my arms and hit
> me about the head.

Edward explained that he managed to throw Cameron off and started up the street, but Cameron and his brother 'caught me by the two arms and bent my back over the rail of a fence'. Edward then managed to fight free and tore Cameron's coat. Cameron, in turn, argued:

> I did not catch him by the coat. I did not strike the
> defendant while he was down. I did not say, 'You b— cow.
> I will bash your brains out on the road'. I did not say, 'You
> are a coward'.

Furthermore, Cameron claimed not to know of Edward's severe wartime injuries prior to the incident: 'I did not know that defendant was a cripple, he gets the same wages as any other man and is able to work as well as any other.'[29] Yet Cameron had known Edward for years; in 1918 he had commented on the Walker brothers' experiences of war.[30] A witness, J. David, corroborated that Cameron was the aggressor and had the 'defendant down and bumping his head on the ground'.[31] Despite this evidence, the police magistrate decided to convict Edward on both charges, fined and bound to good behaviour for three months, a charge that Edward appealed. Instead of being celebrated as a war hero, Edward Walker discovered he was a pariah and not even a second-class citizen back in his own country.

Other soldiers had struggles with the law. In the UK, Louis Lacey had his five-year sentence commuted to one year, but on release with good conduct he was admitted to hospital with a septic foot and sent back to the AIF. Once again, he went absent without leave after escaping lawful custody. His father, Tom Lacey, was concerned with his son's wellbeing and whereabouts, writing to military officials in September 1919:

> I have a son at the front 6086 Private Louis Lacey
> 17th Battalion, and I have received no letters from him
> for the past four months and he said that he thought he
> would be returning to Australia in July, and I have had no
> word from him.[32]

Louis finally sailed for Australia on 22 September 1919. Yet even onboard ship, he took part in a disturbance on the troop deck and received 28 days detention.[33]

Once back in Australia, Louis remained a disturbed individual. It is not known if he re-established a relationship with his family. In the early 1920s, it is recorded that he had embarked on a career in the boxing ring. A Sydney newspaper described him as a 'coloured lad and is built on the lines of a wrestler, with strong arms and legs. He wears his hair like a Hotten-tott. A clever fellow, this son of Ham.'[34] Louis' boxing career, however, seems to have been short-lived. In 1928, he was recorded as living in the Salvation Army Shelter in Melbourne, and in 1932, he was serving two years' hard labour in Long Bay Gaol. Here he was placed under the observation of Dr Hogg, Inspector General of Mental Hospitals, who recorded that his patient made 'conflicting statements as regards his personal history'.[35] Louis varied the location of his birth wildly, from

Ulladulla on New South Wales south coast to Algiers. He also stated that he had served in the Great War on the front line, and (wrongly) claimed to be a member of the Australian Light Horse. Dr Hogg contacted the military for confirmation of Louis' record and received a reply confirming that he had served with the 17th Battalion. At this point Louis Lacey disappears from the historical record. Although we cannot know what his issues were, he clearly struggled with military discipline – and almost certainly with racism both in the army and out of it.

Louis' brother, Ernest, in contrast, appears to have lived a quiet life after the war. When he passed away in 1957, he was described at his funeral as the best known and most respected Aboriginal in Nowra, New South Wales. Over 60 ex-servicemen attended to pay their respects at the Nowra War Cemetery. The funeral was carried out with full military honours and a rousing farewell from the Nowra branch of the RSL. Ernest's casket was draped in a Union Jack with a digger's hat and reversed spurs. A speaker at the gravesite said: 'We would like to remember the deceased as a young man, forgetting all colour of skin; he offered his life for his country along with the rest of Australia.' His community's recognition of his service echoes the limits of mateship extended towards Aboriginal servicemen during the war. As Philippa Scarlett shows, expressions of mateship with Aboriginal soldiers by white soldiers often positioned them as 'white inside', passing over the soldier's Aboriginality, yet still marking it as inferior.[36]

POSTWAR ACTIVISM

Aboriginal soldiers' experiences of war and their difficulties on their return shaped the formative years of the first united all-Aboriginal political organisation to form in Australia, the

Australian Aboriginal Progressive Association (AAPA). In the early 20th century, Aboriginal political mobilisation was catalysed by the revocation of Aboriginal independent farms, and the escalation in Aboriginal child removal by the NSW Aborigines Protection Board. Aboriginal soldiers returning home to New South Wales were faced with the devastating news that some of their families had been forced from their independent farms by the Aborigines Protection Board.[37] Some of these men also learnt that during their absence fighting for their country, their children had been removed from their wives' care and placed into government institutions.[38]

Many prominent leaders of the AAPA, which was created in 1924, were returned soldiers. The experiences they had gained overseas gave them confidence and the courage to take up the fight. As it happened, the AAPA's president, Fred Maynard, did not fight in the First World War. As a wharf labourer in Sydney, he was a part of the Waterside Workers Union, which opposed conscription for overseas service. But Maynard carried a deep awareness of international events from his time on the Sydney waterfront, when he and other Aboriginal dockworkers had developed close connections with visiting international black merchant sailors. Maynard was particularly influenced by Marcus Garvey's Universal Negro Improvement Association (UNIA) in Harlem, which operated from 1920 to 1924. The UNIA had millions of followers, including in Australia, where a chapter was established in 1920.[39] Garvey's message of racial, cultural and historical pride resonated powerfully with the Aboriginal activists. The AAPA adopted many of the demands of Garveyism as part of their political platform. A powerful speech at a UNIA meeting in Harlem in 1922 resonated with the Aboriginal activists' thinking about the dissonance between the supposed aims of the Great War and the reality of Aboriginal peoples' lives:

> You are asked to go and fight the Germans who had done you no wrong. You were told to give the Germans hell, while they were giving your mothers, sisters and sons hell in Mississippi, Georgia, Alabama and the Negro asked, 'Which is better, to make the world safe for democracy, or to make his home safe for his wife and children?' That is what he asked then and what he is asking now.[40]

As AAPA president, Maynard made similar connections between Aboriginal men's service in the Great War and their poor treatment upon return to Australia. In a 1927 letter to NSW Premier Jack Lang, Maynard referenced the key values of Anzac, emphasising the 'loyalty, fidelity and bravery' of Aboriginal men 'when conditions have called for the exercise of such virtues'. This was undoubtedly in reference to the experiences of Aboriginal soldiers in the Great War, including members of the AAPA. He also powerfully recognised the war that had been waged against the Aboriginal population in Australia since 1788.[41] In his letter to Lang, Maynard unleashed his anger at the NSW government's draconian policies, shocking mistreatment and severe control over Aboriginal lives. Maynard clearly carried strong convictions that Australia itself had been a battleground from 1788 into the 20th century.

Maynard also was a very close friend of one of the veterans whose journey has been discussed, Dick Johnson. Like many Aboriginal returned soldiers, Johnson expected that their wartime service would bring about major changes in the treatment of Aboriginal people and communities within

Australia. After the war, many Aboriginal servicemen expressed their disappointment that 'fighting for our King and country' had not resulted in any improvement in Aboriginal rights or living conditions.[42] Some, like Johnson, explicitly linked their soldiering with their activism. At the first AAPA conference at St David's Church and Hall in Sydney in April 1925, with over 200 Aboriginal people in attendance, Johnson referenced Aboriginal military service and loyalty during the war.[43] Months later at the AAPA's first half-year meeting, he was reported in the press as a man 'who wears the returned soldier's badge'.[44] Johnson was a major figure in the AAPA Central Branch and was elected secretary. He witnessed the staggering Aboriginal community response to the formation of the AAPA.[45] Within six months, it had opened offices in Crown Street, Sydney, with a membership of over 600 across 13 branches and four sub-branches around the state. Johnson remained a fixture in the AAPA, attending the major AAPA conferences held in Sydney, Kempsey, Grafton and Lismore between 1925 and 1927. He remains one of the many important, but overlooked, Aboriginal political activists of the 20th century.

A further link between AAPA and Aboriginal wartime service was Tom Lacey, the father of Ernest and Louis. His sons had suffered widely varied experiences during the war: Louis was charged with desertion and jailed, and would suffer ongoing mental health issues and problems with authority; Ernest was prevented from going the front due to medical issues. It is likely that Tom carried the trauma of his sons' experiences with him through the years of the AAPA political fight for Aboriginal rights and justice. A close friend of Fred Maynard, he assumed the position of treasurer when the AAPA was formed and was inspired by the surge for self-determination by oppressed peoples across the globe. In a 1924 letter to Garvey's central branch in Harlem, published in the *Negro World,* Tom Lacey pointed out that he had been a member of the Sydney UNIA branch for four years and had recently been elected as the organiser of the Sydney chapter.[46] Tom pledged to Garvey the support of 10 000 Aboriginal people in New South Wales and 60 000 nationally. He revealed the tight and restrictive controls that Aboriginal people lived under, and that they had trouble reaching 'some of our people, as the missionaries have got the most of them … The authorities won't allow us to see them unless we can give them [the Aboriginal Board] a clear explanation of what we want them for.'[47] Yet Tom Lacey asserted that, given the opportunity, Aboriginal people were capable of gaining the same position 'as the coloured people of the United States of America, who have their own colleges and universities'.[48] Throughout his AAPA years, Tom was regarded with respect. A 1927 newspaper article predicted that he

> will be hailed as a modern Moses. The slogan 'No more slavery in N.S.W.' will reverberate throughout the length and breadth of the continent and will not only have the effect of breaking the chains off the Aboriginals in the prison gangs of West Australia but will straighten out every grievance which the native people are enduring under the respective Australian Governments in general but those of New South Wales particularly.[49]

When Tom Lacey passed away three years later, in 1930, the press described him as 'one of the most forceful advocates of the cause of his people – the Australian Aborigines … His death is a distinct loss to his people, and he will be sadly missed.'[50]

As for the Walker brothers, it was Edward who carried his experience of war into activism. Suffering serious wounds, he should have returned to a hero's welcome, but he was greeted instead by the severe restrictions and blatant racism of the continuing discrimination against Aboriginal Australians. He would become the AAPA secretary of the Clarence River branch of the organisation. A fervent fighter for Aboriginal rights and justice, he joined the organisation only a year after he was assaulted and racially vilified by Cameron. Edward was a prominent figure in the 1925 Kempsey conference and the 1926 conference held in Grafton, though, alas, the press reports tell us little more than his name. Edward Walker died in 1976, aged 82.

ABORIGINAL VETERANS AND THE ANZAC LEGEND

The First World War contributed to the rise of organised Aboriginal political activism in the 1920s. The motives of the Aboriginal men who joined the AIF in 1914–18 were not recorded in any official capacity, but they surely anticipated that their service on behalf of Australia would enhance their claims to full citizenship rights on their return. Instead, they confronted deeply embedded racism, which continued in Australian military service. In the Second World War, for example, Private Russell Amato went AWOL three times from three different units, because he 'couldn't stand the other soldiers making derogatory remarks about Aboriginal people, particularly women, about whom the talk was sexual'.[51] In Amato's court-martial the defending officer reported that Aboriginal soldiers routinely faced such discrimination: 'it appears that there is a certain element in the camps that brings up the colour bar against such men'.[52] The marginalisation of Aboriginal soldiers from the mainstream Anzac narrative was only addressed from the 1990s, with a concerted effort to draw attention to the service of Indigenous soldiers in the prelude to the centenary in the 2010s.

The attitude of Aboriginal veterans to the Anzac legend in the aftermath of the First World War was ambivalent. Pride in their military service and the public display of their medals sat uneasily with the disappointment of rejection, and anger at the inequality in the recognition given to returned soldiers. The fight for Aboriginal rights and justice during the 1920s was driven by this tension between their expectations of war and their subsequent disillusionment. Aboriginal activism challenged Anzac, because it exposed the exclusivity of the mythic narrative and the privileged access that white veterans had to the political and cultural status conferred by military service. The Returned Sailors' and Soldiers' Imperial League might have said each Anzac Day that all veterans were 'in spirit one army', but Aboriginal activism reminded Australians that they were not.[53] The AAPA disappeared from public view after 1929, harassed, hounded and smashed out of existence by a coalition of the Aborigines Protection Board, the missionaries and the police.[54] However, its legacy continued as its members remained active in pressing for Aboriginal rights. At the historic Day of Mourning Protest in Sydney in 1938, over 100 Aboriginal people gathered to protest the Australia sesquicentenary celebrations of white settlement. Dick Johnson was there, and stated:

> We must work full hearted to win our objective. Nothing done half-hearted is a success. We should all work together to arouse the mind of the white men and women of Australia to our awful conditions.[55]

6

BOLSHEVIK ANZAC
THE POLITICS, CELEBRITY AND MYTHOLOGY OF HUGO THROSSELL VC

NATHAN HOBBY

During the Great War, a journalist declared that Captain Hugo Throssell 'is 7 feet [213 centimetres] in height … the tallest man in the Australian army', while a cigarette card from about the same time referred to his 'seven feet of gallant manhood'.[1] Throssell was actually an unremarkable 5 feet 10 inches (178 centimetres) but the exaggeration is apt for a foundational bearer of the Anzac legend. As the first Western Australian to gain a Victoria Cross in the Great War, Hugo Throssell became an Anzac celebrity, especially in his home state. Yet his celebrity status was complicated soon after the war's end by his extraordinary announcement of his conversion to socialism. The son of a conservative politician, he made the announcement when he was the guest of honour in his hometown of Northam, east of Perth, for the Peace Day celebrations on 19 July 1919 to mark the signing of the Treaty of Versailles:

> The war has made me a Socialist … if we want peace … we must do away with the system of production for profit, and reorganise our life in common on the lines

93

of production for use and for the well-being of the community as a whole.[2]

Watching proudly was his wife of six months, novelist Katharine Susannah Prichard, who had been radicalised two years earlier. The speech marked the beginning of a short-lived but significant period of political activism by Throssell, an example of the radicalisation of some returning soldiers at the end of the First World War during the brief period in which it seemed possible that revolutionary change was imminent in Australia. Throssell gave only two more significant political speeches, both on the same day in November 1919, and withdrew from political involvement soon after. Yet biographies by his son, Ric Throssell (1989), and journalist John Hamilton (2012) have connected his suicide in 1933 to his rejection by society because of his political activism. After re-examining the nature of Throssell's activism, this chapter offers a new account of his complicated status as a controversial celebrity Anzac, silenced for challenging the Anzac legend and damaged by his war experiences, yet also still revered.

THROSSELL'S PATH TO SOCIALISM

Throssell gave two accounts of his own political conversion. One was the Peace Day speech, most of which was published verbatim by the *Westralian Worker,* the labour newspaper edited by future prime minister John Curtin.[3] Throssell's speech was focused on making a case for capitalism as the cause of war, and socialism as its solution, with some autobiographical remarks as a preface. The second account was an article, also written in 1919, directly addressing why he became a socialist. It was commissioned by Sydney's *Sun* newspaper after the Peace Day speech, but they then declined to publish it. It was eventually published on 31 December 1920 in the second ever edition of the *Australian Communist,* under the headline 'His eyes are opened'.[4]

Born in 1885, Hugo Throssell was the youngest of 13 living children of George (1840–1910) and Annie (1841–1906) Throssell. Hugo wrote, 'Although my father was Minister for Lands … and was afterwards for a short time Premier of West Australia, I did not take much interest in public affairs. That I heard public affairs and politics a good deal discussed in my old home, however, goes without saying.'[5] The pre-party factional politics that he heard discussed were about personal power, advocating for the local area and regional development.[6]

Hugo Throssell began his Peace Day speech by mentioning that many would remember him as an 'irresponsible lad'; he was also a privileged one, with the 'best of everything'.[7] Educated in Adelaide at the elite Prince Alfred College, after graduating he held an office job for six years in the family business before he and his brother Eric spent several years growing wheat on a family property in Cowcowing.[8] It was marginal land for farming at the best of times and 1914 brought severe drought which, as Ruth Morgan observes, motivated 'many young rural men [to] enter the armed services in order to escape economic hardship'.[9] In debt, with their crops failing, the Throssell brothers enlisted together in October 1914, original members of the newly formed 10th Light Horse Regiment.[10]

Throssell saw active service in Gallipoli in August 1915. On 29 August, he received a gunshot wound to the neck at Hill 60 while seizing and defending a trench all night under enemy fire. He was evacuated to London, where a doctor removed his adenoids, thinking it would fix his hearing problems. After the operation he nearly died from bacterial meningitis, an infection that left permanent effects. He was still in hospital recuperating when newspapers announced on 15 October that he had been awarded the Victoria Cross for his actions at Hill 60, instantly elevating him to celebrity status. A long, laudatory article about Throssell's heroism titled 'The man I want to follow' was published in London's *Daily Mail* on 27 October and reprinted in newspapers across Australia, as well as in pamphlet form in Northam.[11] In the article, Throssell's fellow soldier Sergeant John McMillan testified to Throssell's leadership, courage and masculinity:

> His head was thrown back in the sort of exaltation that you always imagine in the fights of olden days … I can see him now, the very type of the best Australian manhood … the man I want to follow, the man to lead me in a big fight, that is Throssell, VC.[12]

Throssell's status as an exemplar of the Anzac warrior saw him featured in at least three different cigarette-card series; a poem called 'Fighting Jim' (Throssell's nickname) was also circulated on a printed card.[13] In 1916, suffering the effects of his war wounds, Throssell was sent back to Australia to recover and promote recruitment. Visiting Northam in May, he was toasted by two prominent conservative politicians from the district at a civic reception: 'Your father gave to Northam commercial distinction, you have conferred upon it military renown.'[14]

In January 1917, Throssell was sent back to the front, this time to Egypt. He was briefly reunited with his brother, Eric, only for Eric to be killed in action in Palestine on 19 April. In her autobiography, Katharine Susannah Prichard summed up the letters, now lost, he wrote from the front at the time: '[H]e had gone searching for his brother's body, after dark. Crawling over the battlefield, still under enemy gunfire … But he had not found [Eric], or heard how he died… Hugo was broken up by his brother's death.'[15]

Throssell wrote that during his first leave in Australia in 1916, 'the war had more or less got me down, and I did not pay much attention to what was happening at home'. But at the time of his second leave in October 1918, during which he was courting Prichard in Melbourne, 'the increased cost of living surprised me – and the war loan posters'. His 'mind went back to Gallipoli' and the night of intense trench warfare with the Turks; of his troop of 24 men only two 'crawled out whole':

> I realised that those who returned would find that their farms and means of earning a living had not improved, four of the best years of their life were gone, and they were to be taxed to pay the interest on war debts – taxed by the people who stayed at home and lent their money at 4½ per cent while they were fighting. I realised that the men who sold those bombs we threw had made fortunes, that war was a profitable investment for the financiers and wealthier classes, anyhow. These first impressions have been strengthened and confirmed by all that I have seen, read, and heard since then.[16]

Throssell's testimony demonstrates that even if he had been guided by Prichard to his new beliefs, he was able to relate socialist concepts to his own experience, setting the interests of veterans against the interests of capitalists. Frank Bongiorno writes, 'in postwar Europe, soldiers practiced fascist violence, but they also supported red revolution. In Australia their political allegiances seemed similarly unsettled and uncertain.'[17] In Bobbie Oliver's research on the One Big Union movement, she located the Military Censor's observations in 1918 that radicals viewed the 'capturing of [the] returned soldiers or even a portion [of them] as a deciding factor in accomplishing their revolutionary aims, and the most strenuous efforts are being made (and with some little success in that direction)'.[18] In this contest for the political allegiance of veterans, Throssell, with Prichard's help, was making a claim that the left best represented their interests.

Throssell concluded his *Sun* article with the acknowledgement:

> I owe a great deal of my new faith and understanding of the trouble and sorrow in the world to my wife, and that we hope to work together in ways which will make our lives of real service to our fellow men and women.

He had met Katharine Susannah Prichard in 1915 after being evacuated to London; she was working as a journalist in London while establishing her literary career and had just gained fame when her first novel won a major prize. Returning to Melbourne, Prichard corresponded with Throssell while beginning an intimate relationship with Guido Baracchi, a wealthy left-wing activist and theorist who helped radicalise her politics. She came to see the capitalist system as the cause of the war; in 1917 she enrolled as the first student of the far-left Victorian Labor College and welcomed the Russian Revolution as a beacon of hope for a better, egalitarian world. Her sporadic romance with Baracchi ended, but she spent 1918 continuing down a path of radicalism, reading Marx and other texts while she maintained her correspondence with Throssell. Arriving in Melbourne in October 1918, Throssell was determined to marry Prichard despite her radicalism; she wrote, 'I told Hugo my political beliefs and he accepted them with me.'[19] Baracchi's biographer, Jeff Sparrow, notes the way radicalism was romantically 'transmitted' to Baracchi from the poet Lesbia Keogh (later Harford), who introduced him to the labour movement, then to Prichard; the chain continued with Prichard's influence over Throssell.[20]

PARTNERS IN RADICALISM

Throssell and Prichard married in January 1919 and settled in Greenmount on the outskirts of Perth. Throssell had been offered a job as the soldiers' representative on the board of the land settlement scheme for soldiers in Western Australia. They arrived in Perth at a time of ferment and revolutionary expectation. On 4 May 1919, a long-running industrial dispute at Fremantle wharf culminated in Bloody Sunday, a day of violence in which a unionist died of his injuries and was mourned as a working-class martyr.[21] Throssell wrote that the strike 'finally decided any lingering doubts regarding the side I would take for the future'. He had been told that the lumpers (dockers who unloaded cargo) were well paid but 'I visited the port personally, and found the position of the men so misrepresented and so intolerable that they had my entire sympathy'.[22]

As Throssell stated at the conclusion of his article written for the *Sun*, in this initial phase, he and Prichard saw themselves as partners in radicalism, hoping 'to work together in ways which will make our lives of real service to our fellow men and women'.[23] They attempted to proselytise the middle- and upper-class circles of Perth. Prichard wrote in a letter in 1919 of Throssell:

[He] has grown so to my point of view that he usually describes himself as a Bolshevik & certainly has done more explanations of what Bolshevism is than any man I know in this state. Can you hear him explaining what the word means to the State Attorney General?[24]

Describing themselves as 'Bolsheviks' aligned Throssell and Prichard with the Russian Revolution. The immediate effect of the revolution in Australia had been to 'give the Bolshevik Party unassailable prestige as the party of socialism'. Eight major socialist groups were active in Australia and yet 'in the years following October 1917, none of them succeeded in capitalising on the success of the Bolsheviks'.[25] Instead, Throssell's period of activism in 1919 occurred during the interval before the founding of the Communist Party of Australia. In this interval, an Australian radical response was under formation in public gatherings and the publication of books and pamphlets, including Australian titles *Bolshevism: What the Russian Workers Are Doing* by Maurice Blackburn (1918 or 1919), *Red Europe* by Frank Anstey (1919) and Prichard's own *The New Order*, the text of her talk on socialism to the elite women's Karrakatta Club in August 1919 and the first public statement of her radical beliefs.

Throssell and Prichard's involvement was typical of the period: attending a range of socialist gatherings, giving general speeches on socialism, and reading radical literature as activists worked out how to bring the success of Russia to Australia. They travelled into the city on Sunday afternoons for the Social Democratic League meetings on the Esplanade, 'the green flats beside the shining river where the people of Perth gather for such occasions'.[26] At the time, the Social Democratic League was the major group to the left of the Labor party in Perth; after a short-lived existence from 1901 to about 1903, it was revived in 1917 for 'socialists of all shades of opinion'.[27] Prichard wrote in

August 1919, '2 young men of the Social Democratic League are under the impression that Jim & I are brands for the burning', suggesting she and Throssell were not fully committed to the group.[28] After renaming itself the WA Socialist Party in July 1920, the group seems to have ceased activities in 1921, although left-wing gatherings continued on the Esplanade.[29]

Prichard hoped that Throssell would stand for parliament, writing to her friend Nettie Palmer after the Peace Day speech that the state member for Northam, Premier James Mitchell, 'is wondering about his seat. It's the opinion of most people that Jim could have it, as easily as he liked, if he liked. He's so personally popular in that district. But he doesn't want to go into Parliament – at any rate not yet – if ever.'[30] Prichard was unrealistic to think a socialist candidate, even of Throssell's popularity, could win an agricultural seat in Western Australia, but the letter reveals that it was a possibility being discussed at the time. On the strength of his political pedigree and his Victoria Cross, Throssell had been seen as a potential politician before the Peace Day speech. While returning from the front to Australia in October 1918, he was nominated to stand for the by-election for the federal seat of Swan, but he withdrew his nomination on the closing day.[31]

On Sunday, 9 November 1919, in the midst of a federal election campaign that confirmed the Nationalist Prime Minister W.M. (Billy) Hughes in power, Throssell gave his final speeches at two events marking the second anniversary of the Russian Revolution, one in Perth and the other in Fremantle. The Perth event on the Esplanade, 'Justice for Russia', was organised by the Social Democratic League. Throssell spoke alongside John Curtin, who was the Labor candidate for Perth. Throssell's speech, summarised in the *Westralian Worker,* was limited to the situation in Russia, defending the actions and motivations of the Bolsheviks, and denouncing British involvement in the Russian civil war without advocating for socialism in Australia.[32]

The speeches, despite their moderation, were enough to have the Attorney General's Department Investigation Branch – a forerunner of ASIO – open a file on Throssell; the agency feared it was the beginning of a dangerous career of political activism. Instead, it was almost the end of Throssell's political involvement. When the Communist Party of Australia was founded in October 1920, Prichard was tasked with forming a Perth branch. Throssell's name was conspicuously absent from the list of six comrades who were foundation members – although, according to Prichard, he did attend some public meetings with her. After that, Throssell's involvement ceased, while Prichard herself was largely inactive from the birth of their only child in 1922 until 1929.

WHY DID THROSSELL ABANDON ACTIVISM?

Throssell never offered an explanation for his abandonment of activism, and Prichard's brief account of the years of her marriage obscures it by focusing on some minor political involvement Throssell had just before his death. Both Prichard and Throssell were disappointed by the reality of radical politics. Stuart Macintyre writes of the 'ferment of war and revolution' drawing 'middle-class rebels' to communism, only for initial expectations to fade as the party 'retreated into the familiar rituals of a sect on the fringes of the labour movement ... [and] ... lost its wider appeal'.[33] His comments resonate with Prichard's temporary withdrawal in the 1920s and perhaps also speak to Throssell's withdrawal from the movement before the party had even formed. As Macintyre notes, the Communist Party was actually 'formed on the ebb tide of labour unrest', the peaks coming in the great general strike of 1917 and the maritime strike of 1919.[34] By 1920, Throssell may have lost patience with a movement that was not moving fast enough for his liking. He tended towards dilettantism and impulsivity, traits probably worsened by post-traumatic stress disorder and the after-effects of meningitis.[35] His embrace of Prichard's politics seems a sincere one, but he probably did not fully appreciate that he was being asked to make a long-term commitment to a fledgling movement demanding constant sacrifice and offering little reward. Through the 1920s, he became busy with other ventures; his overriding concern was to make a lot of money and build a grander house for the family.[36] When his debts mounted to £4000, he entered into 'innumerable schemes to recover the family fortunes: a wheat-bag loader ... shares in an oilfield in the north-west, which produced only worthless wax; an equally useless steeplechaser ... a mining lease at the Larkinville rush'.[37]

In Prichard's autobiography, she jumps from Throssell's Peace Day speech to his attendance at a peace meeting 14 years later in 1933, obscuring the years of political inactivity. 'Jim attended, with me, the first meeting of a Peace Committee in Perth.'[38] Prichard had re-immersed herself in the Communist Party in 1929, after a new organiser was sent to Perth. In 1933, against the backdrop of the rise of Hitler, the Comintern had been helping set up anti-war groups around the world, which would also serve as communist fronts. Prichard was given the task of establishing a Western Australian anti-war committee, which later became the Movement Against War and Fascism. She placed notices in the newspaper calling specifically on returned soldiers. 'All Returned Soldiers and Ex-Service Men are Invited to attend the above Conference in order to participate in the discussion and register your protest against WAR.'[39] Two hundred people attended the meeting on 13 May 1933, including Throssell. He was one of two Victoria Cross recipients elected to the committee of 45.[40] At the meeting he said he had 'seen enough of the horrors of war, and that he would do his utmost to prevent his own boy from going to war'.[41] Prichard highlighted Throssell's support for the organisation in her autobiography as evidence of his ongoing political commitment – she saw it as an indication of the direction he was headed if he had lived. It is likely, however, that Throssell's attendance was more indicative of his support for her than a renaissance in his political convictions.[42]

Throssell's support of Prichard's return to radical politics was also shown in his encouragement for her to visit the Soviet Union in 1933. He told her, 'We must know whether what we've been told is true.'[43] While Prichard was in the Soviet Union, Throssell launched a scheme to clear his immense debts. He transformed their property into a rodeo show, hoping to make money on admission and sell his properties in Greenmount at the same time. However, the properties remained unsold, his debts worsened and, with Prichard returning soon, after a sleepless night he shot himself with his service revolver on 19 November 1933. The note he left indicates the trauma of war contributed to his suicide: 'I can't sleep and feel my old war head. It's going phut, and that's no good for anyone concerned.'[44] Right back in 1921, an agent noted on Throssell's security file, 'A medical authority informed a friend of mine that he would not be surprised if Throssell went "off his head" at any time …'[45] It is likely Throssell, and many other Great War veterans who suffered ongoing symptoms from exposure to trauma, would meet the criteria for a contemporary diagnosis of post-traumatic stress disorder. The financial strain was clearly another factor. In a warning to Ric in 1945, Prichard wrote, 'Daddy's weakness, & the cause of so much suffering & sorrow to me, was a tendency to spend more than he had or could afford. And so all our troubles began, & mounted until the end – you know.'[46] He was buried with full military honours two days later in a funeral well attended by establishment figures from politics, business and farming.[47]

THE CONSEQUENCES OF THROSSELL'S STAND

Throssell's only child, Ric Throssell, claimed in his memoir that Throssell's Peace Day speech was the root of his later troubles:

> She [Prichard] had not realised just what Jim's public declaration of his change of heart would cost him. He knew that to all of his father's followers, the good conservative farmers and loyal patriots, it would be like treachery … people disowned him in droves … Jim Throssell accepted his ruination with convincing enthusiasm.[48]

Following Ric Throssell's interpretation, journalist John Hamilton wrote in his 2012 biography of Throssell, *The Price of Valour*, that Throssell's 'misfortune began on Peace Day, 19 July 1919', calling his speech 'a disaster waiting to happen'. In his judgement, Throssell was not memorialised in Northam because of it:

> The feeling ran so deep that it was not until 28 August 1999 – just over eighty years since Hugo had made his speech – that a modest cream-brick memorial to him the size of a backyard barbecue was unveiled in Northam by the governor of Western Australia, Michael Jeffery. He said that 'it is probable that rejecting the values of his

peer group was the reason no memorial existed [before] for Throssell'.[49]

In fact, Throssell was memorialised in a significant way on Anzac Day 1925, the ten-year anniversary of the Gallipoli landing. After marching in Perth in the morning, Throssell returned to Northam in the evening for a united church service in the 'packed' town hall to witness the presentation of an oil painting of himself. Businessman Aston Hunter, a friend of Throssell's, had bought the painting from the artist, Duncan MacGregor-Whyte, and was presenting it to the mayor – Throssell's brother, Cecil – who received it on behalf of the citizens of Northam. Although Hunter apparently covered most of the £105 purchase price himself, the Northam RSL had voted to 'aid' him and the council had made a modest donation.[50] Hunter thanked the local RSL for suggesting the service as an appropriate occasion for the presentation. The portrait was to hang in the hall with an existing one of Throssell's father: 'He [Hunter] thought it be very fitting to have on the one side of the stage Capt. Throssell, VC typifying the arts of war, and on the other his father, representing the arts of peace. (Applause).'[51] In 1936, three years after Throssell's death, the portrait was indeed hanging in the town hall and the Northam RSL paid for a brass plate to be attached to it.[52] Northam's public acceptance of the portrait does not fit with the idea that the district rejected him.

However, there were hints of lingering repercussions from his 1919 speech. It was originally suggested that the Northam community cover the cost of the painting, but in the end Throssell's friend had to come up with most of the money. It is also significant that Throssell was not asked to speak at this or any other civic ceremony. His public role had been reduced: in July 1919 he had been placed on the speakers' platform alongside politicians and ministers of religion, 'a scion of the Tory Throssell family' who could be relied upon to reinforce the establishment. At the time, *Truth* newspaper predicted correctly, 'It is safe to say that Hugo will not in future be a "star speaker" at gatherings of Northam Toryism.'[53] And yet, Throssell remained an Anzac celebrity, whose presence at ceremonies was still welcome as a bearer of the Victoria Cross, even though he was silenced because of his critique of war and capitalism.

Throssell's limited involvement with Northam after 1919 may also have reflected the fact he had made his home not there but on the outskirts of the metropolitan area in Greenmount. Rather than being a pariah, he was honoured many times at commemorations in nearby Midland as well as in Perth. On Anzac Day in 1921, he was a special guest at Midland, presenting war medals after two minutes of silence in the solemn part of a day-long sports and community event to raise funds for a soldiers' war memorial.[54] This fundraiser came to fruition in November 1923 when Throssell led a guard of honour at a ceremony to unveil a memorial clock placed on the dome of the Midland Town Hall.[55] Each Anzac Day from 1925 until 1930 he marched in the Perth procession, leading the procession in 1928 and always with a prominent position. His absence was noted in 1932, when only one of eight VCs was in attendance: 'Capt. Hugo Throssell has been a familiar figure in the Anzac Day procession for years, but this time perhaps he took part in the memorial service at Greenmount, where he lives.'[56] On his final Anzac Day in 1933, he was recorded as a guest at the Perth Legacy Club, listening to the speaker Sir J.J. Talbot Hobbs on 'The Lessons of Anzac'.[57]

Not only did Throssell continue to be honoured as a war hero after his 1919 speech – his 'misfortunes' did not begin until much later. For many years he retained his job as the soldiers' representative for the land settlement scheme. In January 1926, the scheme was scaled back, and his position was made part-time. Prichard saw this as the beginning of Throssell's troubles, more than six years after the speech; she wrote to the Repatriation Department after his death: 'When he was first employed as soldiers' representative on the Land Settlement Board, and had a full time job, he never suffered the depression which assailed him when it became one day a week engagement.'[58] There were further troubles about the job in 1930 when the RSL, having grown dissatisfied with Throssell's 'lack of interest' in the scheme, lobbied the premier for the right to replace him as the soldiers' representative. Throssell resigned on Anzac Day 1931 with great bitterness; it is a plausible explanation for his absence from Anzac Day marches from 1931 to 1933. Given the time-lag from Throssell's activist period, it is unlikely the RSL was acting in response to it; they seem to have been genuinely concerned with Throssell's inattentiveness to the position, perhaps partly because they were not aware he was now only working one day a week.[59] Throssell was able to put the hurt behind him enough to propose (unsuccessfully) in September 1933 that the RSL make his rodeo a joint venture, adding 'trenches and a dug-out where war-trophies could be exhibited and the public shoot from the trenches with a periscopic rifle disappearing targets across the creek – a la Gallipoli'.[60]

Rather than being persecuted for his activism, Throssell retained a network of influence and support right to the end of his life. During the Depression in 1931, he rashly resigned from a position at the Agricultural Department in order to go prospecting in a gold rush. He returned empty-handed but his old friend, Jonah Jones, apparently had him reappointed to the job. When that position was made redundant, Jones found him a job as inspector of fertilisers.[61] When Throssell launched his rodeo without proper permissions in 1933, he was granted exemptions at short notice, including being allowed to collect entry fees on a Sunday to cover his costs.[62] Desperate for money just before his death, he was appointed inspector of eggs, again at the Agricultural Department.[63]

Embracing socialism did not lead to Throssell's wholesale rejection by society; it did not cause him to become indebted and nor did it cause him post-traumatic stress disorder. In Throssell's obituaries, there was no mention of his socialist period. Instead, as a typical example, the *Northam Advertiser* devoted two long paragraphs to his actions at Gallipoli and only one paragraph covering his life before and after the war. Throssell's celebrity was conferred on him because of his Victoria Cross, and his political activism did little to diminish it.

Peter Stanley writes, 'Focusing on and invariably celebrating the heroism and success so often a part of the VCs' stories has the effect of distracting attention from the horror and futility that is also part of the broader story.'[64] Despite Hugo Throssell's uncomfortable place in the Anzac story, the glorification of the Victoria Cross has meant that he has been well remembered in recent years, commemorated in newspaper articles and ceremonies. Far from being neglected, he is remembered in multiple ways at the Australian War Memorial, including in the 'After the War' exhibition, which opened in 2018, his portrait displayed under a banner that reads, 'What if your wounds are not visible?'[65] Throssell has been reinterpreted by Hamilton, the Australian War Memorial and others in the light of new sensitivity to the reality of post-traumatic stress disorder. Joan Beaumont writes of the representation of his death at the War Memorial speaking to 'the dominance of the trope of victimhood and trauma' in the collective memory of war.[66] While a focus on the effects of war on the individual psyche is commendable and leads to demands to support veterans properly on their return from war, it stops short of challenging the imperialism and nationalism that led so many like Throssell to enlist. It is symptomatic of this invisible ideology that Throssell's 'misfortune' is traced to the moment he challenged war and the capitalist system, rather than to the traumatic effects of war itself. Throssell's words are too easily forgotten: 'The war … has made me think and inquire what are the causes of wars.'[67]

7

SOLDIER SUICIDE
FIRST WORLD WAR VETERANS' DEATHS IN QUEENSLAND

MARGARET HUTCHISON AND KAREN BIRD

In 2024, the Royal Commission into Defence and Veteran Suicide (2021–24) brought to light something shocking: on average, every fortnight, three current or former service personnel take their own lives.[1] While veteran suicide is widely recognised as a crisis for the current and future Australian Defence Force, there is a longer history of veteran suicide in Australia's military past. An exploration of three First World War soldiers who died by suicide in the aftermath of service, how their experiences were shaped by their transition from military to civilian life, their access to support, and medical understandings of and treatment for what is now called war trauma, provide us with a deeper understanding of the enduring cost of the war and the ongoing challenges many returned men and women, and their families and communities, faced. The lives and deaths of David Molloy, Thomas Beaumont and Victor Wilkins sat outside the dominant narrative of the Anzac legend, at odds both with the Anzac warrior myth established during the war, and the symbol of the revered and stoic returned soldier that later developed.

'SUICIDE CULTURE' AND THE FIRST WORLD WAR

Veteran suicide has conventionally been studied in a medico-legal framework, but if we are to better understand this issue – and address the problem in contemporary Australia – we must reckon with its history more fully. Indeed, suicide is historically and culturally contingent. As John Weaver notes, '[S]uicide is partly situational and history is devoted to situations in time'.[2] Exploring the historical dimensions of suicide allows for the messiness and changeability of society over time. Other disciplines look for neat answers to deaths by suicide, attempting to theorise and categorise issues that are slippery and elusive and often subject to change.[3] However, a historical approach allows us to challenge 'the idea of a motionless world implicit in psychologists' attempts to comprehend suicide through quests for the timeless personality traits of people at risk'.[4] Given suicide is dependent upon the values of any given era, investigating the specifics of place and time are crucial to understanding the experiences of an individual's life and death. Olive Anderson has explained this as 'suicide culture'. She argues that 'what people thought and felt when they found themselves caught up in a situation of which suicide could be the outcome was partly settled by the ways of thinking and feeling about suicide which they had unconsciously absorbed from childhood onwards'.[5] Building on Anderson's idea, this exploration of the deaths of three veterans, David Molloy, Thomas Beaumont and Victor Wilkins, within their early-20th-century context provides an insight into how veteran suicide was understood in Queensland during and immediately after the war.

Ideas about suicide during and after the First World War were influenced by 19th-century morals. Australian attitudes to suicide in the colonial era drew heavily on British responses to self-harm, which were dominated by the Christian belief that suicide was a sin against God.[6] Christian condemnation of suicide generally held sway in Australia until the late 19th century; in New South Wales and Victoria, for instance, those who died by suicide were buried between 9pm and midnight, because of the stigma associated with this form of death. In this era, both medical professionals and the clergy were alarmed by the perceived leniency of coroners' findings of suicide, where verdicts of 'temporary insanity' were more common than *felo-de-se*, or self-murder.[7] As Pat Jalland notes, 'only about 2 per cent of suicides were returned as "felo de se" in 1890s Victoria' and concern over the increase in suicides in this decade fuelled conservative arguments that harsher verdicts should be returned as a deterrent to others contemplating suicide.[8]

At the same time, the late 19th century saw secular views on suicide begin to permeate Australian society. Increasingly, more emphasis was placed on socio-economic factors than religious ones. Such ideas were supported by academic studies in which scientific evidence challenged the authority of religious teachings, including Emile Durkheim's *Le Suicide* (1897), which contended that social integration was a major fact in suicide cases; those less integrated into their community were more likely to die by suicide.[9] While certain events correlated with spikes in suicide, such as the 1887 booms in silver and land, the 1893 bank crashes, and the Federation Drought at the turn of the century, Commonwealth statistician George Handley Knibbs judged that generally suicide was responsible for only 1.13 per cent of all deaths in 1910.[10] The breakdown of these deaths by gender were, according to Knibbs' study, 4.92 male suicides for every female suicide between 1871 and 1909.[11]

During and after the First World War, ideas about suicide were largely informed by theories developed by French scholars in the 19th century, emerging from the disciplines of sociology and psychology.[12] After the war, the dominance of French ideas about the causes of suicide gave way to American ones where, between the 1920s and 1960s, social scientists and psychiatrists in the United States examined the variations of suicide among populations. However, such studies did not necessarily challenge the assumptions that had emerged in the 19th century.[13] While the war stimulated interest in the fields of psychology and psychiatry in Australia, prewar ideas about the hereditary predisposition of mental illness continued to permeate the medical profession in the postwar years.[14] Arthur Butler, author of the *Official History of the Australian Army Medical Services, 1914–1918*, like many at the time, largely conformed to theories that soldiers who suffered from 'war neurosis' were predisposed to psychological conditions.[15] In taking such a line in his official history, he effectively distanced the Australian government from responsibility for soldiers who returned with mental trauma. Although he noted that the war had led to 'the "humanisation" of the treatment of the insane', he did not believe that studying First World War soldiers with mental illness added to the scientific understanding of the issue.[16] Butler's discussion of soldier suicide in his three-volume series was cursory at best.[17] Moreover, he censored much material about shell shock and other mental illnesses, thinking it would be unpalatable to the public and potentially harmful to soldiers.

THE MYTH OF ANZAC AND THE SYMBOL OF THE RETURNED SOLDIER

Butler's approach aligned with that of Charles Bean, Australia's official war correspondent, historian and chief architect of the Anzac legend. Bean's wartime and postwar writings espoused the qualities and inherently Australian virtues that underscored the prowess of the Australian Imperial Force (AIF) soldiers on the battlefield, namely their courage, loyalty to their mates, resourcefulness, inventiveness and endurance, which Bean believed to have developed because of Australia's environment and unique way of life.[18] This myth of the Anzac warrior emerged during the Gallipoli campaign in 1915, but gained traction over the course of the war and was consolidated in Bean's own editing of *The Anzac Book* (1916), a collection of satirical sketches and writings by the soldiers at Gallipoli, as well as his wartime diaries and notebooks and later his editing of the 12-volume official history of the conflict, volumes one to six of which he authored himself.[19] Moreover, the legend was reinforced through the rituals and practices that emerged to commemorate Australia's involvement in the war.

After the conflict, the legend remained a powerful public narrative and served to support the status of the returned soldier, which emerged in this period as a symbol of national unity and sacrifice. As Joan Beaumont puts it, the returned soldier became 'a revered imagined collective' in Australia, and played an important role in shaping veterans' experiences when they returned home.[20] Indeed, the values represented by the returned soldier proved to be a powerful political tool, and the symbol of the returned soldier was used by politicians to bolster Australian patriotism in the immediate aftermath of the war and later as the nation faced the global economic crisis of the 1930s. The power of this symbol became important in this decade, when, for instance, the Scullin government briefly considered reversing the policy of preference for employment of returned soldiers in 1930. Ultimately, in large part due to the work of the Returned Sailors' and Soldier' Imperial League of Australia (RSSILA), veterans retained this entitlement, which was a key component of repatriation policies, and demonstrated the elevated status that returned soldiers enjoyed.[21] Yet, the revered place of returned men in Australian society contrasted with the hardships they faced in their postwar lives.[22]

Some notable veterans were able to amalgamate their war service and the ideal of the revered returned soldier to shape successful postwar lives. Victoria Cross recipient Albert Jacka, for example, became a successful businessman and mayor of St Kilda, and although he died prematurely, his funeral was widely attended by returned soldiers.[23] Alistair Thomson has suggested that for some veterans, the ideal of the valiant soldier spoke to their shared experience and common sense of pride in having fought for Australia.[24] But for many returned soldiers and their families, this image of the heroic Anzac omitted their experiences, both during and after the war. Michael Tyquin argues that it allowed returned men and women a positive framework within which to make sense of their wartime lives, but that at the same time it marginalised war experiences that did not fit the legend, especially of those who returned with mental trauma.[25] Hence, while the Anzac legend was a powerfully unifying narrative for some, for others it proved alienating and papered over their war trauma.

Australia, like many countries that fought in the First World War, was not prepared for the vast numbers of men who returned with physical and mental trauma. As a response to the urgent need to support veterans, the Commonwealth Repatriation Department, or 'the Repat', was established during the war under the *Repatriation Act 1917*. As the first Minister for Repatriation, Senator Edward Davis Millen sought to reinstate able-bodied soldiers into their prewar jobs and help those with war wounds 'regain full participation in the activities of life'.[26] The policies and legislation of repatriation were driven by the idea that returned servicemen would re-establish themselves as independent members of their communities with the means to contribute meaningfully to Australian society. This shaped the evolution of the scheme, which moved from the well-established pensions for soldiers and their dependants – part of the repatriation system from its inception in 1917 – to include labour bureaus for returned servicemen, education and equipment to assist with re-employment, and rehabilitation training for veterans with disabilities.[27] The repatriation scheme also provided free medical and hospital care for returning servicemen who were injured or ill, and the government established hostels and homes for veterans with severe disabilities.

The scheme was generous by the standards of the day. This did not mean it was without its problems, not least the adversarial relationship between the Repatriation Department and veterans, due in large part to the process veterans had to go through to access pension and medical benefits, where the legitimacy of veterans' claims was tested by the department. By the 1920s, approximately 90 000 Australian veterans were receiving war pensions.[28] The Repat was supporting roughly 70 000 more ex-service members than the Canadian scheme (which had tougher appraisals of war-related injuries) by the 1930s. This was a considerable number given the fact that Canada had more returned men than Australia.[29] In August 1931, the

Australian Repatriation Department estimated that around 28 500 men were suffering from gunshot wounds, 6500 from heart conditions, 2900 from tuberculosis, 3150 from the loss of a limb, 129 from blindness, and a further 30 000 from other diseases and disabilities that were attributed to their war service. Around 3250 veterans were suffering from some form of 'war neurosis' or mental illness.[30] Around 12 844 veterans were receiving pensions based on psychiatric grounds in 1931, and by 1939, 4891 cases of war neurosis, which at the time covered shell shock, neurasthenia, epilepsy and alcoholism, were recorded by the Repatriation Department.[31]

Veterans' access to support and treatment varied across Australia. In Queensland, male suicide spiked after the First World War. According to Weaver, while suicide rates increased during the postwar years across most of Australia, especially during the Great Depression, rates of male suicide increased in Queensland to record levels not seen in the previous decades.[32] This was because the state was not only impacted by the global economic crisis but also by a severe drought. Typically, there was greater access to care in Australian capital cities than in rural areas. Treatment for mental illness in Queensland was concentrated in facilities in the south-east of the state around the capital, and regional care for those in the north was slower to develop. Queensland also did not allow voluntary admissions to psychiatric hospitals until 1940 – although, even if voluntary admissions had been available to veterans living in Queensland, the stigma attached to mental illness and such institutions probably remained a deterrent for many returned soldiers and their families.

When seeking support, many veterans and their families preferred repatriation facilities dedicated to returned soldiers over civilian asylums. This was in part due to a concerted effort from the Defence Department to mitigate the shame associated with psychological conditions and their treatment in military hospitals. The department put in place policies to ensure no soldier whose mental illness was considered to be a result of his war service should be 'certified a lunatic'. This term was still associated with the colonial asylum system and carried significant social stigma, connected with paupers, fallen women and others who were considered to sit outside the norms of society. The Defence Department was keen to avoid this stigma for veterans, whom they hoped would be reintegrated into their communities. Nevertheless, if a returned soldier's condition was determined to be incurable or chronic, the term was applied.[33] State lunatic authorities were, in many cases, charged with the care of soldiers whose mental illness was considered to predate their war service, but the care of those whose mental illness was seen to be caused by the stress of active service was overseen in a special military hospital for shell shock – lessening the stigma associated with treatment for mental illness.

UNDERSTANDING VETERAN SUICIDE

For many of the men who returned from the war with physical and mental trauma, and for the families and communities who cared for and supported them, their wartime and postwar experiences fell outside the heroic Anzac warrior mythology. Accurate suicide figures for those who served in the AIF are difficult to obtain. However, based on coroners' reports, a study from 1945 notes that between August 1914 and December 1937, returned soldiers made up 11.6 per cent of deaths by suicide in New South Wales, or 634 of the total 5450 male deaths by suicide in the state.[34] The actual figures were likely higher as not all suicides were referred to the coroner's office for investigation. Yet even these numbers show a high loss of life in this period and directly challenge the Anzac legend.

Veteran suicide was reported widely in the Australian press in the interwar years, with themes of mental illness and coroners' findings of 'suicide while of unsound mind' dominating newspaper articles. Broadsheets, rural newspapers and tabloids across the country published hundreds of articles about the issue, and headlines like 'Ex-soldier's suicide', 'Returned soldier's suicide', or 'Digger's suicide' were commonplace. Such was the extent of reporting on veteran suicide, that in 1919, George Taylor, editor of *The Soldier*, wrote a poignant poem in which he decried the vast quantity of such headlines. Titling the poem 'The suicide', he wrote, 'How oft we see that headline grim. Ah! You who sit and calmly scan that headline think – He was a man … Whose nerves unstrung in noble strife went through Hell in earthly life.'[35] This poem echoed a tendency for newspapers to be explicit in their reportage: Simon Cooke argues that in Victoria between the 1840s and 1920s, deaths by suicide were published in considerable detail in newspapers, with up to four or five on a single page.[36] Newspaper reports of veterans' suicides could be sympathetic to the plight of the men, referring to them as victims of the war and acknowledging the role that postwar difficulties played in their deaths. While newspapers did not use the term, they demonstrate a wider awareness of what is now called war trauma. Well into the 1930s, newspapers linked suicide to a veterans' war service. The kind of war service they saw made no difference. For example, Walter Beer, a 28-year-old man who murdered his wife and daughter before dying by suicide in Sydney in 1926, was referred to in the press as 'a returned soldier who had been in bad health for some time'.[37] Despite his having spent the entirety of his war service in training camps on the Salisbury Plain, press reports implied frontline service and reported (incorrectly) on his being gassed, seemingly in an attempt to make the inexplicable actions of Beer comprehensible. The media identified these men first and foremost as veterans, and despite often also reporting on their postwar occupations and careers and their community connections, understood their deaths to be related to their experiences during the war.

While the official findings of the coronial inquests and the newspaper reportage show how veteran suicide was perceived in Queensland at the time, evidence given at inquests provides poignant insights into how families and communities attempted to understand and come to terms with the deaths of veterans. The individual stories of a handful of veterans can tell us much about how friends and family made sense of the death of their loved one and how they framed their deaths in relation to their war service.

VETERANS' LIVES LOST

David Molloy, Thomas Beaumont and Victor Wilkins all served in the AIF during the First World War and all three died by suicide between 1916 and 1926. These men came from a range of backgrounds, led different lives before the war, and had diverse experiences of service during the conflict. Yet, they are linked by the nature of their deaths. Untangling returned soldiers' deaths by suicide is a complex task. The context within which these men lived and died was shaped by a multitude of interlinking political, social, cultural and economic factors, which were unique to each veteran, and not all of which can be solely attributed to their wartime service. Yet, it is evident when exploring the postwar lives of Molloy, Beaumont and Wilkins, that all three were at odds with the dominant narrative of the Anzac warrior.

In coronial records, veteran suicides were usually ruled as death or suicide while temporarily insane. War service was usually identified in coronial documents, though the extent to which this was attributed to the cause of a veteran's death varied. In some cases, suicides were attributed directly to war trauma. David Molloy's death on 29 February 1920 was ruled a suicide and directly attributed to his poor mental health, which had been caused by his war service in the Middle East. Molloy was an Indigenous man who had been born at Mt Molloy in North Queensland, but was forcibly removed from his community along with his sister in 1903 and taken to the Yarrabah Aboriginal Mission. He enlisted in August 1917 and was posted to the 11th Light Horse Regiment.[38] Arriving in Suez in March 1918, he served in the Palestine Campaign, fighting in the Battle of Semakh in September 1918. In November 1918, he contracted malaria, and a medical report described him as experiencing delusions as a complication of clinical malaria and lobar pneumonia: 'Has delusions he is a major, has signs from above telling him to do certain actions and obeys them'.[39] Evidence given at the inquest noted that Molloy suffered from severe mental illness after this, and his service record shows that he was categorised by military medical authorities as having constitutional – not hereditary – mental trauma as a result of the strain of his service and malaria. He spent the last months of the war in hospital in Cairo where he was put in a 'straight jacket', an episode that severely distressed him.[40] In May 1919, he returned to Australia and in August that year was given a medical discharge.[41]

Molloy's body was found with a gunshot wound to the chest in the Mossman Gorge in Far North Queensland. The coroner ruled his death, at age 24, to be suicide owing to temporary despondency caused by the stress of his active war service.[42] Molloy's death was reported as a 'shooting tragedy', but the media framed this within the context of his military service. The *Cairns Post* explained in detail the way Molloy had separated from his shooting party, the search that had then taken place for him, and the discovery of his body. Although it was not clear whether he had died by suicide at the time the article was published, the newspaper indicated that it was a strong possibility, noting that he had suffered from shell shock because of his war service. The article described Molloy as 'a young man about 24 years of age, who had seen two years of service with the AIF. He was very popular, but at times was despondent, and suffered from shell shock.'[43] Here, Molloy's death was understood as a tragic result of his psychological condition caused by the stress of his war service.

Molloy's death was also understood by his family and community to relate directly to his war service. It was well known among his friends and family that Molloy had suffered from shell shock during the war. He had discussed his time in Palestine, including his treatment in hospital when he had been put in a straitjacket, with his brother-in-law, Edgar Brackenridge, who noted that since returning from the war, Molloy often appeared despondent. He recounted how on the day Molloy died, a party of four had gone out shooting at Molloy's suggestion. They had met another returned soldier, whom Molloy had not seen since the war: 'They spoke about the war ... Before we met Simmonds [the returned soldier] the deceased appeared to be in good spirits and after was very quiet.'[44] Brackenridge, who was part of the search party for Molloy that included the local Indigenous community, noted that it would have been impossible for Molloy to become lost and that there were no footprints around his body. For

Brackenridge, Molloy's death was related to his war trauma, which resurfaced after speaking with a fellow veteran and remembering his war experiences.

It was more common, however, for soldier suicides to be linked to physical war injuries. For instance, Thomas Beaumont, born in Bogantungan, Queensland, was identified as a returned soldier, and his death on 15 December 1916 was attributed to distress caused by his physical condition because of his war service.[45] Beaumont's war was short. He enlisted in January 1916 and joined the 52nd Battalion as a private in Egypt. He was hospitalised with influenza in May 1916, developed a cough and lost a considerable amount of weight – one doctor referring to him as 'wasted' – and was eventually diagnosed as having chronic bronchitis.[46] He was invalided back to Australia in late 1916 and medically discharged from the AIF on 6 December 1916.[47] His service records show that doctors believed his illness was permanently debilitating.[48]

Beaumont's brother, James, understood his death to be related to his bronchitis and described Beaumont as being a physical wreck and very low before he died. His testimony at the inquest shows that he believed Beaumont's chronic illness led him to take his own life: 'I consider it was owing to his physical condition and great suffering from the complaint that caused him to commit the rash act he did'.[49] James noted that there was no tension within the family that might cause his brother's unhappiness and that Thomas had returned home from being discharged in a 'melancholy and dejected mood'.[50] Beaumont's death was reported in the *Morning Bulletin* as being linked to his discharge from the AIF as medically unfit: 'the fact so much prayed on his mind that he took his own life'.[51] During the coroner's inquest, the *Morning Bulletin* again reported on Beaumont's death, relating it to his 'sickly and depressed' condition after he was discharged. His death three days after returning home was reported as a shock to his family, with the newspaper recording that 'he had not said anything that would lead his people to suppose that he had contemplated suicide'.[52] Beaumont's death was constructed as an unplanned, impulsive incident, but nevertheless one that directly related to his physical debility caused by his war injuries. His death is reflective of other suicides by returned soldiers: the evidence suggests that despair over physical injury, disability and chronic pain were key factors in veteran suicides in the aftermath of the First World War.

Not all returned soldiers' deaths by suicide were attributed directly to their war service, although their war service was invariably mentioned and sometimes seen to be a contributing factor. Several reasons were raised at the coroner's inquest to account for Victor Wilkins' suicide. While his war service and status as a returned soldier were raised during the inquiry, his heavy drinking was seen to be the cause of his death. Wilkins, born in Rockhampton, had enlisted in the AIF in July 1915, serving with the 5th Australian Light Horse Regiment. In March 1918, he was found guilty of using false documents to obtain two cases of whisky and given 90 days of Field Punishment No. 2, which entailed hard labouring duties. After contracting malaria in Egypt in December 1918, Wilkins was invalided back to Australia.[53] He had been married with two children before the war, but his wife, Ivy Wilkins, refused to live with him on his return to Queensland. She went to work elsewhere, leaving her children with her mother, and Wilkins took up work as a shearer, sending money to his mother-in-law, Agnes Williams, in support of his children. In 1926, Wilkins was shearing on Ightham Station, in the Barcaldine region of Queensland – far from any mental health or medical support available from the Repatriation Department. He was despondent, drinking heavily, and seems to have recognised that he needed help, although there was little available. He asked his boss, Darcy Irvine, to lock the men's cutthroat razors away as he felt compelled to use them to kill himself. His boss hid the razors in a suitcase but neglected to lock it. Wilkins found the suitcase and used one of the razors to cut his own throat. Agnes Williams believed Wilkins' suicide to be a result of the physical pain he was suffering in his side: 'I think that continuous pain caused him to take his own life', though it is unclear whether this was a war-related injury.[54] There is no evidence of a serious wound or injury to his side on his service record, and much of the inquest was spent documenting Wilkins' drinking habits, which were said to be heavy. It was believed that 'he was suffering from the after effects of drinking' when he died on 3 December 1926. The coroner at Longreach ruled his death, at age 37, a suicide.[55]

Wilkins' family, friends and colleagues had different understandings of his suicide. While Wilkins' mother-in-law believed his death was because of his physical pain, his friends and fellow shearers at Ightham Station understood that he was 'not in his proper senses' on the night he died because of his heavy drinking.[56] William Ward, who had worked with Wilkins for six years at Ightham Station as a shearer, stated he could 'form no idea why the deceased would take his own life', but suggested it was because he was suffering after a heavy bout of drinking.[57] Irvine noted Wilkins' drinking had increased during recent years. He recounted that he had spent three days in Rockhampton with Wilkins who 'was drinking very heavily' a few days before his death. Wilkins himself had admitted 'he felt very much off and blamed the drink as a cause of it'. Irvine also noted that Wilkins had been restless, frightened and scared over several nights and at one point 'imagined he could see different things'. Irvine recounted how Wilkins woke him up saying, 'I think I am going to die, I've got the horrors at last, I can see a man in the corner of the tent with a stick in his hand'. Wilkins asked Irvine to hide all the razors because, as he said, 'I know now why people cut their throats, you have no idea what this is like'. Irvine stayed with him overnight because he believed Wilkins 'was suffering from the DTs' – delirium tremens, a symptom of alcohol withdrawal syndrome that can include hallucinations like those described by Wilkins.[58]

Wilkins' death was reported in the local newspapers and portrayed as a sad accident. An article in the *Longreach Leader*, titled 'Shearer commits suicide: Tragedy at Ightham Station', reported that Wilkins 'was apparently in his ordinary spirits' before his death. His comment that razors should be taken away was reported, but the article largely portrayed his suicide as a surprising, but shocking, tragedy.[59] However, after the coronial inquest, an article in the *Western Champion* contained greater detail about Wilkins' life: reporting the breakdown of his relationship with his wife, his support of their two children, the pain he complained of in his side, and how he caught malarial fever during the war.[60] Notably, neither of the newspapers mentioned his drinking habits, framing his death as a tragic incident, with the *Western Champion* printing his mother-in-law's belief that he died because of the constant pain he suffered.[61]

The inquest also did not make the direct link between Wilkins' war service and his drinking, which seems to have been put down to a personal choice rather than a symptom of pain or mental trauma. Nevertheless, high numbers of returned soldiers suffered from alcoholism.[62] Whether drinking was a coping mechanism for returned soldiers, or a pre-existing condition, medical and repatriation authorities recognised that excessive alcohol consumption aggravated returned soldiers' psychological conditions and could lead them to behave in ways 'that in normal circumstances would be quite foreign to their temperament and disposition'.[63] Many veterans sought to ease their physical and mental pain with alcohol, but deaths as a result of excessive drinking or its after-effects were not often counted in veteran suicide statistics.[64] And, as the example of Victor Wilkins shows, the link was not strongly made in many cases at the time. War service was an ameliorating factor in suicides – drinking was perceived to be a moral failing.

The war trauma, postwar lives and deaths of Molloy, Beaumont and Wilkins were at stark odds with the warrior mythology of Anzac and the symbol of the returned soldier. Within the context of the time, their deaths were understood to, at least in some way, relate to or have been aggravated by their war service and the physical or mental injuries they sustained during the conflict. Tracing the stories of these men can shed light not only on the cost of war to veterans and their families, but also on the way their deaths were constructed and understood in Australia during the postwar years. While the media portrayed the deaths of these men as tragedies, families and communities framed the deaths of their veterans within the broader trajectory of these men's lives, seeing the changes the war wrought in them or the effect that remembering and reliving their wartime experiences had on their wellbeing. Significantly, the deaths of Beaumont and Molloy may yet be honoured within the tradition of Anzac. In 2025, both were under consideration for addition to the Australian War Memorial's Roll of Honour.[65] The Roll of Honour includes the names of veterans whose deaths by suicide are determined to relate directly to their service and fall within the specified period for inclusion, which is usually two years after the end of a conflict. This is an important acknowledgement of the trauma of war, but it does not capture the longer lasting legacies of conflict that can manifest years or decades later.

The archive contains a staggering number of similar stories of First World War servicemen and women whose postwar lives and deaths all sit outside the Anzac narrative. Such stories are not confined to interwar Queensland or those who served in the First World War, but are mirrored across the veteran experience and the many conflicts in which Australia has participated. The continued cost of military service to veterans and their families has become all too evident during the Royal Commission into Defence and Veteran Suicide.[66] The Commission's findings suggest that the values associated with the ideal soldier – such as 'loyalty, sacrifice, and self-reliance' – may also be associated directly or indirectly with suicide risk, as they can implicitly discourage veterans from seeking support.[67] The Commission's recommendations, therefore, present an opportunity for all Australians to finally confront the long history of military and veteran trauma, and address and prevent this issue in the future.

8

'ALIEN TO OUR SPLENDID TRADITION'
THE RELIEF OF TOBRUK, 1941

JOAN BEAUMONT

All memory is selective, and the 'national memory' of war notably so. The collective memory that manifests itself in acts of official and public remembrance always privileges certain narratives from the past to the exclusion of others.[1] In Australia's case, the 1915 landing at Gallipoli undoubtedly tops the hierarchy of battles to be celebrated, since it originally spawned the Anzac legend; but the pantheon of iconic battles also includes two from the Second World War: the Kokoda Trail, 1942; and the siege of Tobruk, North Africa, 1941. The 'Rats of Tobruk', the nickname embraced by Australian troops as a badge of honour after the Nazi propaganda broadcaster William Joyce (Lord Haw-Haw) claimed that they were caught like rats in a trap, were positioned even at the time as exemplars of the Anzac tradition.[2] They have retained this status to this day. In 1983, the 'Rats' were honoured with the third of the memorials installed on the prime memory real estate of Anzac Parade, Canberra.[3] Four decades later, when the last veteran of Tobruk died, the national media resurrected the long-standing claim that the Rats' defence of Tobruk inflicted Hitler's first major defeat of the Second World War.[4] The months-long siege that followed purportedly showed Anzacs at their most defiant and cocky. As the former governor-general Sir Peter Cosgrove said, their attitude was, 'We're Australians and you're not chucking *us* out!'[5]

Yet, the capture and siege are not the full story of Tobruk. Before the siege ended with a British land offensive (code-named Crusader) in December 1941, most of the Australian forces had been evacuated by sea. This relief was carried out at the insistence of successive Australian governments in the face of strong opposition from senior British commanders in the Middle East theatre and by British Prime Minister Winston Churchill. The details of this dispute would be aired publicly by Churchill in 1950, but in subsequent years the relief of Tobruk slipped to the margins of Australian national memory. When mentioned in the public domain, it has been a footnote with little context, or perhaps an episode for which Britain's leaders – ever the popular scapegoat for Australian military defeats – should be blamed. This eliding might be explained by the relief being a minor part of a longer, more dramatic Tobruk narrative, but it surely owes something to the fact that the relief challenges the depiction of the Anzacs as the acme of endurance. Yes, the Rats were not 'chucked out' of Tobruk, but they did leave quietly at night to seek safety and comfort away from the battlefield – if only for a time.

THE SIEGE OF TOBRUK

Australia's Tobruk story starts in January 1941 when the 2nd Australian Imperial Force (AIF) went into action in North Africa, after being deployed to the Middle East to assist in defence of the strategic Suez Canal and British imperial interests in Egypt. The Italians, who entered the war in June 1940, attacked

Egypt in September 1940, but were driven back by a British counterattack beginning in December. On 21–22 January 1941, the Australian 6th Division captured the strategic port of Tobruk, together with some 25 000 Italian troops and massive quantities of supplies.[6]

The British Empire forces then pursued the Italians further along the Libyan coast to Benghazi. But soon the desert war changed dramatically. In February 1941, the German Afrika Corps arrived under the command of Erwin Rommel, with the aim of shoring up the Italian defence. Concurrently, some British forces in North Africa (including the Australian 6th Division) were diverted to support Greece against an Axis invasion. When Rommel seized the opportunity to counterattack, the imperial forces were forced out of the whole of Cyrenaica (the region of north-eastern Libya bordering on the Mediterranean). The Australian 9th Division, the 18th Brigade of the Australian 7th Division, and some British artillery and Indian troops were left under siege in Tobruk, trapped against the Mediterranean coast. The British command thought the trapped forces might be isolated for up to two months, perhaps four. But the siege of Tobruk would last much longer, until December 1941.

On several occasions, and most notably in April and May 1941, German infantry and armour tried to break through Tobruk's fortified perimeter, suffering and inflicting considerable casualties as they did so. The Australian commander of the 9th Division, Major-General L.J. Morshead, in turn, insisted that his troops remain on the 'offensive defence', constantly harassing the enemy with raids and patrols, such as the 1st AIF had become famous for on the Western Front. 'We set out', Morshead later said, 'to besiege the besiegers.'[7] Two British counterattacks in the desert, in May and June 1941, however, failed to relieve the siege – much to the frustration of Churchill, who dismissed the British commander General Archibald Wavell and installed British General Claude Auchinleck in his place on 5 July.

The Tobruk defenders were under constant strain from enemy artillery and air bombardment, and living conditions were primitive. But they were kept supplied with stores, guns, ammunition and medical supplies by sea. The 'Tobruk ferry run' was vulnerable to air attack, especially in the approaches to Tobruk. In all, two destroyers, three sloops and 19 smaller vessels were lost.[8] Among them were two Australian ships, the destroyer HMAS *Waterhen* and the sloop HMAS *Parramatta*, which were sunk in June and November 1941 respectively.

The unfolding Tobruk story gave the Australian press much cause for hyperbole. The Brisbane *Truth* hailed the original capture of the port in January 1941 as '86 hours of Anzac history making':

When it came to the true test of manhood, facing odds, the Italians could not, or did not, stand up to it. Anzac Landing to the Hindenburg Line are the limits each way to battle honors [sic] that the parent battalions of these troops earned in the last war. Bardia [captured earlier in January 1941] and Tobruk are two more that can be proudly embroidered beneath them.[9]

The *Goulburn Evening Post* (among other papers) revelled in the news that an 'Anzac' hat had been placed on a masthead in the centre of Tobruk. The Australians, having ridden 'triumphantly into the town', presented 'an inspiring sight, revealing indomitable cheerfulness despite the fact that they were caked with the dust of the Libyan desert, while many wore torn uniforms after days of fighting'.[10]

The subsequent siege confirmed the belief that the Rats were heirs to the Anzacs of the Great War. The *Sydney Morning Herald*, for example, declared on 2 August 1941:

> Tobruk is destined to be as proud a name as any in Australian history … It was a proud tradition of the old A.I.F., in which General Morshead, who commands the garrison, was an outstanding young Infantry commander, that it made 'no-man's land' its own territory This part of the new A.I.F. is doing the same thing again.[11]

A regional Victorian newspaper even claimed a place for Tobruk in world history:

> Neither in the war of 1914–18, nor in the present war has there occurred anything comparable … Tobruk will always be recalled as the scene of one of the most remarkable and most heroic stands in the history of warfare.[12]

Many papers also ran a letter that that had been written by 'a digger' to his friend:

> I am in my dug-out writing this with a big Italian cigar stuck in my mouth … Hello, the planes, are dropping something and it's not bombs. Hm! Well, well! Would you believe it! He is calling on us, to surrender! What a joke! I wonder what he thinks we are? He will get hell of a shock if he takes us for mugs.[13]

Another 'Song of Tobruk' written by a soldier under siege was featured in August 1941:

> We're the Tobruk Garrison.
> For we are the A.I.F., the same as before
> We will fight with might and come back for more
> No we won't give in.[14]

In sum, the Rats were the second generation of Anzacs, worthy heirs to the traditions of the 1st AIF.

THE RELIEF CONTROVERSY

Yet, many of these diggers, for whom surrender was avowedly unthinkable, were taken out of the war zone from August to October 1941. The relief of Tobruk came about in controversial circumstances. In the aftermath of the disastrous Greek and Cretan campaigns, in which Australia lost 594 dead, 1101 wounded and some 5132 prisoners of war, the Australian government of Sir Robert Menzies was understandably keen to avoid another military disaster.[15] Menzies' hold on power was precarious and he feared the impact on public opinion of more bad news.[16] He also concurred with the argument presented by the Australian Commander-in-Chief, and for a time Deputy Commander-in-Chief in the Middle East, Lieutenant-General Thomas Blamey, that the Australian forces in the Middle East must be concentrated under Australian command. When the AIF had been deployed, a charter had been negotiated with the British stating that all Australian troops should be under a commander with direct responsibility to the Australian government. None of them should be detached or employed apart from the force without that commander's consent. Yet, by May 1941, thanks to urgent operational needs, Australian troops had been dispersed across the Middle Eastern theatre.[17] Blamey, who had failed to inform Canberra early enough of his doubts about the wisdom of the Greek campaign, wanted all of them, including those troops trapped in Tobruk, to be consolidated under his command.

The relief of Tobruk, Blamey claimed, was necessary because the health of the Australian defenders was declining. Many seemed to be losing weight, and the wounded and sick were taking markedly more time to recover.[18]A report by the 9th Division's legal staff officer noted signs of 'lapses in discipline' and mental health issues resulting from the claustrophobic conditions and constant air raids and shelling. There were many cases of desertion and a smaller number of self-inflicted wounds, triggered by 'plain fear' and 'a "bomb-happy" state in much the same manner as shell-shock in the 1914–18 war'.[19] Blamey and Morshead worried that the Tobruk garrison might not be able to withstand another major German assault should Rommel, reinforced with more guns and tanks, take the offensive again.[20]

On 18 July, Blamey proposed to Menzies and General Auchinleck that the Tobruk garrison should be relieved by sea. It seemed a propitious time, given there was a comparative lull in fighting in the desert after Germany launched Operation Barbarossa against the Soviet Union on 22 June. Menzies sent a similar request for relief to Churchill shortly afterwards, stressing that the consolidation of the AIF in the Middle East would 'give immense satisfaction to Australian people [sic] for whom there is great national value and significance in knowing that all Australian soldiers in any zone form one Australian unit'.[21]

The British were initially open to the Australian request. Auchinleck agreed that some of the Australian troops in

Tobruk, the 18th Brigade (from the 7th Division then deployed in Palestine) could be taken out by sea, when a suitable level of air protection could be provided. This evacuation began on the night of 21–22 August. Allied ships came in under the cover of darkness and quickly unloaded supplies and reinforcements before loading some 850 men and taking them back to Alexandria. The departing Australians were replaced by a Polish unit, the 1st Carpathian Brigade.

Auchinleck thought this was enough. He was under intense pressure from an impatient Churchill to resume the offensive in the desert as soon as possible. The commanders of the Royal Air Force and Royal Navy in the Middle Eastern theatre, Admiral Andrew Cunningham and Air Vice Marshal William Tedder, opposed further relief operations; and Auchinleck questioned whether the Tobruk garrison's capacity to resist further attacks had been materially impaired. The 9th Division knew the ground in Tobruk well, he argued, and would do a better job than any new force at defending Tobruk and breaking out to join the planned Crusader offensive, if needed. Beyond that, the logistics of relief meant that Australians could only be relieved in October, very close to D-Day for this offensive.

Churchill backed Auchinleck. For him, Tobruk had become the 'most powerful symbol of British resistance to Hitler since the Battle of Britain [July to September 1940]'.[22] On 5 May he had cabled Morshead, gushing: 'The whole Empire is watching your steadfast and spirited defence of this important outpost Egypt [sic] with gratitude and admiration'. He boasted to the US President Franklin Roosevelt that the repulse of the German attack on Tobruk on 14 April 1941 was the first time that the Germans 'have tasted defeat and they are working on very small margins'.[23] The German attack on the Soviet Union only raised

Tobruk's value, given that Stalin soon insisted that the Western allies launch a second front to take pressure off the Red Army.

For some weeks the British and Australian commanders and governments battled it out, with Arthur Fadden, who replaced Menzies as prime minister in late August, insisting that the relief should continue. Finally, Churchill gave way, but reluctantly and only to avoid an open dispute with the Australian government. He wrote to his minister of state in Cairo, Oliver Lyttelton, on 18 September, 'I was astounded at the Australian Government's decision, being sure it would be repudiated by Australia if the facts could be made known'. To Auchinleck he complained that he was grieved at the Australian attitude, but had long feared the dangerous reactions of Australian and world opinion of seeming to fight all the battles in the Middle East only with Dominion troops.[24] (Australia and New Zealand provided more than half of General Wavell's infantry and a third of his total force.)[25] Auchinleck, no less aggrieved, considered resigning because he had failed to command the confidence of the Australian government – but he stayed until he, too, was sacked by Churchill in August 1942.[26]

Thus, the relief of the Australians at Tobruk resumed from 17 to 27 September. The air attacks that many had feared did not eventuate, and almost 6000 men (including 544 wounded) were evacuated.[27] Two Australian brigades remained in Tobruk, and the British continued to insist that any further withdrawals would handicap the Royal Air Force in its fight for air superiority. 'We feel', Churchill told Fadden on 30 September, 'we are entitled to count upon Australia to make every sacrifice necessary for the comradeship of the Empire.'[28]

This message arrived on the day that Fadden's government fell after two Independents withdrew their support in parliament, but with the approval of the new Labor prime minister, John Curtin, Fadden wrote back insisting that the relief continue. Despite a last-minute appeal from Churchill, it was resumed between 12 and 25 October. On the last day of the operation, enemy attacks damaged the destroyer HMS *Hero* and sank the minelayer HMS *Latona* (with 23 men of the Royal Navy and 14 soldiers becoming casualties).[29] Admiral Cunningham said the relief was too risky to continue, and some Australians – the 2/13th Battalion, two companies of the 2/15th and some men of divisional headquarters – remained in Tobruk. They were still there when the siege was finally lifted by Auchinleck's offensive in early December. They were the only Australians to see the siege through from beginning to end.

THE RELIEF CONTROVERSY EXPOSED

None of this dispute between London and Canberra was known publicly in Australia during the war. The siege continued to be extolled as an exemplar of Anzac heroism. The 1944 film *The Rats of Tobruk*, produced by Charles Chauvel, the nephew of the First World War commander of the Australian Light Horse, General Sir Harry Chauvel, described the 9th Division as being relieved by British and Polish troops, 'scarred but unconquered [after] their 281-day ordeal'. Scenes of men boarding ships in the darkness were followed by a ticker tape parade in Australia (which must have taken place well after the Tobruk relief since the 9th Division stayed on in the Middle East to take part in the second battle of El Alamein in late 1942): 'Now they were heroes! Line on line, to march in triumph, a thrilling conquering company, the 9th was home!'[30] Meanwhile, a 1944 history of Tobruk by war correspondent Chester Wilmot, who spent much of the siege in Tobruk, attributed the relief to 'strong and persistent urging' by Blamey for a single Australian fighting force, and the deteriorating health of the Rats. Their relief was 'a final insult' to Rommel: 'The Australians whom Rommel had threatened to drive into the sea in April [1941] had thrown back all his attacks, defied and harried his forces for over six months and finally had been withdrawn to rest, refit and come back for their revenge at El Alamein in 1942.'[31]

In 1950, however, the controversy about Tobruk's relief was exposed – and by none other than Churchill.[32] His shock defeat in the election of mid-1945 gave Churchill the time to write his six-volume war memoirs and he famously said, 'I shall leave it to history, but remember that I shall be one of the historians'.[33] Churchill's approach was to use a team of researchers to write preliminary drafts before he polished the manuscript, adding his inimitable voice, memories and opinions. Sometimes the Churchillian touch was light, but in Australia's case, he became deeply engaged in the drafting process. He had points to score: not just Australia's failure to follow Britain's example and form a national government, and the accusation of the Curtin government in January 1942 that the evacuation of Singapore would constitute an 'inexcusable betrayal', but also the relief of Tobruk. In volume III, *The Grand Alliance*, Churchill's account of the 'unhappy episode' of Tobruk placed blame on Fadden and Curtin and their preoccupation with domestic politics. Fadden refused to bow to strategic logic because he had a parliamentary majority of only one and was 'confronted in this grievous period by a Party Opposition thirsting for local power'. (Menzies was excused because, although he had clashed with Churchill when visiting London in 1941, the two men had developed a more cordial relationship by the late 1940s. Menzies, too, was more ideologically congenial to Churchill than Curtin.) To bolster his case, Churchill quoted extensively from a series of wartime telegrams, including one to Lyttelton, in which he deprecated the 'Australian resolve to quit the line at this juncture'. 'It has given me pain to have to relate this incident', he concluded, but 'to suppress it indefinitely would be impossible. Besides, the Australian people have a right to know what happened and why'.[34]

The first draft of this account was even stronger than that published in 1950. Given the publication's potential implications for the diplomatic relationship with Australia, the British Cabinet Secretary, Norman Brook, persuaded Churchill to tone it down. When the Australian government of Ben Chifley, who had become prime minister after Curtin's death in 1945, was sent copies of the telegrams Churchill intended to quote, but not the full text, Chifley asked that Australia's views on Tobruk and larger questions of imperial consultation and South-East Asian command be given more space. But Churchill deferred the publication until after the Australian election of December 1949. Once in power, Menzies did not press for more changes. As David Reynolds says, Menzies and the Secretary of the Department of Defence, Frederick Shedden, 'had no interest in defending the reputation of Curtin and the wartime Labor government as pioneers of assertive Australian nationalism'.[35]

When published in early 1950, Churchill's account caused something of a sensation. Some major Australian newspapers (Melbourne's *Herald*, Sydney's *Daily Telegraph*, Brisbane's *Courier Mail* and Adelaide's *Advertiser*) were serialising the whole Second World War history. The press welcomed Churchill's assurances that nothing he said cast aspersions on the valour of the Australian soldiers or the loyalty of the Australian people.[36] But the Returned and Services League (RSL) in Victoria demanded 'a hard-hitting reply'.

> The implication was that Australian withdrew her troops from Tobruk when the general war situation demanded they remain there, and that British servicemen lost their lives unnecessarily in the withdrawal … Our record in war is too glorious to be tarnished by reports of differences based on a political decision.[37]

One Melbourne newspaper, in an article headlined 'Taint on Tobruk', declared, 'The word "quit" is an ugly one, alien to the splendid Australian tradition'.[38] The *Daily Telegraph* (Sydney) featured two AIF officers, unit commanders during the siege, who assured readers that the troops in Tobruk would rather have fought on than be relieved. They had greeted the news of their withdrawal 'with mixed feelings'; pleasure at leaving mixed with 'a feeling of regret that they would not have the opportunity of seeing it through'.[39] The leader of the ALP Opposition and External Affairs Minister during the war, H.V. Evatt, meanwhile, issued a public statement describing Churchill's criticism as 'quite unjustified' and calling on Menzies to publish the messages that Churchill had received from Australia's leaders.[40]

The furore died down, but Churchill's account of the dispute continued for some time to have the status of being authoritative. Only he, and the official historians of the war, had access to the full archival record before the 1970s. In 1952 Paul Hasluck, author of the official history on the Australian government and people at war, did offer a rejoinder to Churchill's critique. Incorporating the views of the Australian War Cabinet, his point-by-point rebuttal concluded that the initial request for the relief of Tobruk had been a matter of 'military judgment' but that 'it was sustained in the face of a plea that was political and emotional as well as military'.[41] But Hasluck's analysis was confined to a nine-page appendix to a 624-page volume that probably few Australians read in its entirety. When later official historians dealt with the operational history of Tobruk, they seemed to have little appetite to revisit the controversy. I.S.O. Playfair, the author of the relevant British official volume dealing with the Mediterranean and Middle East, published in 1960, allocated only a few pages to the relief of Tobruk and did little to unsettle Churchill's version of events. If anything, he confirmed this by emphasising the risks that the relief operation posed to Allied naval vessels.[42] The Australian operational study of Tobruk and El Alamein, published in 1966, concluded with a painfully convoluted passage:

> Either Government might have been proved wrong: the British, if CRUSADER had failed; the Australian, if the German air forces had fought a major battle to prevent the relief. But presupposing the worst possible case, the possible weakening of the CRUSADER offensive that could have resulted from the relief could not have been of such magnitude in relation to the total resources to be employed as to be unlikely to affect the outcome.[43]

Gavin Long's 1973 synthesis of all the official histories consigned the debate about the relief of Tobruk to a bland paragraph.[44] The relief of Tobruk was on its way to becoming a footnote of Australia's war history.

REMEMBERING TOBRUK

The relief had little prominence in the postwar commemoration of Tobruk, although the siege itself continued to be widely celebrated. In April 1948, an obelisk, paid for by the Australian government, was unveiled by Morshead in Tobruk's war cemetery.[45] In the decades that followed, Tobruk memorials sprang up across Australia: from Rockhampton, Mackay, Bundaberg and Brisbane in Queensland, to King's Park in Perth. Some were replicas of a memorial originally built by 9th Division engineers in Tobruk that did not survive the war.[46] Cairns City Council, at the request of the Rats of Tobruk Association in 1956, chose to name its Olympic-sized pool after Tobruk.[47] Townsville had already done the same, completing its baths in 1950. It added a rose garden on the 80th anniversary of the siege in 2021.[48]

Most importantly, the Rats of Tobruk were granted a memorial in Anzac Parade, Canberra, within sight of the national custodian of the memory of war, the Australian War Memorial. This privilege was not won easily. In 1964 the federal government decided to develop Anzac Parade in anticipation of the 50th anniversary of the Gallipoli landing, but the niches were to be reserved for memorials of national significance; for example, 'commemoration of great actions and events in war, involving the whole nation'.[49] The first petition of the ACT Rats of Tobruk Association to install a replica of the Tobruk memorial thus failed. In 1970, Prime Minister John Gorton suggested that the Rats Association work with the National Capital Development Commission (NCDC) to find an alternative site in Canberra.[50]

In the early 1980s, the Rats Association renewed their efforts with additional political support, although the RSL remained uncomfortable with their effort to carve out a unique identity separate from the broader veteran community. Finally, government approval was given to erect a memorial to Tobruk on Anzac Parade.[51] Jointly funded by the Rats of Tobruk Association and the NCDC, it was only the third installation on this important mall, after the Light Horse Memorial (1968) and the RAAF (1973).[52] Like other Tobruk memorials around the country, it was modelled on the original one at Tobruk. Its central plaque was, in fact, the marble one retrieved from the site. It stated, 'This is hallowed ground for here lie those who died for their country'. Some lines from Binyon's famous ode, 'At the going down of the sun', followed. The area surrounding the memorial symbolised the coastline at Tobruk and, so an accompanying plaque explained, depicted the defensive positions that the Rats successfully held against the enemy. An eternal flame was installed in 1984, while a time capsule was placed in the step below the marble stone on 17 April 1991, to commemorate the 50th anniversary of the siege.

The striking thing is the lack of reference to the relief of Tobruk. The focus was on the fighting and the sacrifice of lives. The day chosen for the Canberra memorial's dedication was 13 April, the date on which the Australians successfully held the first German attack on the Tobruk perimeter and Corporal Jack Edmondson won the first Victoria Cross of the Second World War. It was the 'heroism' of the Rats that Governor-General Sir Ninian Stephen praised when unveiling the memorial. It would stand, he said, as a 'reminder to future generations … of what [the Rats] fought for and the freedom which they helped to preserve, not only for Australian [sic] but for people all over the world'.[53]

A similar framing of the Tobruk story has long been evident in the Australian War Memorial. Although its Second World War gallery has evolved over the years, its depiction of Tobruk has remained focused on the defensive battles. In the mid-1950s, it installed a diorama that – naturally enough given this cultural form – focused on the dramatic. It depicted Tobruk harbour full of ships and wrecks, and two half-clad soldiers manning an anti-aircraft gun in the foreground. When the Memorial opened a new exhibition to mark the 70th anniversary of the Tobruk siege, the promotional video invoked all the tropes of the Anzac legend. 'Australian troops added to the already stellar reputation of the digger', with deeds that have become 'legendary'. Their nickname is 'part of our language'. Under the leadership of Morshead, 'Ming the Merciless', they engaged in 'active defence', upholding the traditions of defiance, mateship, humour, endurance and great heroism.[54]

At the time of writing, the diorama is still in the Memorial, vivid as ever after some renovations over the years. It is complemented by a painting of the 9th Division by the official war artist Ivor Hele. This, the accompanying text says, was 'a tribute to the Australians, who, with the British and Polish troops, held out until relieved in December'. Another painting, by John Dowie, depicts a short truce at Tobruk during which Australians recovered the bodies of those who had been killed or wounded in the attempt on 2–3 August 1941 to recapture the strongly held German posts in the section of the Tobruk perimeter known as the 'Salient'. The main text describing Tobruk briefly synthesises the events of the siege, explains the source of the name 'Rats' and concludes that Australian units 'began to be withdrawn from Tobruk in October … An Australian infantry battalion remained in the town until the siege was lifted in December'.

The Memorial's websites continue in the same vein. One mentions almost in passing that 'half the Australian garrison' was relieved in August and the rest in September–October.[55] Another essay on Tobruk references the relief, saying that Australians were evacuated in October for a 'rest' while one battalion remained 'to fight its way out and join with the advancing British 8th Army on the second advance forward'.[56] Visitors to the Memorial, be they online or in person, will leave with no strong sense of the chronology and scale of the relief, let alone the opposition that this action generated among the British. The implication is that Australians spent most – or even all – of the eight-month siege holed up in Tobruk.

A similar impression is conveyed by the popular historian whose writing on Tobruk might aspire to have some role in shaping public memory of war, Peter FitzSimons. His blockbuster *Tobruk*, first published in 2006, was reprinted several times; according to its cover, it has sold over 100 000 copies. Ever a disciple of Anzac, and for a time a member of the Australian War Memorial Council, FitzSimons concludes that Australians had been 'charged with holding Tobruk for two months and had held it for seven'. To be sure, FitzSimons does give the relief of Tobruk some coverage. He acknowledges the political implications of the Menzies government's call for Tobruk's relief. But he positions the dispute within that well-worn trope of Australian popular military history, blaming the British. Auchinleck treats Blamey 'rather off handedly', Churchill responds 'with infinite annoyance'. Blamey 'had at last had a complete gutful of the infernally superior British attitude'.

> [He] didn't doubt that it would have suited the British military leadership to treat Australian soldiers the same way they treated their own soldiers – simply giving them *orders* [sic] and ensuring that those orders were properly executed – but what they failed to understand was that

> Australia was not merely a company of soldiers there to
> do mighty Britain's bidding![57]

Such histrionics, it should be said, were notably absent from the earlier, more balanced and detailed account of the Tobruk relief by Blamey's biographer, the leading military historian David Horner, published in 1998. Horner concluded that the British 'failed to realise that Blamey had a loyalty to Auchinleck as his superior officer, but an even greater loyalty to his own government' and that 'the question remains as to whether the relief was militarily advisable'.[58] Likewise, Graham Freudenberg, in his 2008 study of Churchill and Australia, found arguments for and against both Britain and Australia.[59] However, it is probable that, as so often happens with Australian military history, these more academic accounts did not cut through to the degree that the popular history did.

ELIDING THE RELIEF OF TOBRUK

It should come as no surprise that when the last veteran from Tobruk died in 2024, the media focused on depicting the Rats as Anzacs. Channel Ten's *The Project* enthused about the 'defiant garrison', 'the conditions [that] helped to build mateship' in 'eight long months in Anzac unity'. The Rats embodied the Anzac spirit, displaying 'a uniquely Aussie mix of bravery, grit, humour and aggression'. They 'did *not* surrender. Nor did they retreat'.[60] On Channel 7 news, an Australian War Memorial staff member assured viewers that the Rats held Tobruk 'for *so* long' (emphasis in original).[61] An interviewee of the ABC mentioned, without elaboration, that much of the Tobruk garrison had been relieved.[62]

Perhaps the airbrushing of the relief from the public memory of Tobruk should not surprise us. Memorial facades and public galleries are not the places where the finer details of historical controversy are usually canvassed. Popular histories tend to sell well if they celebrate what soldiers achieved, rather than what they did not. Drama is the essence of military history, and withdrawals and retreats are rarely the stuff of warrior myths – although the evacuation of Gallipoli in December has often been depicted as a triumph of Anzac ingenuity and planning.[63] Being evacuated at night, under the eyes of the enemy, did not necessarily unsettle a celebratory narrative of Tobruk.

The problem with the relief of Tobruk was presumably Churchill's critique. Although Australian historiography rarely concedes this, perhaps he had a case. The Allied situation in North Africa in late 1941 was finely balanced and the desert war would seesaw back and forth until it finally ended in the Allies' favour with the second battle of El Alamein in October 1942. The relief of Tobruk diverted resources that might have been used elsewhere and risked their possible loss. In presenting their case, the Australian leaders certainly gave the appearance of being focused less on the wider strategic situation than on the domestic political ramifications of the Tobruk garrison falling, and the command of the AIF not reverting to Blamey. The evidence that the Rats would break under another German attack was not compelling, particularly as Blamey never visited Tobruk himself.[64] For Blamey, a generally sympathetic biographer concluded in 1973, the health of the Rats was only a secondary argument. His 'cardinal motive was to concentrate the AIF into one force', a motive that was as much personal and political as strategic.[65]

Yet, even if all this were conceded, it was galling for Australia to have been so singled out for criticism in Churchill's globally distributed history. Though he disparaged the Australian politicians and not the Anzacs themselves, it was an affront to the Australian nationalism that was the core of the Anzac mythology. Even the circumspect Hasluck hinted that Australia had been treated as if it were still something of a colony. Churchill, he said, appealed to the Australian government 'to forgo independent judgement and to accept British leadership in the interests of Empire co-operation'.[66]

Furthermore, memory formation, even at the national level, depends upon the interface between custodians of memory at government and community levels. The memorial to the Rats of Tobruk on Anzac Parade, for instance, began with the agitation of the Rats of Tobruk Association, locally and nationally. It would seem, from their public positioning over the years, that the veteran Rats also found the narratives of Tobruk's defence and the relief to be in tension. The first affirmed the Rats as exemplars of the Anzac qualities of endurance, courage and mateship. They would never surrender and would fight their way out by land. But the second attested to their leaving. Admittedly, they did so under orders from their government, but the implications for a valorising mythology that they so cherished were ambiguous. It should come as no surprise, then, that the narrative that challenged Anzac, even only implicitly, lost out in the ongoing construction of the national memory of war.

9

THE INCONVENIENT ENTITY
AUSTRALIAN MILITARY PERSONNEL
AND BRITISH NUCLEAR TESTING
IN AUSTRALIA

MAX BILLINGTON

Between 1952 and 1957, Australia played host to five test series of nuclear weapons that were designed, built and owned by the British government. The detonation of these weapons at the Monte Bello Islands, north of Western Australia's Pilbara Coast, and at the Emu Field and Maralinga test ranges in South Australia, brought nuclear technology to the doorstep of a population that had mostly encountered it only in media coverage of the Japanese cities of Hiroshima and Nagasaki. Despite being a source of national pride at the time of its execution, the test program underwent significant re-evaluation in the late 1970s, in the wake of accusations that it had caused significant environmental and bodily harm. This resulted in the 1984 Royal Commission into British Nuclear Tests in Australia. Reflecting on evidence presented by the British and Australian governments, scientific experts, civilians and former servicemen, the final report of the Royal Commission characterised the British tests as an exercise in scientific and governmental neglect, not only of the environment, but also of the Australian military personnel involved.[1]

151

Despite the report's explicit use of the term 'nuclear veteran' to describe these personnel, the Royal Commission recommended that financial compensation for harms sustained during service at the tests continue be provided under the *Compensation (Government Employees) Act 1972*, rather than under repatriation law (the basis of today's veterans' benefits scheme).[2] This equivalence between civilians and service personnel perpetuated the Australian government's reluctance to acknowledge that the work of the 'nuclear veterans' comprised military service worthy of the symbolic and financial protections offered under the veterans' benefits scheme. The ongoing exclusion of the military personnel involved in the British nuclear testing from Anzac mythology has led to the erasure of soldiers' bodies from histories of Australia's role in the development of nuclear technology. 'Nuclear veterans' and the harms they claim to have suffered are highly *inconvenient* to the state, because they fail to conform to the ideal of bodily harm in combat as the fulfilment of the citizen's duty to protect the nation.[3]

SERVICE AT GROUND ZERO: INDOCTRINATION AND IGNORANCE

An examination of Australian military service at the British nuclear tests is complicated by the lack of academic interest in servicemen involved in the program. The official Australian history of the testing, compiled ahead of the Royal Commission and published alongside its final report in 1985, acknowledges the role of the military in preparing, patrolling and maintaining the test sites.[4] However, it provides scant information regarding the experiences of the individuals performing each task. Similarly, the British government's official history notes the involvement of servicemen from across the Commonwealth and their claims of radiation exposure, but concludes that their allegations misunderstand the science of radiation and its impact on the human body.[5] These histories subsume individual personnel within broader commentary on the organisation of each test and the conspiracies regarding safety that abounded in their aftermath. In doing so, they tend towards what anthropologist Adriana Petryna has termed a 'nonpeopled' approach to the history of British nuclear testing.[6] Consequently, experiential narratives of service at the tests are absent from the 'dominant systems of knowledge' that govern academic understanding of this period.[7]

This erasure of servicemen's experiences of nuclear testing is reflective of the limited public attention given to military involvement in the British program at the time of its execution. The initiation of testing under Operation Hurricane in 1952 was the subject of significant media coverage in Australia, which boasted of the Anglo-Australian defence relationship.[8] However, despite the attention devoted by the major newspapers to the strategic implications of Hurricane, coverage of the Australian military rarely went beyond acknowledging that service personnel would be present on, and in the vicinity of, the Monte Bello Islands. These references to personnel were often buried at the end of articles speculating on the location and timing of Hurricane.[9] Media coverage of Operation Totem in 1953, the first test series to occur on the Australian mainland, followed a similar formula. According to the press, military personnel were present at Emu Field to provide transportation and labour in preparation for the upcoming tests.[10] At the moment of detonation, however, human bodies were absent. Front-page coverage of the first Totem test in the *Canberra*

Times claimed all military personnel were 'evacuated' from the test site 30 minutes before the main event.[11]

While limited in its scope, the media's portrayal of Australian servicemen involved in the British program was not inaccurate; the successful execution of each test relied upon the operational support provided by military personnel. The Royal Australian Navy (RAN) supplied at least 15 ships between 1950 and 1952 in aid of Operation Hurricane, the majority tasked with ferrying resources to, and enforcing an exclusion zone around, the Monte Bello Islands.[12] The Royal Australian Air Force (RAAF) also provided support for cloud-tracking exercises, in addition to taking air samples from the clouds' vicinity.[13] The RAAF maintained its involvement throughout the testing period, while Army personnel joined the RAN to provide labour, transport and security as the tests moved inland to Emu Field in 1953 and the Maralinga range from 1956.

Contrary to the overviews of military involvement offered by media coverage and within academic histories, testimonies submitted to the 1984–85 Royal Commission from soldiers, airmen and sailors reveal that service at the testing sites was rarely confined to basic support duties. Bosun's Yeoman Vincent Douglas (RAN) assisted in the transportation of 'supplies and mail' from Western Australia to the Monte Bello Islands ahead of Operation Hurricane, while aboard HMAS *Hawkesbury*.[14] Douglas noted that *Hawkesbury* then switched from supply duties to 'anti-submarine patrols'.[15] These duties are consistent with historian Petar Djokovic's summary of RAN ship movements in 1952.[16] Douglas stated to the Royal Commission that, in addition to providing security, *Hawkesbury*'s crew witnessed the Hurricane explosion. This was not merely the outcome of patrolling the islands. Douglas remembered that 'shortly prior to the explosion', the crew were issued with 'white plastic film badges', a device for measuring radiation exposure.[17] Douglas's testimony demonstrates that measures were taken to prepare *Hawkesbury* and its crew for exposure to a nuclear explosion. A background report prepared by *Hawkesbury* commanding officer after Hurricane's completion also recorded the commander's intention for his crew 'to witness Britain's first atomic explosion'.[18]

Douglas's account of his experience aboard *Hawkesbury* demonstrates that the necessity of providing operational support for the British program also gave military command the opportunity to place servicemen near ground zero for the explicit purpose of witnessing the detonation of an atomic bomb. The British test program thereby represented a means to indoctrinate servicemen in the benefits of strategic nuclear technology. Australia was following the example set by the United States during its 1951 test series in Nevada, during which troops stationed at Camp Desert Rock performed combat exercises on a simulated nuclear battlefield.[19] By directly exposing soldiers to nuclear weapons, American military command hoped to familiarise its personnel with the concept of nuclear warfare and so psychologically prepare them to fight in its aftermath.[20] Douglas's exposure to the Hurricane blast is an early example of the indoctrination of Australian servicemen during the British nuclear testing.

Statements taken for the Royal Commission demonstrate that the implementation of indoctrination as a formal strategy within the Australian defence forces in the 1950s was inconsistent. This is particularly evident in the varying extent to which knowledge regarding the purpose and risks of service at a nuclear test site were transmitted from the military elite to ordinary personnel.

Many servicemen involved in Operation Hurricane were unaware that they would be taking part prior to the commencement of their duties. Airman William Bovill (RAAF) did not find out that he would be undertaking cloud tracking at Hurricane until a briefing immediately before the flight was scheduled, where 'we were told that the atomic test bomb has gone off'.[21] The briefing did not include 'any instructions about radiation or risks of it', and Bovill did not recall being issued with a film badge. Bovill further claimed that the measuring equipment attached to their Lincoln bomber was faulty, with the crew struggling to determine the location of the cloud based on instrument readings. He performed cloud-tracking duties a second time in 1953, for Operation Totem, and remembered being instructed this time on the use of film badges. However, Bovill could only recall one crew member being issued with a film badge.[22]

Navigator Allen Clark (RAAF) assisted in cloud-tracking operations for Hurricane and Totem and similarly could not recall being made aware of the possibility that the aircraft in use 'might be radioactive'.[23] This was confirmed by wireless operator John Coolahan (RAAF).[24] Assistant squadron gunnery leader Roy Cosgrove (RAAF) was also not provided with any protective clothing or monitoring instruments prior to flying out to photograph the first Totem explosion. He assumed at the time that the crew were not 'in danger because we didn't approach the cloud'.[25] Before commencing an air-sampling flight for the second Totem bomb, Cosgrove questioned the British scientist leading the pre-flight briefing about the level of radiation exposure the crew could expect to receive. The answer he received was vague, prompting him to ask what 'precautions' the crew should take. He was subsequently informed that no protective clothing was available; the crew would have to do without.[26]

Indoctrination of servicemen at Operations Hurricane and Totem thus followed a particular pattern: the direct involvement of personnel in duties that exposed them to an atomic explosion, without the provision of notice regarding the hazards of doing so. Certainly, it was standard practice for servicemen of the lower ranks to be given duties without receiving details about the purpose of their work. However, Australian personnel were aware that they were being excluded from safety protocols that were in place for other members of the test program. Naval aircraft handler Reginald Beaver (RAN) was posted as a driver to the testing range established at Maralinga in 1956 ahead of Operation Buffalo. Upon arrival at the range he received a lecture about the upcoming tests from Sir William Penney, the program's scientific lead. However, Penney 'said nothing about the actual tasks' assigned to Australian servicemen and Beaver was not issued with any protective clothing or monitoring equipment when entering ground zero.[27] Beaver did recall that a decontamination procedure was in place for personnel returning from ground zero, but drivers were excluded from the initial check for radioactive contamination and so were not required to perform the procedure.[28] Batman Leslie Beevers (Army) was escorted into ground zero in between Buffalo explosions 'to witness the damage' that had been caused, but was not issued with protective clothing or a film badge.[29] Beevers stated that he returned to camp immediately after leaving ground zero 'without any checks for radiation'.[30]

Sapper Vincent Cannon (Army) claimed that the security at Maralinga 'was hopeless', with servicemen routinely entering ground zero on weekends 'to relieve the boredom' of daily camp life.[31] Cannon stated that doing so was never considered frightening or even particularly mischievous, 'because really

[we] were in total ignorance of what was happening'.[32] The same appeared to be the case in 1957 during Operation Antler. Canteen attendant Lewis Angel (Army) had no authorisation to enter ground zero but was allowed in to see the craters left behind by the Buffalo series.[33] Angel recalled that personnel were 'supposed to get a lecture' regarding the purpose of Antler but missed out because 'the chap who gave them was not available at the time'.[34]

Taken in isolation from one another, these statements do not necessarily demonstrate deliberate neglect of ordinary Australian personnel. There is evidence to suggest that the type of information that would have enabled the instruction of personnel in radiological safety was not available to Australian military command prior to 1956. Officer Commanding 82 Bomber Wing, I.F. Rose (RAAF), noted in a report compiled in between the two Totem detonations of 1953 that the RAAF did not possess adequate knowledge of the hazards associated with flying in the vicinity of a mushroom cloud.[35] Rose suggested that the British testing administration should have anticipated the possibility that Australian aircraft might become contaminated during cloud-tracking missions, thereby exposing the crew to radiation.[36]

Witness statements tendered at the Royal Commission, however, suggest that the haphazard indoctrination implemented among lower ranks of Australian servicemen was accompanied by a second, organised program catering for the indoctrination of higher ranks from across the Commonwealth. To this end, the 'Indoctrinee Force' (IF) was established in advance of Operation Buffalo in 1956. The IF comprised roughly 250 British, Australian and New Zealand high-ranking military personnel, who attended Buffalo to 'experience the effects of a nuclear explosion' and 'examine the effects of such explosion' on the environment and military equipment.[37] Instructions regarding the creation of the IF specified that personnel were to then 'pass on their experience to other members of the Armed Forces'.[38] The IF would thus be a British version of Camp Desert Rock, with members attending lectures concerning 'the nature and conduct of the trials', witnessing the detonations and taking a tour of ground zero.[39]

A key distinction between the IF and the informal indoctrination of ordinary personnel was the inclusion of radiological safety protocol in the IF lecture program. Brigadier John Broadbent (Army), who participated in the IF, explained to the Royal Commission that he was instructed on 're-entry and safety procedures' to implement when the Force entered ground zero after detonation, as well as on 'the wearing of protective clothing'.[40] Broadbent noted that such clothing – a hooded white suit, gloves, overshoes and respirator – was issued to the IF before entry to ground zero.[41] Significantly, out of the 39 statements submitted to the Royal Commission by witnesses with surnames beginning with A–D, Broadbent's was the only one to state the exact dose of radiation received while present at Maralinga.[42]

The IF was a focus for the Royal Commission due to allegations levelled in the media that its real purpose was to provide the British with human 'guinea pigs'.[43] While the Commission ultimately concluded that this was not the case, the question of human experimentation within the IF remains disputed.[44] An overlooked aspect of the witness statements given by the upper ranks at the Royal Commission, however, is their certainty that the utmost care had been taken to ensure the safety of Australian personnel. Broadbent described the program as 'a well conducted and disciplined exercise' in which all 'precautions were taken for the safety of the persons participating'.[45] Lieutenant Commander Arthur Andrews (RAN), officer-in-charge of decontamination during Operation Buffalo, received specialist training from the Australian Radiation Detection Unit on radiological safety and also claimed to have personally delivered lectures on the subject, which were compulsory for anyone required to enter ground zero.[46] Andrews insisted that all entrants wore protective clothing and film badges, which he collected upon their return to determine each individual's level of exposure.[47]

The testimonies of Andrews and Broadbent suggest that those who had access to the greatest amount of radiological safety information were the most likely to believe that service personnel had been adequately protected from radiation exposure. Such information, however, was concentrated among the upper ranks of the Australian defence forces, such as those invited to participate in the IF. In contrast, ordinary personnel carried out operational support duties in irradiated environments without basic radiological safety instruction. Ironically, Andrews admitted this knowledge disparity between the formally and informally indoctrinated groups in his statement to the Royal Commission. Acknowledging that he was unsure 'precisely' which personnel attended his safety lectures, Andrews thought it 'unlikely that anyone from the motor pool would have attended'.[48] In Andrews' estimation, the duties of lower-ranking personnel such as Reginald Beaver were distinct from those of the higher ranks moving in and out of ground zero; therefore, the mandatory decontamination procedures were not applicable to them.

While servicemen from the upper ranks could confidently identify the safety measures that were in place for military personnel during the testing at the Royal Commission, ordinary personnel were left to question the limited and inconsistent information concerning their own wellbeing during the execution of daily duties. This facilitated the reinterpretation of the meanings associated with 'ordinary' service over the decades as new knowledge regarding the medical and environmental consequences of nuclear testing began to enter the public consciousness from the early 1960s.[49] Such reinterpretation is evident in claims of the New South Wales–based Australian Nuclear Veterans Association (ANVA) that military service at the British testing occurred in hazardous conditions. The hardship suffered by personnel stationed at Maralinga in 1956 was, in fact, foundational to the organisation's existence. Its seven founding members (Beaver among them) had initially met to share memories of the 'appalling conditions' at the range.[50] The founding seven believed that, had they 'been convicts, the law would not have allowed them to be treated so harshly', a view that compelled them to organise social gatherings to preserve the memory of this difficult period.[51] This emphasis on hardship was given new meaning by increasing public awareness of the impact of radiation on the human body and the founding seven's mutual experience of ill-health, both physical and psychological, throughout their post-service lives. By 1976, ANVA's focus consequently shifted from the remembrance of tough conditions to their biological consequences in post-service life.[52] The experience of service at the British tests thus encouraged former military personnel to re-examine their memories in the collective environment offered by ANVA and question whether the tasks they had been instructed to perform had exposed them to radiation.

RADIATION, ILLNESS AND COMPENSATION

A core component of the re-evaluation of service memories was the reframing of physical illness as the outcome of a sacrifice to the nation, or what ANVA described as the 'human consequences' of their service.[53] Nuclear veterans, however, were not eligible to receive repatriation benefits for alleged nuclear injuries. As ANVA's Queensland rival (also known as the Australian Nuclear Veterans Association) explained in its July 1982 newsletter, repatriation law did not cover service performed on home soil between 1953 and 1972.[54] Compensation claims for service at the British tests fell instead under the jurisdiction of the Commissioner for Employees' Compensation (CEC). This resulted in the re-categorisation of former service personnel as Commonwealth employees, effectively undermining the connection between military service and bodily harm in relation to Australian defence involvement in the British program. Furthermore, the burden of proof in CEC claims rested entirely with the individual claimant, who was required to provide official documentation demonstrating his exposure to radiation during the British tests *and* substantiate a link between this exposure and illness. Inconsistencies in the transmission of radiological knowledge during the testing, combined with discrepancies in the records kept by the British test administration, bedevilled 'nuclear veterans'. The CEC reported prior to the Royal Commission that, of the 154 radiation-related compensation claims submitted up until June 1984, just six had been accepted.[55]

The government's refusal to recognise radiological injury as an outcome of military service formed the crux of veteran submissions to the Royal Commission. The witness statements of servicemen described the consequences of illness for their ability to participate in civilian life. They cited their inability to hold down work, deteriorations in their marriages, their inability to conceive children or the frequent occurrence of birth defects in offspring. Leading sick berth attendant at the Maralinga Range Hospital, Stanley Rae (RAN), attributed his collection of 'unexplained illnesses' – ranging from severe abdominal pain and tachycardia to depression and loss of memory – directly to 'Atom Radiation' exposure sustained during his 'compulsory attendance' at Operations Hurricane and Buffalo.[56] Another witness, Vincent Douglas, explained that he developed a 'nervous disorder', which prevented him from gaining regular employment, and noted that he had 'to pay for all [his] medication'.[57] Roy Cosgrove declared that the government's refusal to provide compensation for these types of ill health amounted to a violation of the sacred relationship between the soldier who serves 'our nation' and the government who supports him in post-service life.[58] Nuclear servicemen presented the health problems arising from their radiation exposure as evidence that they had sacrificed their bodily wellbeing so that the British tests could take place. This language of sacrifice was deliberately deployed by those who gave evidence to the Royal Commission with the purpose of staking their claim to the Anzac tradition, and to the welfare provisions that flowed from that quasi-sacred status.

Although the report of the Royal Commission included a stipulation that the government investigate and appropriately respond to the extent of illness among former servicemen, the state remained unwilling to recognise the service of military personnel at the British tests as equivalent to the performance of active military service.[59] The Howard government claimed in 2003 that military personnel had merely 'participated' in the tests, and so should be referred to as 'participants' rather than veterans.[60] This was justified on the basis that wartime service constituted a greater level of bodily sacrifice on behalf of the individual soldier, and thus that it would be inappropriate to dilute the 'special' relationship between the state and the wartime soldier by including the comparatively safe service of soldiers who had undergone nuclear indoctrination in the same repatriation scheme.[61]

Whereas personnel in combat actively sacrificed themselves on behalf of the nation, former nuclear servicemen had passively 'participated' in a program designed to improve their awareness of nuclear warfare. The experience of harm during participation was consequently separated from narratives of sacrifice in wartime, with nuclear servicemen grouped instead with civilians and civil servants who had inadvertently been exposed to radiation. The Australian government not only denied military 'participants' access to financial compensation and social recognition of harms sustained during military service, but ultimately excluded them from the Anzac mythology by refusing them the status of veteran.

THE LIMITS OF SACRIFICE

The relegation of former nuclear servicemen to the category of 'participants' in government legislation cannot simply be taken as gross negligence on behalf of the Australian government.[62] Rather, it is the fundamental circumstances of the sacrifice that 'nuclear veterans' claim to have made that enables their exclusion from Australian warrior mythology. As demonstrated in their testimonies to the Royal Commission, military personnel involved in the tests identified the Australian government as responsible for harm incurred during their service, arguing that it was former prime minister Robert Menzies' willingness to provide support for the British that resulted in the exposure of Australian personnel to hazardous conditions. However, the veneration of the harmed serviceman within the Anzac mythology ultimately requires that the responsibility for such harm resides with an external enemy. As political scientist Matt

McDonald has suggested in reference to the mythologisation of the Anzac landing at Gallipoli in the First World War, the concept of heroic sacrifice enables a state to elide the fundamentally traumatic nature of death and injury in conflict by constructing a narrative that emphasises the harmed individual's commitment to the defence of the nation.[63] Harm incurred in conflict is, therefore, deified as a heroic sacrifice to the nation.[64] The nation reciprocally provides returned personnel with financial compensation in recognition of the symbolic debt owed to those who were harmed.[65] The state thus obscures its own involvement in conflict (through the mobilisation of armed forces) by redirecting attention in military mythology to the apparent heroism of those harmed by the enemy, thereby discouraging doubt regarding the purpose of conflict.[66] This relationship between the state and its military personnel functioned as the primary justification for the establishment of Australia's generous repatriation scheme during the First World War. Wartime prime minister William Hughes described enlistment in the Australian armed forces as creating a 'promise' that the government would provide for those men who 'go out to fight our battles'.[67]

Claims of harm inflicted by a serviceman's own government during the execution of military service threaten the sanctity of the state–soldier relationship enshrined within Anzac mythology because they directly implicate the nation in the use of violence against its own citizens, shattering the portrayal of bodily harm as heroic sacrifice. In the case of 'nuclear veterans', such harm did not result from individuals' active willingness to sacrifice their bodies for the nation, but from the state's decision to place military bodies in danger at ground zero, to enable British experimentation with nuclear weapons. This is illustrated by the circumstances underpinning the informal indoctrination of lower ranks. In the case of Operation Totem, Roy Cosgrove was expected to perform air-sampling operations while being denied information regarding the possibility of radiation exposure.[68] This situation was more explicit in engineer Francis Beitzel's (RAN) statement, in which he claimed to initially have refused the order to witness one of the Buffalo explosions, 'because [he] considered it was dangerous to be near where the bomb was going off'.[69] Beitzel was threatened with a court-martial by his commanding officer and so agreed to attend the test.[70]

'Nuclear veterans' are, therefore, highly *inconvenient entities* for the mythological narrative of Australian military service, as the accommodation of their service within the state–soldier relationship would require the government to admit that military personnel were harmed not in defence of the nation, but in service to it. Moreover, in demanding the government accept responsibility for illnesses attributed to radiation exposure, 'nuclear veterans' threaten to reveal that Anzac mythology is not simply a form of remembrance of those who served in conflict, but a system of state control over the meaning of the nation's involvement in war. Ultimately, the history of former nuclear servicemen's interactions with the Australian government is not indicative of a process of mere exclusion from Anzac mythology. Rather, the circumstances in which these servicemen claim to have performed a sacrifice preclude their accommodation within it. The government's categorisation of these personnel as passive 'participants' in the nuclear program is thus a means of mitigating the inconvenience they represent.[71] Service in the British program is, accordingly, separated from the established meaning of military service in wartime. Although responsibility for compensation for test 'participants' shifted from the Commissioner for Employees' Compensation to the

Department of Veterans' Affairs (DVA) in 2017, this separation has been perpetuated by the DVA's policy of allowing 'anyone' present in a test area, be they civilian or servicemen, access to government support.[72]

'Nuclear veterans' have, in their campaign for inclusion, inadvertently exposed the rigid nature of Anzac mythology. They have found themselves displaced, not only from histories of the British nuclear testing period, but from Australian military history itself. This is not to say that former nuclear servicemen are responsible for perpetuating their own historical homelessness through their efforts to achieve recognition and financial redress from the Australian government. Rather, the government's relegation of former nuclear service personnel to the category of 'participants' demonstrates that Anzac mythology does not regard military service as the basis for inclusion in existing structures of national remembrance.

The basic tenets of Australian strategic policy, which made Australian troops available for use in the British nuclear program in the 1950s, continue to define the nation's approach to defence. International relations theorist Clinton Fernandes describes this as a 'subimperial' approach, in which Australian soldiers are offered willingly in support of the national interest of great power allies.[73] The AUKUS agreement, which proposes to grant the Australian military use of nuclear-powered submarines, is not simply a reflection of the British test program but a logical outcome of the 'subimperial' approach.[74] Under AUKUS, the Australian government will once again make military bodies available to operate nuclear technologies that are central to the security of a superpower ally. The experience of the first generation of Australian 'nuclear veterans' indicates that any occurrence of harm in service to AUKUS will be quietly separated from official political and historical narratives. Therefore, it is necessary to ask: in excluding the military bodies present at ground zero, is Australian warrior mythology about Australian warriors at all?

10

'NO MORE SILENCE ABOUT SEXUAL VIOLENCE'
FEMINIST PROTESTS AT ANZAC DAY, 1977-87

CHRISTINA TWOMEY

In 1977, women led the Anzac Day march in Sydney for the first time. In honour of the 75th anniversary of the formation of the Australian Army Nursing Corps, veteran nurses took pride of place at the front of the march. Journalists reminded readers that First World War diggers once knew the nurses as 'old grey mares', a reference to the colour of their uniforms. As the nurses marched, other veterans called out, 'Hello you beauty'.[1] The gendered language was a clumsy attempt to elide the discomfort of male combat veterans falling in behind women, and an effort to render the strange familiar. Behind the scenes, there were more profound changes taking place that would make the novelty of women leading the march seem like child's play. A younger generation began to look to Anzac Day not so much for its exclusion of women as for its silence about the impact of war on them. In the same year that nurses led the march, the Sydney Rape Crisis Collective were 'disgusted' that the Custodian of the Cenotaph in Sydney had refused them permission as part of official proceedings to lay a wreath in memory of women raped in war.[2] Collectives of women throughout the country, inspired

169

by women's liberation movement campaigns against sexual violence, were soon on a collision course with the custodians of Anzac. In the decade from 1977, Anzac Day became a flashpoint for tensions between feminist protestors, march organisers and veterans. The most radical of the women's groups wanted to abolish Anzac Day altogether.

Despite commencing in an era when Anzac Day had waned in popularity, protest tactics at the annual march that drew attention to the links between militarism, sexual violence, patriarchy and the subjection of women were controversial.[3] 'It would be a national tragedy if this day of all days were to be desecrated by minority groups who seek to turn it into a day of protest and by so doing undermine our national pride and heritage', the Returned Services League (RSL) complained to the Minister for the Capital Territory in early 1981.[4] Nothing provokes defence like attack, and so it proved with the commemoration of Anzac Day. The RSL, conservative legislatures in some jurisdictions, the judiciary and police circled the wagons to protect an institution from groups of women dressed in black, carrying banners and wreaths, and singing songs. Attempts to control feminist activists drew public attention to their cause and swelled the ranks of their supporters and, more significantly, their opponents. Feminist lawyer Jocelynne Scutt saw it coming. 'Since the protests by feminists began,' she wrote in 1984, 'an Anzac Day that was dying … has revived with a vengeance.'[5]

There have been many theories advanced subsequently about why Anzac Day underwent a renaissance in the 1980s, including but not limited to the RSL's ability to adapt by being more inclusive, the desire for a sacred ritual in a secular society, and a political need to focus on a national day that sidesteps the issue of Aboriginal dispossession as a foundational act.[6] All of these factors contributed to its increased appeal. Yet Scutt put her finger on one other reason that is less often factored into the equation – new understandings about war as a traumatising event, building since the 1970s, that used affect and emotion to inspire greater empathy for its victims. Feminist protestors added a gendered dimension by suggesting that war's unheralded victims were women. Male veterans, with significant support from Anzac's custodians, were determined to prioritise that status for themselves.

WOMEN AGAINST RAPE COLLECTIVES

The women's groups that began to appear at Anzac Day from 1977 had their origins in anti-rape activism. The women's liberation movement, both within Australia and internationally, had focused attention on male sexual violence, especially the lack of support for rape victims, legal impediments to the conviction of rapists, and cultural attitudes that shamed victims and tolerated perpetrators.[7] Contemporaneous with similar developments overseas, rape crisis centres, designed to help women victims, were established in major Australian cities from the early to mid-1970s.[8] Melbourne Women Against Rape began as the Rape Action Crisis Group in 1973 and opened the Collingwood Rape Crisis Centre the following year.[9] In Adelaide, women who worked in the Rape Crisis Centre had formed a Women Against Rape group by early 1978. Lyn McKenzie, a member of the Melbourne Women Against Rape collective, asserted: 'We are feminists, and do stem from the Women's Liberation Movements, and as such we are constantly aware of the ramifications of rape for all women.'[10]

The early public activities of Women Against Rape collectives prefigured the form and shape of later Anzac Day protests. Apart from providing support and counselling for victims of rape, Women Against Rape collectives were initially focused on law reform. By 1976, they were protesting on the steps of Victoria's Parliament House, demanding an inquiry into rape laws.[11] Similar moves were afoot in the United Kingdom, where street theatre typified campaigns against judicial decisions such as a suspended sentence for rape on the grounds that a young man's promising army career would be destroyed if it were enforced.[12] Australian women's groups began to take their protests about women's safety to the street, as did feminists in the UK, the US and Europe. A Melbourne group called the Campaign Against the Causes of Rape marched on 12 February 1977, in the wake of the rape and murder of two women in Easy Street, Collingwood. Protestors carried signs including 'Rape: No Women Are Safe' and 'Cops Rape Black Women'.[13] Reclaim the Night marches began in the UK in 1977 and appeared in Australia at around the same time. The Adelaide Women Against Rape group marched down Rundle Mall on the eve of International Women's Day in March 1978, demanding women's right to go anywhere, at any time, without fear of rape.[14]

The language of war inflected political activism around rape. The acronym of Women Against Rape – WAR – was ripe for the picking. A year after its formation, the London chapter of Women Against Rape published the pamphlet *Women at W.A.R.*[15] Australian Women Against Rape groups also began to be known as WAR from about 1978. Yet this was no mere acronym – women's collectives conceived of rape as male war on women and of themselves as engaged in a war to defeat it. *War on Rape* was the title of an advice pamphlet for sexual assault victims published in Melbourne.[16] It reflected the influence of Susan Brownmiller's 1975 book *Against Our Will: Men, Women and Rape*, and quoted her most famous line: rape was a 'male ideology' and a 'conscious process of intimidation by which *all men* keep *all women* in a state of fear'.[17]

In Australia, in the context of a culture that had profound links between masculinity, war and nationalism, Women Against Rape's conceptual and metaphorical focus on war soon became more literal. Brownmiller's book, written in the shadow of Vietnam and the mass rape of Bengali women in the Bangladesh Liberation War, devoted a chapter to a historical examination of the use of rape as a weapon of war. The absence of recognition for women's suffering in war was especially conspicuous to feminists in Australia, where one of the most significant national days is a commemoration of sacrifice in armed conflict. In 1977, women from the Sydney Rape Crisis Centre were the first collective to gather on Anzac Day carrying a wreath with a ribbon bearing the words, 'In memory of women who suffered rape in war'. They had not been deterred by the Custodian of the Cenotaph's exclusion of them from official proceedings. To their minds, Anzac Day ignored the cost of war to women and glorified masculinity. They stressed that rape, an assertion of male power over women, was 'a deliberate technique of war used to humiliate the enemy'. Drawing attention to contemporary examples, they carried banners declaring 'US Soldiers Admit to Mass Rape in Vietnam' and '300,000 Women Raped in Bangladesh War'. The mainstream press chose to ignore the protest – only the communist *Tribune* published photographs and commentary about it. Police ultimately allowed the women to place a wreath after the ceremony, on the proviso that the 'offensive' ribbon mentioning rape was removed.[18] The next year, Women Against Rape again appeared at the Sydney Anzac Day march, this time wearing black T-shirts emblazoned with 'In Memory of Women

Raped in War' on the front, and 'Women Against Rape' on the back. A T-shirt with a slogan was a very 1970s way to draw attention in a march that was curated for uniforms and medals, and wreaths with ribbons. No police officer worth their salt would attempt to pull off a woman's T-shirt in public. 'These, at least, would not be forcibly removed', one participant remarked.[19] They also had the added benefit of forming a striking image in black and white newspaper photographs.

In the late 1970s, Women Against Rape activities on Anzac Day were designed to at once mourn women raped in war and to insist on the pervasiveness of the threat of rape to women in everyday life. A banner at the Sydney march in 1978 read: 'In Memory of Women Raped or Murdered by Men in Peace and War'.[20] In Canberra the same year, women and children carried a banner to the Australian War Memorial proclaiming that 'Rape is War Against Women'.[21] They, too, were wearing the T-shirts. Members of the Rape Crisis Centre, the Women's Electoral Lobby, the Women's Information Centre and the Campaign Against Crimes Against Women made up the numbers in Canberra, underscoring the breadth of links into the women's movement.[22] 'Rape in wartime is not isolated from the occurrence of sexual assault in peacetime', insisted Kim O'Sullivan from Sydney WAR.[23] Melbourne Women Against Rape appeared at that city's march in 1979 wearing black robes with 'Remember the Women Raped in War' painted in bright red letters. They caught the attention of a brigadier who, after some debate, allowed them to lay their wreath in the shape of a women's symbol made from crepe paper in the women's suffrage colours of purple, green and white. Foreshadowing a debate that would come to engulf the Melbourne protesters, there was some internal dissent in the collective that the women had not been 'radical enough' in their comments to the press. 'It is not an easy thing to confront a mass of marching men, some of whom are younger Vietnam veterans, and watching a crowd of women who may have lost husbands and fathers in war', the editor of the Victorian Women's Liberation newsletter remarked, in sympathy with a more moderate approach.[24]

The RSL was uncomfortable from the outset about the presence of Women Against Rape protestors on Anzac Day. The Cenotaph was not the place to commemorate rape, nor was Anzac Day the time to do it, insisted James H. Neilson, Secretary of the Sydney RSL, in response to the first attempted wreath-laying in 1977.[25] Despite denigrating such activities as 'exhibitionism', Neilson did express a modicum of empathy. He acknowledged the 'terrible sadness' he felt for rape victims and that there should be nothing but 'loathing and contempt of the offenders'.[26] By 1979, the grudging tolerance that was still on display in Melbourne had evaporated elsewhere. Protestors upped the ante and started to paint graffiti on the walls of RSL clubs and war memorials. An implication that there were rapists in veteran ranks was evident in placards exhibited during the march asking, 'How many women did you rape in the war, Dad?' and 'Heroes rape women too'.[27] The response at Townsville in 1979 was typical. When a women's collective laid a wreath in the shape of a 'feminist fist' in memory of women raped in war, then raised a placard 'Women raped by victors: The war crime that's never mentioned', onlookers were outraged. In the cognitive dissonance that can occur when emotions run high, RSL members contradicted themselves, shouting both, 'You lot sure wouldn't get raped' and 'The Japs would have raped you – we saved you from them'. They then incinerated the women's wreath.[28]

The first arrests took place in Canberra. On Anzac Day in 1980, 14 women were arrested there for obstructing police under the *Australian Federal Police Act 1979*. After the main body of the march had passed, they commenced walking towards the Australian War Memorial and singing songs, until a dispute broke out with police.[29] They were alleged to have disobeyed a police instruction not to march behind the procession because there was potential for an 'imminent breach of the peace'.[30] One of those arrested claimed that when she was being charged at the police station, one officer said: 'Anzac Day is for men not wimmin'.[31] He probably didn't spell it that way, but the point about the intrusion of a gendered critique into a largely masculinist institution was clear. The case was heard in the Canberra Court of Petty Sessions in September 1980. Special Magistrate Nichols found all 14 protestors guilty, and sentenced three of them, Anne Forbutt (19), Elizabeth Blake (20) and Sara Jane Henderson (21), whom he deemed to be on a path to becoming 'social anarchists', to a month's jail. Their ages were broadly reflective of the demographic involved in the protests, with all but one of the other women who received a $200 fine aged in their early twenties. Nichols objected to the 'disgusting' nature of the placards, which included one that stated: 'Soldiers are Phallic Murderers'. He considered that the protestors had been engaged in 'social mutiny'.[32] The convictions were later overturned on appeal to the Supreme Court of the ACT.[33]

Canberra activists were energised by the brewing conflict with authorities. The Canberra Anzac Day March Collective planned a 'non-violent women's march' in Canberra for Anzac Day 1981, to show that 'we are not intimidated'.[34] The flyers prepared for distribution at the march contained quotes from Brownmiller and other writers on the prevalence of rape, and some comments directed more squarely at the military. One was a rhetorical question about the 20th-century wars in which

Australian soldiers had participated: 'Australian troops fought "honourably" … How many women did Australian troops rape?'[35] While this was still not a critique of Anzac Day itself, the material distributed by the collective certainly did raise questions about the behaviour and morality of Australian soldiers in wartime. On Anzac Day, they planned to follow rather than disrupt the march and to lay a wreath at the Australian War Memorial's Stone of Remembrance. They instructed members, 'at the risk of sounding heavy', to refrain from carrying any placards or wearing T-shirts with anything other than the two main messages they wished to convey: 'In Memory of Women of All Countries Raped in All Wars' and 'Rape is Standard Operating Procedure in War'. Women watching the march would apparently be 'more inclined to identify with these simple messages and less inclined to freak out'.[36] Perhaps this anxiety about provocation was why the Canberra group were no longer gathering under the auspices of Women Against Rape. It was also of a piece with some Melbourne women's concerns about winning the argument without alienating the audience.

THE RSL REACTS

The RSL was very inclined to 'freak out', particularly since it was fully aware of the Anzac Day March Collective's plans and literature. There is a folder, labelled 'Wimmin Against Rape', in the RSL's archives, which contains copies of the collective's flyers. Several were forwarded by Mrs Bev Cains, a Member of the ACT House of Assembly and the Australian Family Movement, who described herself as 'very concerned with the activities of the radical women's movement'.[37] It is clear from internal correspondence that while they were grateful for the reports from

Mrs Cains, the RSL had already infiltrated the Anzac Day March Collective and was aware of its plans as they unfolded. The RSL considered itself 'in a confrontation situation with radical feminist groups' who had no interest in anything but 'an organised assault on society'. 'There is no doubt that this assault on the tradition of Anzac Day is backed by Marxist-Lesbian groups', Alf Clarke, the President of the ACT RSL concluded.[38]

Armed with this kind of information, the RSL convinced the Coalition government's Minister for the Capital Territory, Michael Hodgman, that drastic action was necessary. In 1981, in the ACT, it became an offence to disrupt Anzac Day celebrations, or to engage in conduct which was 'offensive or insulting' or likely to offend or insult someone taking part in the ceremony. Furthermore, the Australian Federal Police were now entitled to make an arrest if there were 'reasonable grounds for believing' that a person was likely to disturb the march.[39] The Minister had used the extraordinary power vested in the Governor-General to issue ordinances for the ACT by executive decree. There had been no consultation with any legislative body in the preparation of the ordinance, including the ACT House of Assembly, which had no legislative powers in any case, or with the federal parliament, which did have the power to overturn such ordinances. As innocuous as the *Traffic (Amendment) Ordinance 1981* might sound, it effectively handed power to the Australian Federal Police to prevent anti-rape protesters from conducting any activity on Anzac Day, in large measure because the RSL didn't want them there.

This blatant attempt to outlaw dissent generated new momentum.[40] In the Senate, Susan Ryan, Labor Senator for the ACT, led the criticism of the undemocratic nature of the ordinance. Ryan considered Hodgman's claim that the protesters were Marxist lesbians who were attempting to sabotage the solemn remembrance of Anzac Day as 'crazy' and 'hysterical'. The Minister was trying to curry favour with the RSL and 'exploit the prejudices that exist in the community about the women's movement', Ryan claimed.[41] Ken Fry, the ALP Member of Parliament representing Fraser in the ACT, said he was 'ashamed' to be a member of the RSL and thought denying women the right to march was an infringement of their civil liberties.[42] The RSL unsuccessfully tried to ban him from representing the ALP Opposition at the wreath-laying ceremony, although his wife refused to attend and joined the marchers instead.[43] On Anzac Day itself, hundreds of people gathered in a side street, their numbers increased twenty-fold since the previous year. They were prevented from leaving the area by a police blockade, and when they tried to do so, a total of 64 people were arrested, 60 of whom were women.[44] One of them was Ken Fry's daughter.[45] The controversy surrounding the ordinance's interference with freedom of assembly led to it being repealed and replaced within a year by the *Public Assemblies Ordinance 1982*.[46] The repeal meant that when the cases of those charged reached the ACT Supreme Court, they were summarily dismissed.[47] When a new Labor government was elected nationally in 1983, it repealed the ordinance altogether.[48]

Although there were no special ordinances passed in New South Wales that directly addressed the Anzac Day march, in the early 1980s the judiciary and police used their existing powers to limit the participation of feminist protesters. The Wran Labor government's *Public Assemblies Act 1979* (NSW) had been designed to liberalise existing laws, strengthen the right to march, and move to a scheme where notification, rather than permission to assemble, was required.[49] The organiser of a public assembly had to notify the Commissioner of Police about details of an event, and the Act also allowed the Commissioner to confer with the organisers before seeking a Supreme Court Order to prohibit the assembly. The relaxation of regulations had worked: only one public assembly had been prohibited under the Act before 1983. That year, the Sydney Women Against Rape Collective (SWARC) notified their intention to march on Anzac Day, prior to the official procession, to mourn and remember all women raped in all wars. Justice Lee agreed with the police and the RSL that the women's march should be prohibited because it could not take place without affront and the possibility of violence. A protest that he construed as centred on the rape of women by servicemen in war amounted to provocation and held the potential to throw a 'slur' on veterans participating in the march. He further described the proposed march as akin to 'mourners at a funeral procession honouring a loved one' being joined by 'strangers honouring another'.[50] The *Legal Services Bulletin* described Justice Lee's decision as 'a giant leap backwards in the judicial interpretation of the right to march'.[51] The following year, 1984, SWARC was again prohibited from marching, with Justice Hunt continuing the analogy that their presence would be like strangers arriving at a funeral and alleging that the deceased was a rapist.[52] SWARC member Erika Sabina commented that 'the full force of patriarchal society was turned upon us, represented by the judiciary, the police and the Returned Services League'.[53] It was the last time that SWARC bothered to notify authorities about their intentions.

SWARC members were unbowed and remained committed to non-violent forms of protest. In 1983, organisers including Sabine Willis, Lynette Ariel and Rosemary Pringle responded to their prohibition by encouraging women to assemble in Macquarie Place on Anzac Day.[54] About 500 women gathered and participated in a ceremony in memory of all women raped in all wars. The group then marched silently along Sydney streets and towards Martin Place, where they faced 70 police officers lined across the street. Told to disperse, the group began singing and walking towards the police, resulting in the arrest of 161 women. They were charged with 'serious alarm and affront' under section 5 of the *Offences in Public Places Act 1979*. Even if Justice Lee had authorised the march, it would have afforded the protestors no protection from the charges that were brought against them.[55] Ultimately the prosecutions were dropped and no women were arrested in Sydney in 1984, despite again being prohibited from marching and again doing so anyway. By 1986, making a virtue of necessity, SWARC declared their opposition to being part of the main march: 'We don't want to be incorporated into the main body and have them say "Right, rape ladies over there, section seven, you may lay your wreath after the Scottish Highlanders"'.[56]

Feminist protestors were never a homogenous group, but there were often links to unions, students and women staff members on university campuses. As debates between radical and socialist feminists in the women's liberation movement grew more intense, the Women Against Rape collectives began to fracture. In Melbourne, for example, by the early 1980s the group coordinating protests on Anzac Day were no longer Women Against Rape: they had become the 'Anti-Anzac Day Collective'. Reflecting the influence of feminist historians and philosophers, who were examining the conceptual links between masculinity, citizenship and militarism, and their manifestations in Australian nationalism and Anzac mythology, the Melbourne group concluded that they did not want to be coopted into a misogynist tradition.[57] Anzac Day was an embodiment of patriarchy. Instead of seeking a place at the table, symbolised as laying a wreath at the Shrine of Remembrance, the Anti-Anzac Day Collective were campaigning for the abolition of Anzac Day itself. They argued that Anzac Day equated manhood and nationhood, excluded and silenced women, and perpetuated violence against them. In 1984, 17 women were arrested for invading the ceremonial area of the Shrine of Remembrance carrying a banner proclaiming: 'Abolish Anzac Day. No more silence about sexual violence'.[58]

Moves by the police and politicians to stymie the protests increased both the public profile of Women Against Rape and the number of participants willing to join them. While the numbers of women involved in the protests in major cities swelled to hundreds in the mid-1980s, so too did the strength of reaction to them. The street theatre aspects of some protests – the unknown rape victim on a bier dressed as a black-clad woman wrapped in white lace, with red flowers on her body to symbolise blood, the banners, the singing of songs – made for dramatic nightly news reports on the television and attention-grabbing photographs for the front pages of newspapers the following morning. In an era when there had been a huge amount of soul-searching about the relevance, appeal and future of Anzac Day, the feminist protests represented a major injection of drama and vitality. The old adage that no publicity is bad publicity certainly held true in this case, where Anzac Day found itself back in the headlines, even if it was only to declare that 'DEMO WOMEN' were desecrating it. Reporting was driven by the clashes, not just between protestors and police, but between veterans, onlookers and members of the collectives.

The virulence of the response in some quarters demonstrated that the pervasive threat of violence to women that lay at the heart of the feminist critique was far more than rhetorical ploy.

Fred Farrall in uniform, sent as a postcard to his aunt. Farrall explained in his interview after his service: 'I had an idea that war and everything connected to it was wrong'.

Fred Farrall

Ern Morton in uniform. He 'turned against the war'
after encountering a wounded German officer.

Ern Morton

The grave of Private Nicholas Permakoff in Esquelbecq Military Cemetery, France, which was used as a burial ground for soldiers who died at the 2nd Canadian and 3rd Australian Casualty Clearing Stations (CCS) from April to September 1918. Permakoff died from a gunshot wound on 14 June 1918.

The War Graves Photographic Project

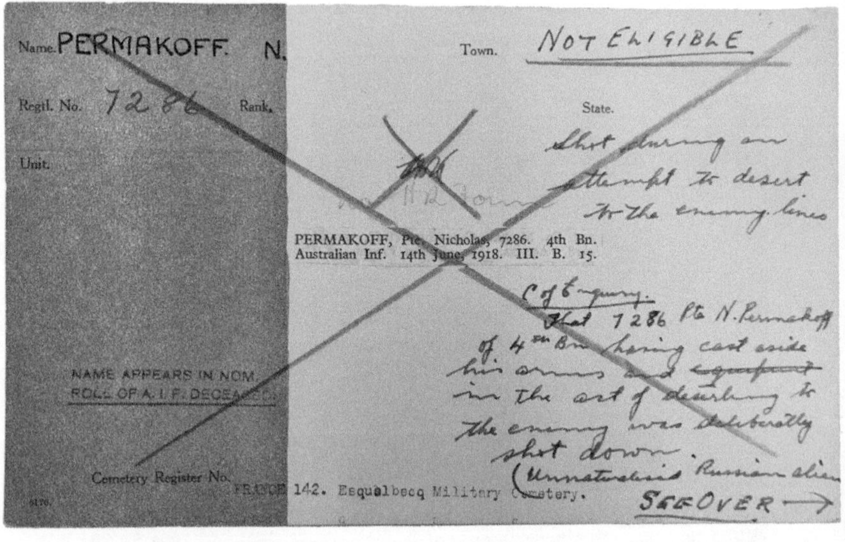

Permakoff's Roll of Honour card entry. His exclusion from the Roll is made clear. Permakoff remains one of only four Australian soldiers who died during the First World War not commemorated on the Roll; the three others were convicted and hanged for murder.

Roll of Honour Cards, 1914–1918, Army, Australian War Memorial, AWM 145

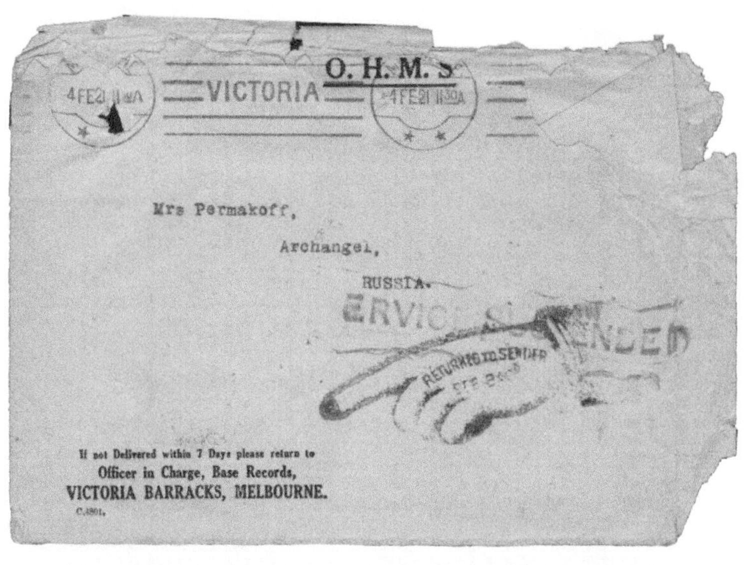

Base Records in Melbourne attempted to send Permakoff's mother photographs and particulars of his grave in France.

Service Record of Nicholas Permakoff, B2455, National Archives Australia

DIGGERS' GRIEVANCES.

PROCESSION TO PARLIAMENT.

OFFICERS NOT WANTED.

Returned soldiers to the number of several hundreds yesterday afternoon attended a meeting at His Majesty's Theatre, called by the "Heresy Committee" of the Perth Branch of the R.S.A., for the purpose of discussing specified and general grievances. Officers were not invited.

Mr. J. N. O'Neill, the chairman of the Heresy Committee, explained that that body had been duly elected by the Perth Branch, and after sitting daily for three weeks, had drawn up a report to be submitted to the next meeting. It had decided on holding a mass meeting, and had asked the president of the branch to call it, but he had refused, so the committee had been compelled to act. It was for members to choose between the officers of the R.S.A. and a few "dinkum diggers" who were working to get a fair deal for their comrades.

Mr. Fanton, who was voted to the chair, said that, in his opinion it was useless carrying resolutions. What was necessary was for members to decide whether they were content with the association, which was an organisation for the assistance of returned soldiers in name only, or whether they would form an association which would do real work for members. Senator Millen had absolutely refused to give the returned soldiers representation on the repatriation committees; and the association had no legal standing to enforce the payment of proper wages to members, as an industrial union had; so it really had no status to do anything for its members. At present the position of the returned soldier was little better than it was after the Crimea and the South African war. No proper scheme of repatriation had been started, either owing to incompetence, or as a deliberate attempt to flood the labour market and bring down wages. The returned soldiers had come back to pay their share of the war taxation, and of the many high salaries paid to Defence and Naval officers, who had not been on active service, while blind soldiers were dependent on charity for a sufficient living. If that was what the association stood for, then the sooner it was burst up the better. He had nothing against any of the members of the R.S.A. executive, who had held commissions, but they did not understand the conditions under which the manual labourer lived and worked, as they had never been through the mill themselves.

Mr. Needham moved: "This meeting of returned soldiers emphatically protests against the non-fulfilment of the promises made to the soldiers by the Federal and State Governments." He said that what was wanted was some manufacturers. The men had been workers before they became soldiers, and they wanted work to do again. They had no wish to go down to the Repatriation Department and have charity doled out. They should go in their thousands, and demand their rights from Parliament.

Mr. O'Neill, in seconding the motion, said the State and Federal Governments had failed to make good their promises of four years ago, and would continue to do so unless the soldiers showed a determination to secure their dues. If the returned men stood together they would have their grievances rectified without firing a shot.

Mr. Shakespeare said that when the Repatriation Bill was before the Legislative Council the latter could not find a quorum. That showed how much attention was being given to returned soldiers; and it would be necessary for them to use their weight in order to alter such a state of affairs. He moved to amend the motion by adding that the returned soldiers should march to Parliament House, and demand that their representatives be heard at the Bar of the House.

The addition was accepted, and the motion as amended was carried unanimously.

Mr. Purtell moved—"In view of the large number of unemployed soldiers we call upon Federal and State Governments together with employers generally to shoulder the full responsibility of immediately placing these soldiers in their former positions or positions suitable to their physical condition." As an instance of the manner in which returned soldiers were treated, he said he had been a member of a party which went mining for base metals, and seemed to be doing well, until it came to marketing their product. Then, for tungsten which was quoted at over £4,000 per ton in America they received £169 per ton. On bismuth, the quotation for which was about £2,000 per ton, they did somewhat better, receiving £400 per ton. He urged that returned soldiers should be settled in the pastoral areas, where 1,000 men could easily be placed. They were mostly miners or back woodsmen who would certainly make good.

Mr. Norton, in seconding the motion, castigated in turn the Federal and State Governments, the employers and the Returned Soldiers' Association, for failing in their duty in dealing with the problem of finding work for the returned soldiers.

One speaker touching on the tramway question, contended that the strikers had themselves to blame, for having chosen the wrong moment to strike. Another, who was a member of the Tramway Union, urged that if the tram men were given the opportunity of earning a living wage in six days instead of having to work seven, there would be work on the trams for 20 or 30 more returned men. A third speaker complained that the Repatriation Department sent men to do work for which they were not physically fit; while a fourth added that if a man refused such a job because he was unable to do it, his sustenance was cut off, and he had no right of appeal, except to Melbourne which was useless.

The motion was carried unanimously.

The chairman moved—"This meeting is of the opinion that all pensions should be standardised and increased to meet the high cost of living now prevailing in Australia." In taking exception to the big difference between the pensions of officers and those of rankers, he pointed out that it cost just as much to feed the an ex-private and his wife and children as it did to feed an ex-officer and his family.

The motion was carried unanimously.

Mr. Donnes moved—"In view of the present deplorable condition of the labour market, we emphatically protest against the closing down of public works, such as the Henderson Naval Base." He said that the A.W.U., the members of which were chiefly concerned on the naval base works, had a good award, which would expire shortly, and the Government was endeavouring to use the unemployed returned soldiers to bring wages down in the new award. The site had already been reported upon by a number of engineering experts, and now the Government was bringing out Admiral Jellicoe, who probably knew nothing about civil engineering. During the week since work had been stopped, £1,000 worth of work had been washed into the sea, and £100,000 of the taxpayers' money would inevitably vanish in the same way, before the arrival of the Admiral. The place should be employing 1,000 men.

Mr. Monsfield, in supporting the motion, said the returned soldiers did not want to see men with families who had not been to the war, sacked in order to find work for them.

The motion was carried.

A good deal of discussion took place on the following motion, for which Mr. O'Neill was responsible:—"This meeting is of opinion that it would be in the best interests of returned soldiers generally that all official positions in the R.S.A. should be held by members who have not held commissioned rank." He said that everywhere, by tradition, training and treatment, the man with a star was in a class apart, and even though he was the best man in the world he could not be a pal of the ranker. The R.S.A. was run by the ex-officers, and stood condemned in the eyes of the "dinkums." There were 12 ex-officers on the executive, and it was no good the "diggers" trying to get anything through. Ex-officers held all the paid positions, and there was no possibility of any one else getting such a position. The president (Major Lamb) had even repudiated that meeting, because it was a meeting of "diggers."

A number of other speakers strongly expressed similar views.

On the other side a one-armed officer just back on 1914 leave, demanded to know why it had been necessary for him to attend uninvited. He contended that in civil life, as on active service, the interests of the "diggers" and himself were identical. They had fought for freedom, and they intended to have it. He asked members to consider well before splitting the association. Let them change their executive if they liked, but stick together.

This speaker had several supporters, one of whom declared that the motion was an insult to many good fellows who had proved themselves to be men right through the war. There were plenty of men with two or three "pips" on their shoulders who were as good "diggers" as the best.

The motion was carried by a large majority.

A motion declaring that Senator Pearce was totally unfit to deal with demobilisation matters, and calling on the Federal Government to recall him, was carried unanimously.

Dick Johnson, here in uniform, went on to become a leading figure in the Australian Aboriginal Progressive Association and wore his returned-soldier badge to meetings.

Provided by the Johnson family

Edward Walker, another soldier and leading figure in the Australian Aboriginal Progressive Association, photographed here in the *Queenslander Pictorial*, supplement to *The Queenslander*, August 1917.

State Library of Queensland

Hugo Throssell, James Woods and Thomas (Jack) Axford,
all Victoria Cross winners, at a 1928 Anzac Day ceremony.

State Library of Western Australia, Truth *Newspaper
Collection 047700PD*

Hugo Throssell, his wife, Katharine Susannah Prichard, and their, son Ric, c. 1925.
Throssell's suicide note eight years later asked that his family get a war pension.

Katharine Susannah Prichard Writers' Centre

AFTERMATH OF WAR SERVICE

Anzac Commits Suicide

SYDNEY, Monday.—Ermerald Schick, 39, who was an Anzac at 17, came from Lord Howe Island to march in the Sydney celebrations Anzac procession on April 25.

Yesterday he was found shot at his parents' home in Willoughby. A note found near the body stated that he was sorry, but he was unable to stand the mental torture any longer.

He suffered shellshock at the war, and it frequently made him ill. Schick was found dead sitting in a chair with a repeating rifle between his knees and a bullet wound in his forehead. He left a widow and four children.

Headline in the Adelaide *News*, demonstrating how reportage of suicide linked soldiers' deaths with their war service and Anzac status.

'Aftermath of war service – Anzac commits suicide', News (Adelaide), 20 June 1938, 2

DEATH OF THOMAS BEAUMONT.

Mr. S. J. M'Kinlay, J.P., held an inquiry this morning into the circumstances surrounding the death of Thomas Beaumont. Evidence was given by James Beaumont, Emma Quinn Beaumont, and Constable P. Hogan. It showed that the deceased, who was thirty-three years of age, and resided near Rannes, enlisted in the Australian Imperial Force and went to Egypt. From there he was invalided to Brisbane and last month was discharged as medically unfit, the certificate showing his complaint to be chronic bronchitis. He arrived at Wowan in a sickly and depressed condition, and about 10 a.m. on the 13th of December—three days after he returned home—he went outside and his mother soon afterwards found him with his throat cut. He died shortly after. He had not said anything that would lead his people to suppose that he had contemplated suicide.

Headline in the Rockhampton *Morning Bulletin* reporting on the suicide of Thomas Beaumont, who cut his throat after being invalided out of Egypt.

'Death of Thomas Beaumont', Morning Bulletin (Rockhampton), 6 January 1917, 14

Tobruk war cemetery, c. 1943, in which 559 Australians are buried. This memorial was replaced with a different one in 1948, but the original became the model for the 1983 Rats of Tobruk memorial in Canberra, and other memorials to the Rats elsewhere in Australia.

Australian War Memorial P11259.004

The Rats of Tobruk memorial on Anzac Parade in Canberra. Installed in 1983, at the initiative of the Rats of Tobruk Association, it was the third memorial on this mall.

Photo by Margaret Hutchison

Service personnel working shirtless to clean up the
rubble in the vicinity of an atomic blast at Operation Buffalo.

*Image taken from a video of Operation Buffalo,
held at Imperial War Museum London*

'Women Against Rape', Canberra, 1982.

NLA MS7930, Jack Waterford Papers

'Women Rally! No to the Anzac Myths', Melbourne, 1986.

F.J. Riley Ephemera Collection, State Library of Victoria, ECPO278

Gerry Binder, bringing his anti-war protest into Santiago Sierra's performance art work, *Veterans of the Wars of Afghanistan, Timor-Leste, Iraq and Vietnam Facing the Corner*, part of *13 Rooms* at Kaldor Public Art Project 27 (2013). Gerry stands in the corner of a white room, facing away from the exhibit viewers, wearing a 'War is Terrorism' T-shirt.

Gerry Binder

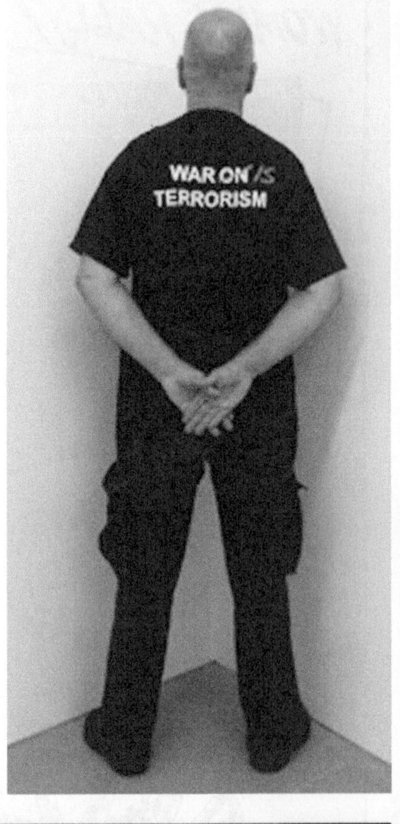

Ben Roberts-Smith cheers another soldier drinking from a prosthetic leg, taken as a war trophy from the body of a slain Afghan man. In the *Ben Roberts-Smith v Fairfax Media* defamation case, Roberts-Smith's lawyer admitted that 'hundreds' of images exist of Australian soldiers drinking from the leg.

Fairfax/Nine

The warrior of the future:
a Ukrainian soldier prepares to launch a drone.

Oleksandr Volosyanskyi, in Oleksandra Molloy, Drones in
Modern Warfare: Lessons Learnt from the War in Ukraine,
Australian Army Occasional Paper, no. 29, 2024, 25.

Anzac Day dawn services are often held in awe-inspiring locations, as this image, taken at Kings Park overlooking the Swan River in central Perth, illustrates. Returned soldiers remarked in the decades after the war how the slopes leading up to Kings Park from the road snaking along the Swan River reminded them of what they faced when they landed at Gallipoli.

Photo by Gnangarra

A sense of the sacred pervades the dawn service ritual.
As darkness gently transmutes into light on 25 April 2005,
a large crowd gathers at the forecourt of the Australian War
Memorial for the Anzac Day dawn service.

Photo by Peter Ellis

When protestors were arrested for putting stickers on the door of the Anzac Memorial at Hyde Park in 1985, some onlookers chanted 'choke the bitches'.[59] Veterans in Melbourne attempted to physically intimidate members of the Anti-Anzac Day Collective, setting fire to their banners and making obscene gestures to them. After witnessing the activities of the collective, a First World War veteran told a journalist: 'I reckon they should line them up and bloody shoot them'.[60] In response to the chant '1, 2, 3, 4 … Anzac Day glorifies war', veterans shouted back at the sound of 'four': 'Kick all dykes to the floor'.[61] Cartoonists, too, had a field day, adding to the vilification, with Les Tanner depicting dungaree-wearing spiky-haired women beneath an 'Anti Anzac' banner being observed by an old digger commenting: 'I wonder why we bothered'.[62]

REFRAMING THE VETERAN AS VICTIM

As Jocelynne Scutt predicted, the revival of Anzac Day in the early 1980s was driven in part by the effort to defend it from the affrontery of women who pointed out the links between militarism and sexual violence. The hostility of the leadership of the RSL to such protests might have been predicted, the rallying of Vietnam veterans to defend the institution and old diggers possibly less so. Motivated to join their fellow veterans in the face of what they saw as an unwarranted critique, Vietnam veterans in this period also began to consolidate a narrative of their own about verbal abuse by anti-war protestors during the 1960s and 1970s. Ann Curthoys challenges this characterisation and suggests that one incident, in 1966, when a woman smeared in paint interrupted a Sydney homecoming march, has exerted an outsized influence on collective memory. She can find no further evidence of interruption to homecoming marches, and instead asserts that government policy, rather than individuals, was the object of anti-war protests. Moreover, memories of Vietnam veterans being called rapists during that conflict were most likely a conflation of the activities of anti-war and later feminist protestors.[63]

While, in one sense, the feminist protestors and Anzac Day defenders came from opposing points of view about the occasion's meaning and significance, in another they shared an understanding about the impact of war that had gained momentum since the 1970s. War as 'horror' began to replace an earlier emphasis on heroism and glory. The closing decades of the 20th century, both within Australia and internationally, saw a growing fascination in western, liberal democratic cultures with stories of misery and suffering. In Australia, this was reflected in a growing body of literature, beginning with Bill Gammage's *The Broken Years* (1974), which focused on the experiences of the ordinary soldier to show 'the horrors of war'.[64] Patsy Adam-Smith's popular study *The Anzacs* (1978) made the point that 'not one of the soldiers glorified war'.[65] A recasting of war as horror was accompanied by new empathy for its victims, which had been revolutionised by the recognition of post-traumatic stress disorder (PTSD) in the *Diagnostic and Statistical Manual of Mental Disorders, Third Edition* in 1980.[66] Physical disability arising from war service had long held legitimacy as the basis for repatriation entitlements. The mental suffering of veterans had been the subject of far greater ambivalence. Earlier assumptions that those who experienced 'war neurosis' had a predisposition to weakness, were malingerers, or motivated by financial gain gave way to new conceptions of trauma that invested events themselves, rather than the mental predisposition of their victims, as the primary cause of suffering. As a consequence, the horror of war and the physical and mental toll that it could place on veterans emerged as a primary narrative in writing about its impact. Anzac Day had always been a solemn affair, but the traumatised or psychologically scarred veteran had not previously been front and centre of commemorations. Yet from the 1980s, these veterans gained more and more prominence. Vietnam veterans with PTSD were one such group; former prisoners of war were another.

By focusing on the civilian female victims of war, and specifically those who had been subjected to rape, feminist protestors were both literally and metaphorically displacing an emerging focus on the soldier himself as victim. Misogyny and grievance about the implications that veterans themselves might be rapists drove some opposition to the feminist protestors, but the more profound objection was that a focus on the raped woman displaced recognition of veterans themselves as victims of war. There were echoes in Australia of Susan Jeffords' contemporaneous analysis of the 'remasculinization' of American culture, wherein the challenge to patriarchal power posed by women's and civil rights groups in the previous few decades was negated, in part, by figuring Vietnam veterans as victims too.[67] When a Vietnam veteran interrupted Anti-Anzac protestors in Melbourne in 1985, stood beneath their banner and waved his prosthetic leg in the air and declared, 'You can't be proud … Because they say you are a war monger, but I am proud', his actions made headlines around the country. The lost leg was 'the most brilliant anti-war banner of all' and his protest put paid to the 'chants and heckling'.[68] In reports of the event, the displacement of the female protestors restored the veteran as the rightful focus and object of empathy. A shared antipathy to the 1980s protests was one of the factors that inspired a growing rapprochement between the RSL and

Vietnam veterans, and in 1987 Vietnam veterans led the march in Sydney for the first time. Later that year, the 'Welcome Home' parade for Vietnam veterans consolidated the sense that the ambivalence and tension that had typified the response to them had been overcome.

THE CONTEST FOR VICTIMHOOD

By the late 1980s, the Women Against Rape and feminist protests had petered out. Women Against Rape in Canberra was one of the first groups to withdraw, in 1985. They felt that their inclusion in the official program in 1984 legitimised their concerns: 'We have made our point.' 'The community now makes the connection between rape and war and Anzac Day', a spokesperson said. Their energies would now be directed to other ways of highlighting issues to do with rape: 'It's not just a "one day of the year" thing for us, we live with it every day of our lives.' They were uninterested in making it a civil liberties issue, or an 'Abolish Anzac' issue.[69] The peak years of Melbourne protests, where the focus was on a broader critique of Anzac Day itself, were the mid-1980s. By 1987, only about 60 people gathered under the 'Abolish Anzac Day' purple banner, and spokesperson Leslie Hall said her group was gathered there to focus on the 'wider perspective of war', not just rape.[70] They attracted little attention from veterans at the march. Tensions about tactics, and political differences among members of the collective, meant that participation in protests on Anzac Day had fallen away by late 1980s.

The comments of the Canberra protest organisers that their point had been made might appear sanguine, yet there is evidence to suggest they could be correct. In Australia, government funding of Centres Against Sexual Assault from 1988 led to the disbandment of many Women Against Rape collectives. Within a decade, the claims of women subjected to military sexual slavery by the Imperial Japanese Army in the 1930s and 1940s, and the use of sexual violence as a planned instrument of war policy in the former Yugoslavia in the 1990s, and during the 1994 Rwandan genocide, led to recognition of rape as a crime against humanity and a war crime in the Rome Statute of 1998. And there were men who recognised the women's courage in speaking out. Throughout the peak years of activity, women's groups reported that some men who had been horrified by the behaviour of their fellow soldiers reached out to them to offer admiration and praise for drawing attention to the crime of rape in war.[71] In 1987, members of the Blacktown RSL club were interviewed about their views on a range of matters, including women protestors at Anzac Day. Earl O'Sullivan, a 71-year-old veteran, commented that 'protestors might offend some people, but they have a case'.[72] On further reflection though, some scholars and participants themselves offered pause for thought. They suggested that Women Against Rape universalised the experience of women and, in the Australian context, overlooked the sexual violence that accompanied colonisation.[73]

The Women Against Rape and Anti-Anzac Day collectives may have faded away by 1990, but Anzac Day was a very different institution in the wake of their protests. The renewed enthusiasm for Anzac Day, after decades in the doldrums, was not merely a reaction to the depredations of a gendered critique. Nor was it, as journalist Paul Kelly put it in 2011, 'the triumph of the people over the intellectual class'.[74] One relatively overlooked element was a new emphasis on the traumatising effect of war on its victims, and the emotive power of this narrative to draw an audience back to Anzac in an era when cultural interest in victimhood and suffering was soaring. The Women Against Rape protestors had their origins in the 1970s women's liberation movement but they also reflected that era's emphasis on identifying victims over heroes. These broader cultural forces at first blunted, then ultimately usurped, the feminist critique. Men previously alienated from the march saw themselves as victims, too. They began to rewrite the script of Anzac for a new era, insisting on their own suffering, and reasserting the centrality of the male veteran to Anzac commemoration.

11

ANTI-WAR VETERAN ACTIVISM FROM VIETNAM TO THE WAR ON TERROR

MIA MARTIN HOBBS

Mia: I contacted Australian Veterans for Peace last year, hoping to find Australian VFP Vietnam veterans who had returned to Vietnam postwar … I would be very interested in speaking to any Australian Vietnam veterans in the VFP.

Gerry: Sadly, AVP [Australian Veterans for Peace] only ever attracted passing interest from only a very small number of veterans, none of whom ever became members per se, so I'm the sole 'member' … I got the distinct impression that Australian Vietnam veterans who were opposed to war were reluctant to speak out about it or join anti-war groups.[1]

This is part of an email chain between me and Gerry Binder, a Vietnam veteran and the sole member of Australian Veterans for Peace. I contacted Australian Veterans for Peace in 2017 for my doctoral research with veterans who had returned to Vietnam after the war. In my fieldwork, I had interviewed dozens of staunchly anti-war American veterans, but among the Australians, I repeatedly encountered contempt for the anti-war movement, pride in service and a strong adherence to Anzac narratives of war. I was attempting to diversify my interview pool when I first contacted Gerry, thinking that I was approaching a whole organisation. But Gerry revealed that he was the only member: Australian Veterans for Peace is a one-man blog, which Gerry has maintained since 2004. There were anti-war Australian veterans out there, Gerry claimed, but they were 'reluctant to speak out'.[2]

There are only a handful of Australian veterans, from Vietnam to the War on Terror, who spoke out against war. Interviews, veterans' memoirs, artworks, blogs and newspaper articles show how veterans faced implicit and overt pressure – from the veteran community, politicians and the Australian media – not to state anti-war views. These sources suggest that veterans who developed anti-war views often avoided speaking publicly and, in some cases, avoided being identified as veterans at all. Since the 'Anzac revival' began in the late 1980s, veterans who question war or criticise the militarism that underpins the Anzac legend have been isolated and marginalised. The Anzac legend itself stymies anti-war dissent.

TURNING AGAINST THE WAR IN VIETNAM

The anti–Vietnam War movement in Australia began as an anti-conscription movement, grounded in Australia's history of volunteerism in the First World War, which has led to a common assumption that anti–Vietnam War soldiers must have been unwilling conscripts. However, interviews show that many anti-war veterans initially supported the war, and their later anti-war feeling stemmed in part from the dissonance between their pre-deployment beliefs and the disillusionment they experienced during the war.[3] Gerry Binder came to Australia as a refugee from Romania, fleeing the Soviet occupation, and was raised in an intensely anti-communist family. He joined the Australian Army reserve in 1964 and regular Army in 1967: 'by this time, the Vietnam War was going full tilt, and I was full tilt anti-communist'.[4] Gerry deployed with 9RAR in 1968. Similarly, although he was conscripted, Rob de Kok remembered that he was willing to go to Vietnam because he believed:

> all of Menzies' bullshit, and you know, if you don't stop them now in Southeast Asia they'll come here, they'll kill your wife and rape your children or vice versa, you know, this is a terrible thing and we have to go fight the communists, all that shit, the Cold War business, meant that I actually went in willingly.[5]

Their support for the war effort was underpinned by a desire to undertake a rite of passage and live up to the family name. 'I have to say, my mum and all the rest of the family were so pleased when I got drafted, because finally something would make a man out of me', Rob remembers.[6] He deployed with 4RAR in 1971. Terry Burstall, who wrote about becoming anti-war in his memoirs, joined the Army 'in order to help stop the communist aggressor from the north. I had a wistful feeling about joining a long list of family forebears who had made this trip to war before me'.[7] He enlisted in 1965 and deployed the following year with 6RAR.

Yet once at war, Rob and Terry quickly found they opposed it. 'Either the first time you're shot at, or the first time somebody you know actually gets hit', Rob explained. 'You don't have to stay long in a war before you actually think, "This is just ridiculous. This shouldn't be happening."'[8] Terry, similarly, reflected that the Battle of Long Tan marked a major turning point for him: 'Nothing takes the supposed glory out of war more quickly than the sight of dead mutilated friends … I had gone to Vietnam for all the right reasons but found that none of them fitted the cause.'[9] Anti-war veterans were particularly disturbed by the destruction inflicted upon Vietnamese civilians. Terry remembered a particular operation:

> Operation Enoggera, to search and destroy the village of Long Phuoc, and when I say destroy I mean fuckin' destroy … We just absolutely destroyed the whole bloody lot. We pulled it to the ground and burnt it and blew it up. There was absolutely nothing left of Long Phuoc when we left, absolutely nothing.[10]

Gerry, similarly, remembered a particular incident where his unit had discovered a pit and a rifle in the home of two elderly Vietnamese, and decided they were Viet Cong:

> So what did we do? We told them to move away. They took them away as prisoners. Then the tank blew their shack to shithouse. Just destroyed it, just disappeared in a shower of sparks and flame. And I was not happy with that. I thought, these people are just harmless peasants.[11]

Gerry reflected that if he was in that situation, he would dig a pit to hide in and find a rifle to defend himself. 'That doesn't mean they're bloody a Viet Cong or enemy or any of that sort of shit. It just means they're terrified people living in a war zone.'[12] The needless mistreatment of local Vietnamese led him to question the logic of war when 'we were theoretically there, the propaganda was, to win the hearts and minds'. He remembered asking his lieutenant one night:

'I'm just saying, "What are we doing here, sir?" I remember that I was questioning him. He gave me a typical military answer. "Oh, we are saving the country", or whatever. He certainly didn't go, "Yes, actually, I was wondering that myself."'[13]

These veterans returned to Australia disillusioned with war. 'When we left in June I don't know what I took with me. Anger. Disillusionment. Disappointment. I certainly wasn't going to be able to join the exalted ranks of my family forebears', Terry reflected.[14] Rob experienced a loss of faith, abandoning his Catholicism: 'I thought, how can anybody sit down and watch this from above? And then how can anybody believe in it? Yeah! Yeah, I just thought, OK, I'm just not gonna trust you again, you sold me down the river.'[15] However, neither spoke up or spoke out about their doubts about the war. Terry reflected that it was hard for soldiers to speak out against the war because it would upset those who had lost their loved ones:

> When you lose a son or husband in a war, there has to be at least a Cause – he died for his country, or defending our freedom, or something. In Vietnam none of these rationales could be used. Many of us who had been there knew this, but it was better not to rock the boat while other boys went off to risk their lives and parents and wives grieved.[16]

Instead, both Rob and Terry isolated themselves from the Army and the war. 'From the moment I came back, I did my best to dissociate myself from everything', Rob explained. He moved to Adelaide, got married and trained to become an English teacher:

'I thought there's more to life, and I'm picking it up from here, and I'll make a better man of myself.'[17] Gerry, meanwhile, remained in the Army for seven years after returning. Although he still believed deeply in the anti-communist cause, he had begun to question 'the wisdom of the war'. By the mid-1970s, he was made an instructor for new recruits at Kapooka, but felt uneasy about training recruits to kill: 'I couldn't tell these people, yeah, you know, go kill people. I just couldn't do it anymore.' Gerry left the Army in 1976.

VIETNAM REFLECTIONS AND THE ANZAC REVIVAL

It took years for Vietnam veterans to speak out against the war. The early 1980s saw a surge of public interest in the Vietnam War and its legacies, with popular culture representations, veteran activism and commemorative events that encouraged veterans to reflect on the meaning and purpose of the war. For some veterans, this reflective milieu opened the door to overt criticism of war. Terry returned to Vietnam in 1986 to learn about the Vietnamese experience of the war. Meeting with Vietnamese victims of Australian warfare clarified his anti-war views and emboldened him to state them publicly in his memoir, *A Soldier Returns*:

> The Australian Army in Vietnam followed policies that created enormous hardship and suffering for the local people of Phuoc Tuy. Granted, war itself is an atrocity, but there was no need for the mindless brutality toward the civilian population. Our war was to fight the VC, not the people. If we say the VC were the people, we are then admitting that we were fighting against our own beliefs, as our rationale was to help the people.[18]

After his return trip, Terry became much more active. He was interviewed by Stuart Rintoul for *Ashes of Vietnam* (1987), a collection of veteran stories that emphasised 'the savagery and arbitrariness of the war', and in 1991 wrote an article, 'Policy contradictions of the Australian task force in Vietnam', for *Vietnam Generation,* an American anti-war academic journal.[19] This public anti-war testimony coincided with a surge of Vietnam War commemoration in the US and Australia, which positioned the war as a mistake, or 'quagmire'.[20] Terry indicated that he finally felt his views were shared by many veterans: 'After twenty odd years I can talk openly of the uselessness because it is apparent now to all.'[21]

Terry's sense that the 'uselessness' of the war was 'apparent now to all' was mirrored in a surge of artwork by Vietnam veterans beginning in the early 1980s, some of which was overtly critical of conflict. In 1988, Vietnam veteran and art student Peter Daly asked the Australian War Memorial about its policy regarding the acquisition of art by veterans. He was told that where war events had been 'adequately covered' by war artists and photographers, 'we do not seek examples of pictures painted from memory'.[22] In response, Peter Daly and fellow veteran Archibald Zammit-Ross co-curated 'Dog Tags', a travelling exhibition of veteran art that coincided with the dedication of the Vietnam Forces National Memorial in Canberra in 1992.[23] The exhibition positioned the war as a tragic waste, emphasising themes of 'the mass media's complicity in wartime propaganda, the superficiality of patriotism, the depersonalization of the individual by the military, and the sacralisation and commemoration of the war dead'.[24] Peter Daly's contributions centred on exposing the 'patriarchal values of dominance and winning ... I want to make a statement in my art that hopefully will contribute to a progressive awareness'.[25]

Yet while the reflective milieu around the war in the 1980s and 1990s inspired these artists to create and exhibit their work, the wider commemoration of the war also fed into the growing Anzac revival. The war was increasingly remembered with a jingoistic tone, stifling expressions of uncertainty and doubt with the narrative that Australia's war in Vietnam was 'the legend of Anzac upheld'.[26] Anti-war veteran-artists recognised that the Vietnam War was increasingly being exploited by politicians. One of the veteran artists from the 'Dog Tags' exhibition, Terry Eichler, was a conscript who deployed with the 1 Australian Reinforcement Unit and then 9RAR in 1968–69. He was the subject of a student film in 1999, in which he reflects:

> the legacy is a war hero, and that's absurd, I mean it's not reality, it's not sane reality, it's propaganda for a particular view of Australian identity. And if people realised, if people had actually been in war, they'd realise immediately that's bullshit, it's just bullshit, and it's dangerous bullshit.[27]

While the Australian War Memorial acquired some artwork by anti-war veterans in the 1990s, the works collected were those critical of conscription or expressing survivors' guilt, rather than those that criticised the war or militarism, and they have rarely been exhibited. Referencing the works of veteran artists including Peter Daly and Terry Eichler, in 2007 scholar Kate McCulloch observed that 'there is a severe lack of this kind of art in the Australian War Memorial'.[28] In 2011, a retrospective in *Art Monthly Australia* observed that 'the AWM has so far shown limited interest in subversive or "outsider" art by veterans'.

Referring to the artworks in the 1992 'Dog Tags' exhibition, the essay argued that 'this is a history that is scarcely acknowledged by our official institutions'.[29]

By the 1990s, new technologies also allowed different narratives about the war to reach veterans who still believed in the war cause. In the early 1980s, Gerry had become a store manager with McDonald's. He bought a computer to help him run the stocktake. 'So that's how I got into computers', he explained. 'I sort of grew into computers as computers came along.' By the 1990s, he was spending time on early internet forums:

> and, you know, I'd be stupid enough to say I was a Vietnam veteran. And some people would try to educate me about what was wrong with that war … Because it's text-based, they would quote a whole lot of shit at me, and so I looked that stuff up.

Gerry began 'reading stuff and realising I was not educated about Vietnam … and I realised, oi. [He sighed]. And then I got very angry that I'd been- Angry with myself for allowing myself to become so brainwashed and angry at the system for brainwashing me.'[30]

Yet, as anti-war veterans were developing their views, the wider veteran community was increasingly influenced by the Anzac revival, which positioned Australian soldiers as exceptionally tough, brave and irreverent. These Anzac themes manifested in a spate of memoirs and non-fiction histories written by veterans in the 1990s and 2000s.[31] For example, Long Tan veteran Bob Buick published a memoir, *All Guts and No Glory* (2000), in which he described killing a wounded Vietnamese soldier, a 'poor bastard lying there with half a metre of his gut spread over the ground'.[32] Fellow Long Tan veteran Terry Burstall wrote of so-called 'mercy killings' in *A Soldier Returns*:

> I do not condone the killings, but I understand how they happened and I will state here that I would have done the same thing … at that time I wanted to kill every VC or Vietnamese in Vietnam … We must make sure this sort of thing will never happen again.[33]

A decade later, when Bob Buick's memoir came out, Terry was disturbed that it went 'into graphic detail about killing a wounded enemy soldier, which is completely and utterly against the Geneva conventions … if it was a mercy killing, would he have done the same to an Australian? Because it was only – we were only 15 minutes from a hospital by helicopter.'[34] The 'war of words' between Long Tan veterans was aired on ABC's *7.30 Report* on the anniversary of Long Tan that year, with the book framed as 'a no-nonsense memoir by a no-nonsense soldier'. Bob Buick was described by other veterans as 'one of the heroes of Long Tan', someone whom 'any reasonable army' would want leading their soldiers. Bob shrugged off the concerns by saying that 'mercy killing' was 'part of soldiering', and that 'war is not nice at all'.[35] Terry's concerns, both about the 'mercy' killing when medical aid was available, and about the cavalier tone in which it was described, were thus implicitly diminished. Other veterans and the Australian media both framed Terry as oversensitive or 'upset', while Bob was a 'no-nonsense' hero.

STAND FAST AGAINST THE WAR ON TERROR

The Anzac narrative was also invoked to justify Australia's involvement in the War on Terror, with Prime Minister John Howard drawing on the theme of mateship to frame Australia's support for the US in Afghanistan and then Iraq.[36] Gerry found it deeply troubling to see Australia once more following the US into war: 'Okay, we'll go all the way with LBJ all over again. That's what I heard … Well, it's now all the way with George W. Bush. It's rubbish. But there we are. By this time, I'm realising that we are nothing but a puppet state of America.'[37] Gerry had heard about two Navy veterans handing their medals into Greens leader Bob Brown to protest against Australia's involvement in the Iraq War, and he decided to do the same at the Stop the War rally in March 2003. 'They gave me these medals in the last stupid war we fought and I'm going to give them back to John Howard', he announced.[38] Shortly after, he began his blog, Australian Veterans for Peace, which he has maintained for 20 years, 'to give a voice to Australian war veterans who are strongly opposed to war'.[39] As a result of his blog, a younger veteran from Timor, Chip Henriss, contacted Gerry asking to join his 'movement': 'he thought I had a movement going. He didn't realise I was the only member of Veterans for Peace. It was not a very large movement!'[40]

Chip was a former US marine who later joined the Australian Army and served in East Timor in the late 1990s. He was 'profoundly proud' of Australia's role in the INTERFET mission, but began to suspect that Australia's motivations for involvement were not humanitarian. In 2002, Australia and Timor negotiated new maritime boundaries, which extended Australia's claim into Timorese territories with vast petroleum reserves, leading to accusations of Australia 'bullying' Timor.[41] Chip joined the Timor Sea Justice Campaign, and his Timor activism led him to create Stand Fast in 2007, a group for anti-war veterans in Australia. The name references the drill command of holding attention, 'challenging the idea that an anti-war activist is in one box and former military personnel are in another', and echoing a longstanding trend in US-veteran activism that positions anti-war protest as a continuation of patriotic service.[42] He was joined by another Timor veteran, Hamish Chitts, who had served 'basically at the lowest level of Australia's intelligence community' in the early 2000s. In his blog, Hamish wrote that in the lead-up to the invasion of Iraq, he and other intelligence officers:

> knew it for the farce that it was. We started sending around joke emails to each other about [politicians'] reasons ... our superiors soon clamped down on any dissent but the point is there was no failure of intelligence. Everyone knew there were no WMDs, everyone knew that Al Qaeda had no significant presence in Iraq.

As a result of the Iraq War, Hamish sought a discharge: 'I did not want to be a part of or contribute in any way to this nor did I want to risk my life again, especially for the sake of big business.'[43]

Gerry, Rob and Hamish joined Stand Fast, although Gerry explained that they 'never really got more than three or four people', communicating online.[44] Nonetheless, the group generated anti-war action. In the early 2000s, Rob had backed out of speaking at several rallies against the Iraq War, but the support of Stand Fast empowered him to finally make a public protest, on Anzac Day, in 2010 at the Australian War Memorial.[45]

Rob wrote about the experience for the *Australian* newspaper's *Weekend* magazine: 'On Anzac Day, clutching anti-war leaflets, you don't expect much, except resistance.'[46] Rob's leaflets were titled, 'I am a Vietnam veteran not marching today', and begged passing Australians to 'question Australia's ongoing support for the wars in Iraq and Afghanistan … wars we started for false reasons and continue for false patriotism and misdirected fear'.[47] He was 'ready to quit' when an interaction with an Afghanistan veteran changed his mind. Rob shared that he hated seeing 'kids being groomed for war', while the younger veteran shared that he was mourning his best friend, lost to suicide. '"You look after yourself, mate." As I watched him walk to his unit I knew I was going to stay, to hand out every leaflet, get them to whoever would take them … We were brothers. Somewhere inside we shared a scar.'[48]

Rob's story of quiet connection over anti-war sentiment has been echoed by other anti-war veterans. Vietnam veteran Noel Turnbull gave his first Anzac Day speech in 2017, which questioned the wisdom of the wars in Vietnam and Iraq and challenged the idea of soldiers dying for the flag. Afterwards, a younger veteran approached him, and 'as he came near, he extended his hand and I took it and we shook. Then he leant in and said quietly but with passion, "I have just been down at the Service listening to all the fucking crap. You told it as it is."'[49] These stories suggest some anti-war feeling, or at least sympathy, among the broader veteran community, including those who march on Anzac Day.

WHY HAVE ANTI-WAR VETERANS STRUGGLED TO ORGANISE IN AUSTRALIA?

Quiet opposition to war is much more widespread among the ranks than many would believe. It came up repeatedly in conversations with Vietnam veterans across the political spectrum: 'I did not agree with being there for sure', one veteran, Les Vincent, said, 'I don't think I was unique.'[50] Many felt the war in Vietnam was a case of fighting 'other people's wars', an 'insurance policy' for the US alliance. 'Most people now see the folly of our involvement in the Vietnam War', Graham Edwards reflected. 'I think most people now see it as having been a political war.'[51] The majority of interviewees explained they would willingly defend Australia from attack but do not support Australia's participation in wars overseas. They attributed this change to their experiences in the military and war. Wal Cameron explained that serving in Vietnam 'changed my views, greatly. To this day I still think we should be bringing all our troops home from around the world.'[52]

This is a view shared by many former and currently serving members I have spoken to, across different time periods and conflicts: 'I was in the service to defend Australia, not to attack other people', one told me.[53] 'I signed on the dotted line to defend Australia', another said, 'not to go to war on behalf of the US'.[54] Others suggested that all war should be avoided, at all costs. 'Anyone who's ever served,' said John Abernethy, 'we do not believe in war. There's better ways to resolve issues than killing.'[55] Another Vietnam veteran, Brian Cleaver, agreed: 'There has to be diplomatic ways of resolving problems before the first shot is fired.'[56]

Yet despite sharing anti-war sentiments, these veterans were uncomfortable with being labelled as anti-war. Brian shied away from labelling his statement as pacifist: 'That's a big word. It has a lot of meanings to it.' Brian here alluded to the idea that the anti-war movement was hostile, even abusive, during the Vietnam War: 'flinging shit at the veterans and the service personnel'.[57] The apocryphal story of a hostile homecoming was created in the US by the Nixon administration in an attempt to discredit the anti-war movement and draw attention away from the fact that many returning soldiers were turning against the war.[58] The memory myth of the abusive anti-war movement then became a recurrent trope in Vietnam War films in the late 1970s, and began to appear in veterans' memories in both the US and Australia, coinciding with the surge of Vietnam War commemorations in the 1980s.[59]

This myth has come to dominate Australian memory of the Vietnam War, and continues to shape the way politicians, the media and the Australian public talk about military service. Negative depictions of the anti–Vietnam War movement have been deployed time and again, to diminish the anti-war views expressed by soldiers and veterans. In the lead-up to the Gulf War in Iraq in 1990, the US veterans' lobby deliberately invoked a 'support the troops' campaign that situated anti-war protest as anti-soldier.[60] This narrative was also apparent in Australia: in 1991 seaman Terry Jones went absent without leave as HMAS *Adelaide* was preparing to depart Perth for the Gulf War in Iraq. 'I am not a coward and I would be prepared to fight for my country, but I am taking a political stand because this is not our war', he declared.[61] Media coverage scolded him, with a *Canberra Times* editorial arguing that support for Terry Jones equated to characterising willing service personnel as 'uninformed and lack[ing] in intelligence. Attitudes based on this conception are likely to make the sailors feel as unwelcome as the Vietnam veterans felt on their return to Australia.'[62]

These same claims were repeated a decade later when Australian soldiers once again prepared to deploy to Iraq. The protest of Magnus Mansie and Brett Jones, the two Gulf War veterans who inspired Gerry to return his medals, was reported in the *Sydney Morning Herald* with the headline 'Support the troops, PM tells protesters'.[63]

The public perception that anti-war activism is offensive to soldiers has been reinforced by the refusal of mainstream veterans' organisations to engage with anti-war veteran campaigns. In 2005, Chip Henriss joined forces with Second World War veterans who had served in Timor to put out an advertisement on Anzac Day, denouncing the Howard government's handling of the Timor Sea maritime boundary dispute and reminding the public of the 'Australian notion of a fair go'. The ad was pulled after criticism from the RSL president that it was 'offensive' to 'use the Anzac spirit as the basis for criticising the government'.[64] Similarly, in 2012, an organisation calling for parliamentary oversight of the deployment of Australian troops was established, reflecting the sentiment of almost every Australian veteran I have interviewed. The Australian War Powers Reform campaign included a 'Veterans' Appeal', which sought support from current and former Australian Defence Force personnel.[65] Yet the campaign organisers reported that 'there seemed to be resistance from some [veterans'] orgs that we approached to them helping circulate information about the appeal'.[66]

Anti-war veteran activists are also treated differently from other veterans by the Australian media. The coverage of anti-war veteran activism is sparse, and lacking in biographical details. For example, Gulf War veterans Magnus Mansie and Brett Jones were barely discussed in Australian reportage of the March 2003 protests. Short articles in the *Sydney Morning Herald,* the *Age* and *ABC News* online acknowledged their protest, but only the first included the fact that they had 'tried to hand their medals to Prime Minister John Howard at parliament, but say they were told he was too busy to receive them'. They handed their medals to Bob Brown instead. The articles included quotations from the veterans – Magnus Mansie explained that 'it is my personal opinion that this is an illegal war and a war that shouldn't be occurring' – but did not go into detail about how they came to serve, what their experiences were, and how that factored into their opposition to war.[67] Similarly, brief reportage of a Stand Fast protest at Victoria Barracks in 2010 did not even acknowledge that 'spokesman Hamish Chitts' was also a veteran who resigned from the Army in protest against the Iraq War.[68] This is in stark contrast to the usual pattern of reporting on veterans, which tends to be highly detailed and sympathetic, describing both the veterans' experiences as soldiers and their post-service lives.[69] The absence of the usual personal details suggests that Australian media outlets are unsure of how to depict veterans who oppose war, or reluctant to give them a sympathetic airing.

In recent years, following repeated Anzac Day scandals, there have been signs that the Australian media is hesitant to publicise veterans' anti-war statements, with even centre-left media outlets avoiding rather than courting controversy on Anzac Day.[70] For instance, in 2018, Chip Henriss was interviewed for Anzac Day by SBS journalist Yu Xia, and stated: 'I don't think we should celebrate the fact that we went to war … the German Army during World War II, can't imagine any of them celebrating their military service.'[71] Chip's interview was conducted in English, but the segment was broadcast only on SBS Mandarin, with his criticism mostly spoken over by the journalist in Mandarin. Consequently, it did not make headlines that a former Australian

Army soldier was comparing Anzac Day to Germans glorifying the Second World War.

Because media articles tend to aim for 'balance', they often seek out a military or RSL perspective on anti-war veteran activism, leading them to reproduce the idea that anti-war activism is anathema to military values typified by the Anzac digger: a stoic larrikin with an easygoing nature. These Anzac traits, highly prized as the ideal of Australian masculinity, do not sit comfortably with anti-war complaint. As a result, anti-war veterans have been implicitly represented as weak or cowardly. For example, Terry Jones, the Gulf War seaman who went AWOL, was branded a 'whinger' by his commander for opposing the war and accused of leaving his mates 'in the lurch'. These comments became the headline in media coverage of his protest, rather than his statement that 'this is not our war'.[72] The media also tends to situate anti-war veterans as the odd men out, rather than as individuals who served their country and who speak from experience. In 2010, Stand Fast held protests outside Brisbane's Gallipoli Barracks and Sydney's Holsworthy Barracks. Hamish Chitts led the Brisbane protest and although he claimed to have received 'good media coverage, with as many journalists and camera crews present at the start as there were protesters', the reportage itself diminished the activists: 'media outnumber activists at war rally'.[73]

The sensitivity around anti-war protest, the hostility to anti-war veterans within mainstream organisations, and the diminishing of anti-war protests all dissuade veterans from publicly expressing their anti-war views. One interviewee acknowledged that 'if I knew then what I knew now, I'd be a protester'.[74] This was also the only veteran, of more than 50 interviewed, who asked to be kept anonymous. Gerry suggested that the potential for backlash deterred many veterans from engaging in anti-war campaigns: 'When you're talking to them privately, you might get a lot of anti-war sentiment being expressed, but publicly, they won't go public. They don't want to go public.'[75]

Openly, anti-war veterans also avoid participating in veterans' groups and commemorations, making it harder for them to find each other and organise themselves, and limiting the sharing of anti-war views in traditional veterans' spaces. Gerry has considered going back to Vietnam, but knew that 'I might have to rub shoulders with vets who go there who are still "true believers" in the propaganda that sent us there', and was worried that 'I might say something which might trigger violence from them'.[76] Some had attempted to connect with the veteran community, but found it alienating. The anonymous interviewee attended an Anzac Day march once, but the people he knew there 'were as pissed as parrots, and I was embarrassed, and I thought, "I don't really want to be part of this" … So I walked away from it.'[77] He has avoided RSLs and parades ever since. Others drop the identity of veteran completely. Rob explained:

> I didn't want to be a Vietnam vet, I didn't want anybody
> to know about it, I certainly wouldn't have gone to a
> Welcome Home parade and I didn't keep in touch with
> the association, 4RAR, or RSL or anybody like that …
> My only impression of veterans were people who were sort
> of loud and proud about their deeds. And still thought it
> was the best part of their life, which is a bit sad.[78]

Rob believes that there are many veterans like him who do not identify with the label 'veteran' at all, hiding their experiences even from those who know them well. He had 'a friend who's really – all sort of the same as me. He's very quiet about being a vet, and we talked together for many years before knowing it [about each other].'[79]

Even once they find one another, anti-war veterans have not always agreed on methods of protest. Gerry wanted other veterans to turn their medals in like him, but they refused; Rob and Chip organised anti-war protests on Anzac Day, which Gerry opposed, while Hamish acknowledged disagreement 'among some in the anti-war movement that these actions [protesting outside barracks] are somehow attacking soldiers'.[80] Gerry explained that it was difficult for him to be around younger activists who advocated for 'basically, armed rebellion'. He is still, to this day, angry that the Australian government made him 'a participant in mass murder. Not happy about that. But they're lucky that somewhere along the line I also became a sworn pacifist.' His non-violence is a direct response to his soldiering experience:

> I got really angry. I thought, shit, if I put this anger into practice, because of what I know, I can go and kill a lot of people that I'm angry with, and I'm going, 'I can't do that' … I realised I could only be a pacifist or else I'm just the other side of the same coin.[81]

Gerry's experience with violence meant that when he hears ostensibly anti-war protesters advocating violent agitation, he assumes: 'You're probably an ASIO plant, or you're an idiot. Either one.'[82] Gerry's discomfort with the wider anti-war movement's strategy reflects the difficulty of organising an anti-war group from a very small population of veterans. In Australia it is very difficult for anti-war veterans to find even a handful of others with whom they agree and feel comfortable.

Finally, anti-war Australian veterans and soldiers have focused more on criticising US imperialism than they have on Australia's contribution to 'illegal wars', viewing as they do the US as the lead belligerent and Australia as a blind follower: 'corporate Australia and further up the chain, corporate America', in the words of Chip.[83] Terry Jones opposed the first Gulf War on the basis that 'we are just following the Americans. I am prepared to die to defend my country but not to protect United States oil lines.' Gerry says to people who try to thank him for his service: 'I did not serve you. I served American interests. You want to thank me for that, get lost.'[84] Aside from the anti-capitalist elements of their critique, these comments echo wider Australian criticism of the US alliance and so-called 'insurance policy'. [85] In fact, these statements reflect a deep-seated anti-Americanism among Australian soldiers and veterans, which is a key aspect of the Anzac legend: any wrongdoing in war is attributed to our bigger, more powerful allies.[86] In contrast, veterans rarely make public statements about Australian war conduct; for example, the revelations in the 2020s about Australian war crimes in Afghanistan and Timor.[87] Echoing a widespread critique of Australian foreign policy in radical terms, rather than focusing on Australian war conduct, makes it easy for other Australians to agree with and yet disregard anti-war Australian complaint.

HOW ANZAC INHIBITS ANTI-WAR VETERANS

Tracing these stories of anti-war veterans in Australia reveals that, while some soldiers develop anti-war views during war, most do not feel comfortable speaking out during their service. Instead, anti-war veterans found their views and their voices in reaction to changes in Australian politics, society and culture:

commemorations around the Vietnam War, the Anzac revival and the War on Terror were all key inciting events. This gradual unfolding of anti-war sentiment echoes similar patterns among anti-war veterans in the US and UK. However, while veterans from allied militaries successfully organised anti-war groups and received sober consideration in the mainstream media, Australian veterans struggled to find one another and come together in protest; when they have taken public stands, they have been diminished by Australian politicians, media and the wider veteran community.[88] Part of this may be the lack of a tradition of anti-war protest among soldiers in Australia, unlike allies in the US and UK, who have such traditions to draw inspiration from.[89] Yet Australia has its own historic outliers. Another factor is the negative association with the anti-war movement in Australia, widely perceived to be hostile to soldiers and veterans. Yet a similar negative narrative about the anti-war movement is equally pronounced in the US. Why, then, have anti-war Australian veterans had such difficulty gaining traction?

The stories of these anti-war veterans show that Anzac itself plays a key role. The Anzac revival entrenched the notion that 'politicising' Anzac Day by questioning the purpose of war is offensive to veterans. Consequently, Australian media have downplayed or even avoided reporting on anti-war veteran activity to avoid the scandal of causing offence. The Anzac digger also remains a central ideal of Australian masculinity, and the one to which soldiers and veterans still aspire. The easygoing, larrikin digger who does his job and helps his mates is at odds with the sole, worried soldier voicing moral concerns. As a result, many veterans with anti-war views are uncomfortable voicing them, and openly anti-war veterans avoid mainstream veterans' environments. Yet the Australian military has its fair share of critical or questioning members. One of my hopes for this collection is that it encourages more open, critical reflection by soldiers and veterans on Australia's participation in war – both in the past and in the future.

12

CRIMES CLOAKED IN ANZAC
AUSTRALIAN SPECIAL FORCES
AND ALLEGATIONS OF ATROCITIES
IN AFGHANISTAN

MIA MARTIN HOBBS

In the wake of the *Inspector-General of the Australian Defence Force Afghanistan Inquiry Report*, commonly known as the Brereton report, in November of 2020, some believed that allegations of Australian atrocities in Afghanistan had well and truly proven the Anzac legend to be hollow. Five years prior, sociologist Samantha Crompvoets had been charged with a review of Australian Special Forces, in response to debate within the Australian national security community about the potential use of Special Forces in domestic counterterrorism settings.[1] The new commander of Special Operations Command (SOCOMD), Major General Jeffrey Sengelmann, was concerned about 'serious endemic problems that are plaguing SOCOMD', highlighting issues such as binge drinking and bullying that indicated deeper operational issues.[2] Hired to investigate Special Forces' function and capability, Crompvoets also uncovered allegations of atrocities.[3] Her report triggered the Brereton inquiry, which after four years of investigation found that at least 25 defence personnel were involved in the 'unlawful killings' of 39 Afghan civilians. For Crompvoets, the 'most distressing'

212

part of her review was that the acts of violence were 'normal and reoccurring' within Special Forces.[4]

This is a story that should not fit the Anzac legend. 'The digger mythology is in crisis', Andrew Probyn, ABC defence editor, proclaimed upon the release of the Brereton report.[5] War correspondent Mark Baker stated that the allegations 'cast a shadow over the reputation of the entire Australian Defence Force (ADF), its proud legacy in two world wars and multiple other conflicts and its claim to be the repository of the hallowed Anzac spirit and a standard bearer of the Australian character'.[6] Andrew Tillet, defence editor of the *Australian Financial Review*, predicted that the consequences 'will be carried by a generation of soldiers'.[7] In the years that followed, journalists, defence commentators and academics anticipated that the Brereton report would generate soul-searching, not only within the ADF but across the nation, about the spirit and character of Australia.[8] The Special Forces were previously heralded as the pinnacle of Anzac, 'larrikins yes, murderers no', but the allegations had 'devastated the Australian Army's reputation as a model military institution' and 'shattered the Anzac myth'.[9] After Australia's most decorated living soldier embroiled himself in a defamation suit that only corroborated allegations that he had committed war crimes, Chris Masters, Fairfax journalist and one of the lawsuit's defendants, argued that allegations of atrocities 'allows us a reset on all things Anzac'.[10]

Yet the alleged war crimes were not the challenge to Anzac that so many anticipated. First, because the report revealed that alleged perpetrators saw themselves as living up to the Anzac legend: enacting warrior rituals, positioning transgressions as anti-establishment and enforcing their code of silence through mateship. While some soldiers spoke out against atrocities, the acceptance of misconduct by the majority, and the elevation of perpetrators by higher command, demonstrates that the perpetrators were not a 'rogue element' but in fact embodied the values and ideals of the Special Forces.

Second, while the Brereton report and ensuing media coverage decried the 'warrior-hero culture' that permeated the perpetrators' units, this culture reflected a revived emphasis on the martial themes of the Anzac legend, driven by Australia's participation in the so-called War on Terror (2001–21). The public perception of the Special Forces as the modern embodiment of the fierce, fighting Anzacs was reinforced in wider Australian culture throughout Australian deployments in Afghanistan and Iraq, exemplified by the elevation of Ben Roberts-Smith, awarded the Victoria Cross in 2011.

Finally, as the fallout of the Brereton report continued, public reactions to reports of Australian wrongdoing immediately drew upon themes from the Anzac legend to make sense of the allegations. Commentators drew on both older, martial themes of the soldier as a formidable warrior, and more recent themes of the veteran as a traumatised victim, blending together old and new ideas about Anzac. The immediate impulse of many was to highlight the honour and professionalism of the Special Forces, emphasising their courage and endurance across long and repeated deployments. Commentators employed the theme of betrayal to position the accused as persecuted victims. As Roberts-Smith's defamation case presented him in an increasingly poor light, the narrative of betrayal switched to emphasise the traumas suffered by Special Forces more generally. After the publication of the Brereton report, Australian service personnel, defence commentators and the media increasingly placed blame on the higher command. Thus, rather than dispelling Anzac, allegations of Australian atrocities have been situated in ways that cohere with the legend.

A 'WARRIOR-HERO CULTURE'

The Brereton report revealed that Australian Special Forces saw themselves as supreme fighters and explicitly adopted rituals associated with a 'warrior-hero culture'.[11] These warrior rituals work to separate the soldier from civilians and mark him as superior. For example, the inquiry found a practice of 'blooding', or committing an unlawful kill, to initiate a junior soldier into the warrior brotherhood. The tradition of marking a 'first kill' as a rite of passage into manhood is found in warrior mythologies across the world, and is paralleled in the narrative that the Anzac experience at Gallipoli was a 'baptism of fire' for Australia.[12] The Brereton report found the practice of blooding to be explicit and top-down: 'junior soldiers were required by their commanders to shoot a prisoner, in order to achieve the soldier's first kill'.[13] Patrol commanders reportedly discussed their 'aim to "blood the rookie" before a mission in 2009'.[14] By 2012, blooding was incorporated into mission-readiness training practices in Australia. A new soldier in the unit would be ordered to simulate executing a prisoner, with another soldier 'role-playing as a prisoner, on his knees facing a wall'. Afterwards, the trainer would explain to the 'rookie': 'that's how it's going to be when we get over there'.[15]

Similarly, practices of trophy-taking and corpse desecration show how Special Forces reveled in their warrior identity. During the defamation proceedings, it emerged that buried in Roberts-Smith's backyard, inside a child's lunchbox, were USB drives loaded with videos and images that documented these practices. One image shows an Afghan man, dead from a bullet wound to the head, lying on a woven mat with regimental souvenir coins covering his eyes.[16] This 'bizarre practice' was 'derived from the old myth about paying the ferryman for the journey to the underworld', reflecting a view among perpetrators of themselves as agents of death.[17] Such trophies were not limited to photographs. In *Rogue Forces* (2021), ABC journalist Mark Willacy reveals how Special Operations soldiers at a training session about biometrics became fixated on justifications for severing body parts from killed insurgents, joking with a visiting sergeant about 'bringing back a hand'. Willacy's source explained that 'the Australians were not asking permission to cut off hands or digits. Corporal L says they were already doing it.' According to Corporal L, the practice began with the Special Operations Engineer Regiment and spread through the Special Forces. Perpetrators carried secateurs, machetes and small axes to collect these trophies. 'It was because they were enjoying it. It was fun. Like "one-up-me"'.[18]

The evidence of trophy collection reveals how Australian perpetrators situated their mistreatment of the dead as a form of irreverent humour. In April 2009, at a site known as Whiskey 108, 2 Squadron of the Special Air Service Regiment (SASR) executed an old man with a prosthetic leg. That leg was taken back to the 2 Squadron mess as a souvenir and repeatedly used as a drinking vessel at the 'Fat Ladies Arms', an unofficial bar on the Afghanistan base.[19] The widespread participation in this practice illustrates a culture that used perverse humour to foster mateship between soldiers.[20] In the defamation proceedings, one soldier admitted that drinking from the leg 'helped me decompress, let off steam, bond', and admitted that 'soldiers of all ranks drank from the leg and he had cheered them on'.[21] The same soldier acknowledged that the leg was brought back to Australia and framed, with souvenir glasses created in its shape and distributed among soldiers. An anonymous source in the Brereton report observed that 'some soldiers believed quite passionately that an Australian soldier is expected to "muck up" on operations. It seems as though many soldiers felt that they were almost obliged to live up to a rogue, irreverent and scruffy stereotype (a distorted view of the larrikin).'[22] As Crompvoets notes, among the Special Forces, 'skylarking' was blurred 'with the normalization of deviance'.[23]

The ideal of the Anzac digger as being anti-authority appears to have encouraged disregard for the Rules of Engagement and motivated the widespread cover-up of crimes. Crompvoets observed that Special Forces had created a culture that was both 'very disciplined in the combat environment yet rules are ambiguous, bent and broken'. Joint Operations Command lawyers were so concerned about the actions of the Special Forces that they changed the Rules of Engagement, but the soldiers 'just got more creative in how they wrote up the incidents'.[24] The use of 'throwdowns' (placing foreign weapons or equipment on a corpse to frame the dead person as an enemy killed in action) is illustrative of this: originating as a practice to avoid scrutiny after mistakes in the heat of battle, throwdowns became a strategy for 'concealing deliberate unlawful killings'.[25] The Brereton report notes that incidents of throwdowns occurred 'at a much smaller and more discrete level' in 2008, but by 2012, had become an 'organisationally routine practice'.[26] The practice was so widespread that soldiers in Australia would 'joke about how the same serial number [of a gun] was in every single photo of a dead Afghani'.[27]

The evidence shows that these warrior rituals were widely known and if not universally participated in, tolerated and often celebrated within the Special Forces. Allegations of blooding spanned a duration of at least four years (2009–12). While Willacy's source acknowledged that dismembering was done by 'probably just a handful' of soldiers, he was explicit that 'everyone knew that this was going on, including the commanders. It was done for fun.' Trophies were sometimes brought back to the 'geeks' who provided soldiers with the intelligence for that specific mission: 'It was their macabre way of saying, "This is the fruits of your labours, guys. Congratulations."'[28] This demonstrates that such warrior rituals were accepted and recognised even by those not on the battlefield. Similarly, in Roberts-Smith's defamation suit, his own lawyer acknowledged that there existed 'images of hundreds of soldiers drinking from the leg'.[29] Beyond the battlefield, as public interest in the Brereton report grew, 'current and former' Special Forces soldiers set up an Instagram account, 'State Sanctioned Violence', which celebrated violence as a core part of the Anzac legend. The Instagram account offered merchandise for sale, including stickers bearing the slogan, 'Make Diggers Violent Again', and shared photographs of those stickers affixed to personal items at Canberra's Royal Military College in Duntroon.[30] These rituals, and the celebration of violence inherent in them, reflect Crompvoets' initial finding that in the culture of the Special Forces, unsanctioned violence was equated with being a good soldier.[31] Her findings are supported by the fact that the few soldiers who did speak up 'were ostracised and attacked. The leadership didn't applaud them – it tore them down.'[32] That same leadership elevated those known to be perpetrating crimes: 'not only were some of the soldiers who were doing the wrong thing not punished, they were decorated. What message did that send to the younger, less experienced and more impressionable operators?'[33]

Those who opposed these rituals faced entrenched resistance. The code of silence was enforced through the Anzac virtue of mateship.[34] Major General Jeffrey Sengelman acknowledged that 'mateship was prioritised over leadership, resulting in an undermining of the chain of command and a confused notion of what was acceptable'.[35] The sanctity of mateship repeatedly stymied efforts to uncover the truth of what was occurring within the Special Forces. Chris Masters described it as 'a kinship of silence. It was commonly pressed on the operators that the reputation of the regiment overrides everything else. Appalling, but there it was. The sin of not having a mate's back was greater than the virtue of exposing war crimes.'[36] Even as rumours of misconduct spread, military historian Tom Frame observes that not a single former or serving soldier 'availed themselves of whistleblower protections to make a formal report'.[37] 'People don't want to dob in mates', an interviewee of Masters explained.[38]

These threads of Anzac, woven through the allegations of Australian atrocities, are all underpinned by a sense of exceptionalism. There is a pronounced undercurrent in Australia of the Special Forces soldier as inherently superior, implicitly justifying his actions. As a former Defence intelligence analyst told me, 'From the moment I stepped foot onto Campbell Barracks [SAS base], they were like, "We do things differently here". And that led to, well, if you're told that you do things differently, if you're told that you're allowed to blur the lines to get stuff done, where do you stop?'[39] The Special Forces are treated differently within the ADF: allowed to alter their uniforms, wear facial hair and make demands for equipment outside the regular ADF chain of command. Some soldiers have argued that this is the 'root of many cultural issues – we're special in what we do, we're different, we're better, therefore the rules don't apply to us and we can basically do whatever we like'.[40] In fact, in a letter to then Chief of Defence, Angus Campbell, Sengelmann acknowledges that Special Forces 'retain an image that is iconic and popularised in a way analogous to that of the ANZAC's. That they are seen as hero's [sic] … represents an uneasy balance between deserved recognition of sacrifice and inflated expectation of standards.'[41]

THE 'ANZAC AVATAR'

The aura of exceptionalism surrounding the Special Forces and their embrace of 'warrior-hero culture' are best evidenced by the rise and fall of the most notorious soldier associated with war crimes, Ben Roberts-Smith. As a young man, Roberts-Smith idolised the military and 'looked up to the first Anzacs' as his heroes.[42] Enlisting in the Army in 1996, Roberts-Smith first served in East Timor, and was selected for the Special Air Service Regiment in 2003. After operations in Iraq in 2005–06, Roberts-Smith deployed to Afghanistan six times between 2006 and 2012, and 'formed impeccable connections up the chain of command'.[43] He was awarded the Medal of Gallantry in 2006 and the Victoria Cross in 2011.[44] He left the Army in 2013 as a 'poster boy' for the ADF, feted by the Chief of Defence Force as 'an exemplary soldier who has demonstrated extreme devotion to duty and most conspicuous gallantry in the face of danger', and 'a first-class ambassador for our nation and the Australian Defence Force'.[45] After leaving the army, 'the legend came alive'. In his book *Flawed Hero*, Masters describes Roberts-Smith as an 'Anzac avatar': 'the myth of the classic Anzac, seven-foot-tall and bulletproof, found in human form'.[46] In a 2017 article on why the military 'is such a good breeding ground for people', the Brisbane *Courier-Mail* asked its readers to 'imagine for a moment being Ben Roberts-Smith. You're the embodiment of masculinity … a bloke built like a superhero.'[47] A 2019 review of the media landscape by *Crikey* found that together, the *West Australian* and NewsCorp outlets had published over a hundred articles on Ben Roberts-Smith, all 'glowing' and 'gushing' over the Victoria Cross winner.[48]

Yet this public elevation of Roberts-Smith by the ADF might have broken the bonds of mateship that previously protected him. Masters observes that 'while outside the ADF his reputation continued to grow, within the organisation it was in further retreat. In special forces, a veteran who cashes in on his fame can quickly become persona non grata.'[49] Roberts-Smith's willingness to buy into the idolatry being built around him led to a nickname, 'Achilles', used by 'a few of the non-believers, who mocked the warrior self-image, seeing it as a façade masking serious character flaws'.[50] Roberts-Smith's association with warrior identity eventually became his downfall with the so-called 'Spartan kick': an event in which he allegedly kicked an Afghan civilian, Ali Jan, off a cliff, and later coerced an Afghan soldier to execute him. The kick emulated the ultra-violent action film *300*, about the Spartans – 'the finest soldiers the world has ever known', according to the film's lore – in their battle against the Persian 'Godking'. In an iconic scene, a Persian messenger is kicked in slow motion across a precipice by the Spartan king, Leonidas.[51] In the aftermath of the murder of Ali Jan, colleagues apparently began to use the nickname 'Leonidas' for Roberts-Smith. The defamation suit he brought in 2018 was based on this nickname: Roberts-Smith argued that he was known as 'Leonidas' because of the Spartan tattoo on his ribs.[52]

The image of the Special Forces soldier as the modern-day embodiment of Anzac was not isolated to the ADF. Masters argues that while Ben Roberts-Smith certainly pursued celebrity, it would not have been possible without it being 'wished upon him by a cheer squad of myth makers and an idol-hungry nation'.[53] While since the 1980s the dominant narrative of the Anzac legend had had been 'transformed' by films such as *Gallipoli* (1981) to emphasise 'tales of trauma and suffering', Australia's participation in the US-led wars in Afghanistan and Iraq revived public interest in the martial elements of the legend.[54] While the wider ADF largely deployed in support or humanitarian roles that spoke to the modern, gentler themes of Anzac, Special Forces operated 'outside the wire' on 'kill-capture missions'.[55] Crompvoets observed that Australian reportage of the War on Terror repeatedly presented the Special Forces soldiers 'as heroes and as hooligans'.[56] There was a sustained public investment in these men as the true epitome of the digger, which cannot be divorced from their crimes. The Brereton report highlighted that 'the hyperbole surrounding the contribution of Australian soldiers in Afghanistan makes the soldiers feel entitled to be treated almost as Roman gladiators'.[57]

Furthermore, even after the rumours of atrocities emerged, the very journalists who published the allegations did so in a way that revered the Special Forces soldier for his capacity for violence. In fact, the Brereton report acknowledged that 'books and accounts covering Special Operations in Afghanistan and Iraq tended to foster a "warrior-hero" culture'.[58] Masters acknowledges that his first book on the Special Forces, *No Front Line*, was 'inspired' by the belief he shared with an Australian Army general: 'There is something about the Australian character that is suited to things soldiers are asked to do.'[59] He even admits that his admiration for the Special Forces stifled his journalistic ethics: his initial coverage of the incident that afforded Ben

Roberts-Smith a Medal of Gallantry – an incident that would go on to be associated with the execution of two teenage Afghan civilians – 'fell short of a more complete truth'.[60] Similarly, in *Rogue Forces*, Willacy (responsible for the award-winning *Four Corners* episode 'Killing Field') lionises the 'exquisite violence and elegant unpleasantness' inflicted by Special Forces, who have a 'preternatural lethality', skilled in the 'art of exquisite unpleasantness' with the 'delicate mission' of being 'both door-kickers and protectors. Hearts and minds are their mission – winning some, putting bullets into others'.[61] Even as they revealed the depravity of Australian conduct in war, these journalists revered those who inflicted it.

Thus, not only did perpetrators view themselves as Anzacs, the Australian Defence Force and media also positioned Special Forces in this way. The elevation of Roberts-Smith as a poster boy for the ADF – when his crimes were widely known throughout the Special Forces and rumoured throughout the wider ADF – demonstrates institutional acceptance of Special Forces as modern-day Anzacs *because* of what Justice Brereton described as their 'warrior-hero culture of killing'.[62]

UNDERSTANDING ALLEGATIONS THROUGH THE LENS OF ANZAC

Given the framing of Special Forces as the ultimate inheritors of Anzac, perhaps it should not be surprising that when reports of atrocities began to emerge in the 2010s, many refused to acknowledge they might be responsible for any wrongdoing.[63] Tom Frame notes that 'the strong presumption was that Australian soldiers would never kill unarmed or disarmed people'.[64] As a result, in her 2016 report, Crompvoets observed that 'many atrocities have been documented in the media and yet seem to disappear shortly after they surface'.[65]

Yet as the leaks became a flow of allegations in 2017, even the staunchest supporters of Anzac had to respond. A key approach was to humanise Special Forces as honourable, presenting them as fundamentally good men doing a hard job, beyond the purview of civilians. Headlines implicitly deflected the need for inquiry: 'We need rough men to keep us safe', 'You can't judge decisions taken in the heat of battle from the comfort of home', 'Do we really need to know?', 'War is messy, mistakes are made'.[66] Leading proponents of Anzac, including the Director of the Australian War Memorial, Brendan Nelson, and Australia's oldest living Victoria Cross recipient, Keith Payne, expressed the same sentiment: 'war is a messy business'.[67] This phrase worked to simultaneously evoke the endurance and masculinity of the digger and dismiss the concerns of civilian journalists as overzealous and uninformed, a sentiment that echoed across right-wing media: 'unaware of the battlefield complexities, the ABC questions our brave soldiers' honour'.[68] Even the journalists who broke the stories about alleged atrocities maintained a reverence for 'Australia's reputation for civilised soldiering, for toughness and fairness'.[69] This reportage held up soldiering as the peak of masculinity. 'Soldiers are obliged to become philosophers', mused Masters. 'To reconcile the challenge of inflicting harm with the purpose of doing good is an eternal task.'[70]

Other themes from the Anzac myth also made their way into the defence of the Special Forces. Prior to the release of the Brereton report, a slew of articles by defence commentators emphasised the endurance of Special Forces in the face of 'high operational tempo' in Afghanistan.[71] Military psychologist Nick Doran drew attention to the 'esprit de corps' that encouraged soldiers 'to go over there and play your important role with the lads and do your job', which meant that in some cases, 'people push themselves to the limit or perhaps beyond'.[72] Although the report itself determined that tempo was a contributing rather than causal factor, the *Australian* asked: 'Will anyone be held accountable for keeping a core group of Australian soldiers on an almost constant cycle of deployment and redeployment – some for the better part of a decade – with little real rest in between?'[73]

The element of the Anzac repertoire that was drawn on most commonly in response to allegations of atrocities by Australian soldiers was that of betrayal. While the original betrayal of the Anzacs is popularly thought to be that committed by the British leadership, who sacrificed the Australian soldiers at Gallipoli and elsewhere, since the 1980s the theme of betrayal has centred on harm inflicted on soldiers by civilians, who cannot understand their sacrifice and suffering. As Christina Twomey discusses in chapter 10, this reorienting led to the depiction of the Anzac digger as a traumatised victim. The emphasis on trauma and victimhood was particularly apparent in the defence of Roberts-Smith. Nelson decried journalists 'tearing down our heroes', while right-wing press launched a pre-emptive defence: 'with headlines including "Inquiry risks making SAS feel betrayed", "War hero 'will be cleared", and "Leave Ben alone"'.[74] The national broadsheet published a detailed response to the publication of Masters' *No Front Line* in 2017, which began:

Australia's most decorated soldier had to phone Leigh Locke-Thomas this week and tell it to her straight: the 10th anniversary of the death of her husband, Sergeant Matthew Locke, on October 25 will coincide with the release day of a Defence-facilitated history of our special forces in Afghanistan that Roberts-Smith considers damaging to 'the legacy of an Australian hero killed in action', his dear mate Matthew Locke.[75]

Letters to the newspapers demonstrated the breadth of faith in, and sense of betrayal of, the Special Forces in Australia: 'what an absolute disgrace that some armchair author denigrates the actions of Australia's SAS heroes'; 'few civilians would have any concept of the challenges of military campaigns'; 'this disservice makes me sick in the guts'; 'nothing short of utter contempt for those sent to partake in a war in which we ought never to have been involved'.[76] Masters and his fellow journalist Nick McKenzie received threats from veterans 'who didn't know Roberts-Smith but believed our reporting to be a treasonous attack on the Anzac legend itself'.[77] Even after Roberts-Smith launched his defamation case in 2018, suing the newspapers that had reported allegations of war crimes, the narrative continued that Roberts-Smith was the one in need of defence. The West Australian branch of the Returned and Services League threw its 'full support' behind Roberts-Smith, who was 'being tarnished without a shred of evidence'.[78] A Change.org petition, 'Stop the witch hunt. Support the SAS and Ben Roberts-Smith', was created in 2019, which drew on themes of Anzac courage and endurance to emphasise the pain of the betrayal:

> Their job is to deploy into the hottest of hot spots to take the fight to people deemed to be a threat to this country. SASR members are family men, who routinely deployed to Afghanistan and other extremely hostile places in order to do a job that the vast majority of people cannot do … These heroes should not be subjected to this harassment,

second guessing and 'armchair quarterbacking'. They
should be recognised as the heroes that they are, doing
a tough job under difficult circumstances, putting their
lives on the line repeatedly for the guy beside them, for
their mates and for all Australians. You want men like
this defending the country. Stop the witch hunt. Support
the SASR.[79]

As of 2025, this petition has over 25 000 signatures. Multiple Facebook groups also promise their support for Roberts-Smith.[80]

Roberts-Smith himself explicitly drew on the theme of the betrayed Anzac victim to bolster his cause. Before he identified himself as 'Leonidas', Roberts-Smith cautioned Australians that 'we should be looking after our soldiers, not persecuting them'.[81] Upon launching the defamation suit, the 'betrayed hero' line became his core narrative. Making use of the support of 2GB radio, NewsCorp, and Seven West (controlled by Roberts-Smith's legal benefactor, Kerry Stokes), Roberts-Smith put out a constant stream of plaintive accounts: 'I am appalled that the service of my colleagues and my service to my country and my regiment is being traduced in such an irresponsible way'; 'I just want a fair go. Why can't I expect that?'; 'They're calling me a murderer: war hero Ben Roberts-Smith'.[82] Roberts-Smith indicated that the allegations were more traumatising than his 17 months in Afghanistan, stating that he 'can't sleep and gets up every morning dreading the allegations'.[83] In the courtroom, he contrasted his years 'fighting for my country' against allegations based on 'rumour and innuendo'. It 'breaks my heart', he said, 'I did everything I possibly could to ensure I did it with honour' and now 'there are moments in my life in the last three years that I just didn't think it was worth it'.[84] As the case dragged on, the emphasis on betrayal and trauma became increasingly explicit: 'It's actually quite traumatising', he testified to his barrister. 'I feel betrayed and humiliated.'[85] Roberts-Smith also implied that his accusers were not living up to the ideal of mateship, which was 'unfair not only to me, but all members of the ADF, whose service to our country is being attacked by individuals who choose to hide behind anonymous leaking'.[86] Roberts-Smith 'choked back tears as he recalled trying to defend himself against "cowards" who had attacked "from the shadows" and "crushed" his soul in their effort to destroy his reputation'.[87]

In 2023, the lawsuit ended with the presiding justice, Anthony Besanko, dismissing Roberts-Smith's claims of defamation on the grounds that the allegations published by the newspapers were substantially true. This judgment did far more damage to the reputation of Roberts-Smith than the original reportage. He sank from 'from a national hero to a virtual pariah'.[88] The case exposed further allegations about multiple murders and assaults in Afghanistan, bullying of other soldiers, domestic violence and intimidating witnesses.[89] Yet a small but vocal group of Australians continue to support Roberts-Smith. Immediately following the judgment, a new petition was launched to 'grant a pre-emptive pardon to Ben Roberts-Smith VC MG concerning any violations that may have occurred during his tour of Afghanistan so that our most decorated living soldier can live the rest of his life without fear of prosecution for his service to the nation'.[90] Mining magnate Gina Rinehart condemned journalists for 'gloating' over the judgment, while NewsCorp and Seven West outlets continued to run headlines questioning the legitimacy of the finding.[91]

Yet, because the defamation suit focused on allegations about Roberts-Smith's character *specifically*, it had the effect of muting discussion about any collective Australian wrongdoing in Afghanistan. Crompvoets thought the furore around the disgraced soldier operated as a distraction, when there was 'so much more that was wrong' in Special Forces.[92] Media coverage and defence commentators increasingly blamed Roberts-Smith for tarnishing the reputation of the broader Special Forces, particularly once news leaked that prosecutors were building cases against him and another soldier.[93] Reporters emphasised the trauma of soldier witnesses to war crimes, who were also 'victims' of Australia's war in Afghanistan.[94] They were 'Pawns in a Deadly Game' now living with 'the horror of "moral injury" suffered in the line of duty'.[95] The betrayal shifted from that of Roberts-Smith by the public, to a betrayal of the ADF and Special Forces by Roberts-Smith himself.

With this shift, a narrative emerged that there were two kinds of Special Forces: the honest, moral majority and the aberrant few. Days before the release of the Brereton report in November 2020, an anonymous article titled 'They are not one of us' in the *Sydney Morning Herald* claimed to speak for the wider Special Forces in denouncing the crimes, declaring 'our commitment to truth' and separating allegations of atrocities from the 'professionalism of the extraordinary men and women who do extraordinary work under extraordinary circumstances'.[96] In the wake of the report, an editorial in the *Australian* argued that 'the culture of the SAS is basically sound. That is why so many members provided vital evidence to the IGADF inquiry – a measure of moral courage and integrity.'[97] This line echoed the immediate response from the ADF, which now framed those few who dared to speak out as 'the personification of the Regiment ... applauded for their moral courage'.[98] Prominent veterans, such as Western Australian Liberal politician Andrew Hastie, insisted that fault lay only with 'a small number of soldiers', warning against condemning 'warrior-hero culture' because a 'positive warrior culture' also existed: 'humble, quiet … tough as nails. Supremely competent at arms. The sort of bloke that you'd want next to you in a gunfight.'[99] This also became the line of argument in the ensuing work by the key journalists who originally revealed the allegations. In *Flawed Hero*, Masters was at pains to separate Roberts-Smith and a handful of his close allies from the wider Special Forces: 'I want most of all to recognise the soldiers who had stayed the course – to pay tribute to their physical and moral courage in speaking what had been a punishing truth.'[100] The disgraced war hero thus became the foil for his fellow Special Forces members, who were presented as the true inheritors of Anzac. This narrative of courageous soldiers holding one another to account elides the fact that Crompvoets, the Brereton report and Masters' own journalism (among others) had revealed how Special Forces soldiers collectively bought into the 'warrior-hero culture' over many years, and that the very few who spoke out were bullied and shunned while the perpetrators were rewarded and celebrated.

Increasingly, Australian commentary centred on how higher command had abdicated responsibility for the atrocities, reflecting the Anzac theme of betrayal of frontline soldiers by superiors. The Brereton report had emphasised that responsibility lay at a patrol commander level, but many felt that the generals had made scapegoats of those on the ground. Sources for the key journalists explained that soldiers were 'grasping for operational clarity in a fog of strategic ambiguity'.[101] Reporters warned of 'growing disquiet in the ranks … that the "higher ups" will avoid punishment for the darkest stain on the country's military in living history'.[102] Special Forces veteran Mark Wales reflected that it 'was politically expedient to overuse special forces in combat, to the point of systemic and moral failure. Now we are looking at punishing some of those who returned from the failed mission.'[103] Consequently, Brereton's recommendations for collective punishment for Special Forces were met with widespread hostility among the veteran community. The recommendation that Roberts-Smith's squadron be disbanded was 'a symbolic sham: an act of ritualised hypocrisy … it would run a dagger through the heart with all who have served with pride and sacrifice'.[104] The Chief of Army's decision to withdraw the 'meritorious group citation' for the Special Operations Task Group in Afghanistan was 'hurtful and groundless' and 'not fair on thousands of our soldiers who served with distinction and deserve the thanks of a grateful nation'.[105] That decision was later revoked by Defence Minister Peter Dutton, who insisted that 'we shouldn't be punishing the 99 per cent for the sins of the one per cent'.[106] In 2024, Labor's Defence Minister Richard Marles' decision to strip mid-ranking officers with 'moral command responsibility and accountability' of their medals was met with similar outcry: the 'government has sought to punish and publicly humiliate Australian commanders by removing awards after the war is over'.[107] As Crompvoets observed in her book, Australian focus shifted 'from the details of alleged wrongdoing, including murder, to concerns about the loss of medals, the legacies of the SASR veterans from World War II, and a personal, professional and symbolic betrayal of Australia's veterans, diggers and elite "dogs of war" by Defence's top brass'.[108]

REDEEMING THE ANZAC LEGEND IN AFGHANISTAN

In 2025, a new documentary, *Bravery and Betrayal*, was released by Wandering Warriors, a charity established by SAS Queensland in 2013 to support Special Forces veterans. This sought to tell 'the true story of the SAS in Afghanistan', which 'won every single fight, achieved nothing but strategic success' and is 'carrying scars that you can't see', betrayed by generals who were 'there for themselves'. The documentary highlights the 'great unknown' about the SAS, which is 'how poorly we've been treated'.[109] *Bravery and Betrayal* thus offers a very different narrative of Australian warfare from that revealed by the Brereton report five years earlier. The documentary was promoted on Sky News by host Erin Molan (daughter of the late Liberal politician and senior ADF officer, Major General Jim Molan), who despaired that 'somehow, over the past few years serving your country, putting your life on the line for the sake of this nation, has become almost demonized instead of honoured and celebrated'. Molan introduced the documentary as an effort 'to reclaim the narrative, to give a voice to the overwhelmingly brave majority who did nothing wrong but fight for their country'.[110]

Meanwhile, the Afghanistan Inquiry Reform Plan concluded its work in 2023. The final report agreed that Special Forces was ready 'to rebuild the trust of Government, Defence and the public', and concluded that they were ready 'to put the response to the Afghanistan Inquiry behind it. It is time to move forward and to consolidate the reforms under firm and watchful leadership.'[111] As a senior officer working on the Reform Plan told Chris Masters, 'the general mood is that it has been squibbed'.[112]

Beyond the newspaper editorials and responses from the veteran community, it is hard to measure what the broader feeling in the Australian community is about the war crimes allegations. Reactions in letters to editors and membership in social media support groups tend to come from those who are most invested in the story. It seems likely that while Roberts-Smith has been disgraced, the wider Special Forces and ADF are still seen as heroic victims of an unjust war and ungrateful community. In her review of the Special Forces, Crompvoets observed that 'the obscure nature of culture lends itself to convenient truths'.[113] The Anzac legend is core to all discussions about the military and war in Australia, and so inevitably shapes stories around it. The desire of politicians and military leaders to uphold the Anzac legend, and the compulsion among sections of the public to continue to believe – despite evidence that undermines its key tenets – reveal the difficulty of challenging Anzac.

The warrior mythology that Anzac articulates is not unique to Australia. Countries around the world praise the same traits and promote the same narratives about their soldiers: they are honourable, virtuous, formidable, brave, martyrs.[114] Within the War on Terror, Australia's allies in the United States and United Kingdom have similar notions of their own soldiers, and have seen similar defences mounted in response to war crimes in Afghanistan and Iraq.[115] In this light, the reworking of Australian atrocities into the Anzac legend speaks to a broader need to make sense of information that challenges national identity and core beliefs. In the final chapter of this collection, Carolyn Holbrook explores the social need for myths such as Anzac, and why they persist in light of these repeated challenges.

13

THE ANZAC WARRIOR IN THE AGE OF AUTONOMOUS WARFARE

BIANCA BAGGIARINI AND JOAN BEAUMONT

Since the landing at Gallipoli in 1915, the Anzac legend has held a central place in the national memory of Australia's wars. However, its content and meaning have never been static.[1] Over the generations, this mythic narrative of war has evolved from celebrating the Australian soldier as a natural fighter – even killer – to revering the veteran as a traumatised war victim.[2] Always, Anzac has served, in public discourse at least, as a powerful trope of Australian nationalism. At times, its evolution has reduced the legend to the vapid: to quote Prime Minister Julia Gillard, speaking at the 60th anniversary of the Battle of Kapyong, which was fought on 23–25 April 1951 during the Korean War, Anzac is a story of 'ordinary Australians who were asked to do extraordinary things'.[3] Yet some core elements of the original Anzac legend have persisted to this day. These are the values of courage, endurance, mateship and sacrifice – the words inscribed on the four pillars of the memorial erected in 2002 at Isurava, an iconic battle site from the Second World War on the Kokoda Track, Papua New Guinea.

How might the construction of the Anzac legend be affected by the growing role of autonomous systems in future warfare?

How will these weapons, which have the potential to transform the interface between Australian defence personnel and their enemy, change the way military service is remembered? In recent decades, Western armed forces have adopted autonomous systems that appear to remove the soldier from danger entirely. Defence personnel have inflicted violence on their enemy from a great distance, without placing their own lives at risk. In such situations, the term 'autonomous warrior' might seem to be a contradiction in terms. Yet early evidence suggests that even soldiers operating far from their enemy are at risk of harm, though it might be 'moral injury', in the form of trauma, rather than physical injury. Furthermore, in wars of attrition, such as that between Russia and Ukraine, drones have made soldiers on the ground even more vulnerable than before. Stories from that front line echo the powerlessness and terror of earlier battle fronts. It seems, then, that the dominance of the battlefield by ever more precise weaponry will not exclude the requirement of 'sacrifice' during warfare, and that soldiers of the future will continue to manifest the values of endurance, courage and even sacrifice – albeit in different ways from those of the past. Beyond that, even if the conduct of future warfare should change to the point where the Australian Defence Force (ADF) of the future bears little resemblance to fighting forces of the past, we should not assume that the Anzac legend will cease to play a role in the Australian political culture and society. As Carolyn Holbrook argues in chapter 14, it serves a sociopolitical purpose that might ensure its continuing place in the Australian imagination, whatever the character of modern fighting.

UNDERSTANDING AUTONOMOUS WARFARE

First, how do we define autonomous warfare? The meaning of the term 'autonomy' is debated, but the Australian Army definition will serve our purposes: autonomy is 'the ability of a machine to perform a task without human input … once operated [it] performs some task or function on its own'.[4] As this definition suggests, autonomous systems can take various forms and cover a wide range of interconnected technologies. These include uncrewed weaponry, self-learning machines, and systems able to make sense of their environment using artificial intelligence (AI). This the Australian Army defines as 'a collection of techniques and technologies that demonstrate behaviour and automate functions that are typically associated with, or exceed the capacity of, human intelligence'.[5]

Autonomous warfare systems are best thought of as being positioned along a spectrum in which the degree of control by human operators diminishes as the autonomy of the weapons increases. The most controversial weapons are those at the end of the spectrum, where weapons apply lethal force with little, if any, human control. These weapons can select, and attack, targets triggered by software sensors that match what they detect in the environment with a 'target profile' – which could be the shape of a military vehicle or the movement of a person.[6] In such a scenario, it is the target that triggers the strike, not the weapon. Key to such autonomous weapons systems are predictive machine-learning algorithms that 'know' what constitutes, for example, a military vehicle or a person.[7] The algorithm acquires this knowledge through repeated exposure to training data. Owing to their 'learning' abilities, machine-learning systems can often program themselves – in ways that sometimes confound computer scientists – while humans merely shape the initial parameters of the learning process.[8]

At the time of writing, the most publicly visible autonomous weapons systems are drones. These unmanned aerial vehicles (UAV) can be controlled at a distance by a human operator or can operate autonomously using software-controlled flight plans that work in conjunction with global positioning systems (GPS). Large drones became widespread after the September 11 attacks on the United States in 2001. In the so-called 'first drone age', the defence forces of the US, the UK, Australia and other nations became more entangled in counterinsurgency fighting and began to deploy remotely operated drones with more regularity. This was largely for counterterrorism strikes, intelligence, surveillance and reconnaissance.[9] But drones were also used, more controversially, and notably by the United States' Central Intelligence Agency (CIA), to target individuals identified as terrorists in undeclared war zones.[10] These drones were remotely piloted, involving multiple people often working from bases inside the US or otherwise far from the scene of combat.

Take the functioning of a lethal Predator or Reaper drone (a weapon that Australia considered buying but then decided against, presumably to divert the funding to other priorities).[11] This weapon is popularly thought to be operated without a human pilot but, in the case of the US, its operation has required up to 80 people, collaborating in fast-paced media and intelligence environments, sometimes in the same room but normally in different locations. Chatting to each other via instant messaging, these 'soldiers' have many overlapping tasks and responsibilities, including identification and discrimination of targets and deployment of weapons. A pilot commands other personnel while moving and controlling the flight of the unmanned aircraft (although aspects of this will be automated). Seated next to the pilot is the sensor and radar operator who controls the cameras mounted to the drone and focuses them, while maintaining the aim of the missile if the pilot decides to launch one. A mission intelligence coordinator accesses computer databases of intelligence information containing archived data and coordinates human intelligence analysts at remote locations through audio and text communications. Finally, the group deploying the drone includes imagery analysts who collect, disseminate and report real-time visual intelligence from various regions of conflict to multiple agencies.[12]

After two decades of the so-called War on Terror, we entered what some call the 'second drone age'. This has witnessed the proliferation of AI-enabled systems and a growing number of heavily armed state and non-state actors competing for dominance in a drone and AI arms race. To this end, at least 113 countries and 65 non-state actors have weaponised drones.[13] Some actors are actively involved in trialling these new technologies in conflict zones. In 2023, the Israeli Defence Force (IDF) deployed a new AI system called Habsora (Hebrew for 'the Gospel') to produce new bombing targets at rapid speeds that far outpace human-led target generation.[14] The IDF is also using drones, such as the Lanius, a small quadcopter capable of manoeuvring in small spaces, to map, navigate and explode targets within Hamas's labyrinthine underground tunnel system.[15] Other non-state actors effectively wielding drones include the Houthis, an Iran-backed Yemeni militia. Since 2021, they have been deploying Iranian drones, including the Shahed models, to attack commercial shipping vehicles.[16] At roughly $50 000 a piece, these drones reveal the increasing affordability of entering a conflict and continuing to engage in one. Authoritarian regimes such as North Korea are also testing new AI-equipped suicide drones.[17] Moreover, advances are being made in AI-enabled support tools for strategic-level decision-making, such that the decision to go to war may one day soon be outsourced to, or at least highly influenced by, machine intelligence.[18] The second drone age, therefore, is marked by advances in drones and AI across strategic, operational and tactical levels of conflict, with both state and non-state actors exploiting these advances for both non-conventional and conventional war.

The impact of drones on the conduct of war came into full view when Russia invaded Ukraine in 2022.[19] In this conflict, drones have enabled Ukrainian forces to launch air strikes that have disrupted Russian attacks on land, while naval drones and unmanned sea vessels have compensated for Ukraine's lack of an operational navy. The unmanned surface vehicle Sea Baby 2024 can deliver an explosive warhead over 1000 kilometres using a guidance system that includes passive sonar identification and direction finding.[20] Naval drones have damaged the Crimean Bridge and forced the Russian Black Sea Fleet to retreat.[21] Ukraine has also developed a range of uncrewed airborne drones capable of avoiding Russian air defences and of launching operational and strategic strikes against oil refineries, ammunition dumps and other targets, some well within Russian territory.

Yet, if Ukrainian drone operators have proven to be innovative and adaptive across all combat domains, so too have the Russians. They have developed technically sophisticated drones, including, at the time of writing, fibre optic drones. With their video and control signals transmitted through a physical fibre optic cord, not through radio frequencies, these UAVs cannot be jammed by electronic interceptors.[22] Russian drones have proved able to scout into covered positions on the battlefield and strike small targets, even individual soldiers. Here, then, autonomous weapons have done nothing to reduce the risk of death and injury for the fighting soldier. In fact, they have increased it by establishing many kilometres of surface area that are deadly no-go zones. Soldiers describe being stalked by drones, 'constantly buzzing in the air, ready to strike as soon as they see movement'.[23]

Meanwhile, Russian drones have rained destruction on Ukrainian cities, posing 'one of the deadliest threats to civilians in frontline areas'.[24] The capital city, Kyiv, was attacked in September 2025 by more than 800 drones, the largest single aerial bombardment since the war began. Some estimates suggest that Russia is aiming to be able to deploy 2000 drones per day.[25] Russian forces are also trying to alleviate manpower and training requirements by developing AI-enabled drone swarms (that is, multiple drones sharing data, moving in a synchronised fashion and handling complex tasks with precision).[26]

The drones of the future will kill in ways that seem almost Orwellian. Drawing on biometric data extracted from social media, smartphones and security cameras – already sold by private companies and shared with governments – some militaries have the capacity to equip autonomous drones with AI-powered facial recognition technology. Such systems can search out specific members of an enemy's force and make individualised attacks.[27] The development of DNA-linked bioweapons might even enable militaries to target individual soldiers with viruses specifically designed to disable or kill them.

Thus, in 2023, the United States Air Force announced it had developed facial recognition technology for use with drones, while in 2021, the UN claimed that Libyan troops had equipped Turkish-made Kargu-2 drones with this technology for autonomous targeting.[28] Israel, too, has used facial recognition technology in

Palestine (primarily at checkpoints) for segregation, social control and mass surveillance of Palestinians.[29] It is now combining AI with facial recognition software to match injured or obscured faces with real identities, and to search for Israeli hostages and Hamas fighters.[30]

Given such developments, ethicists and human rights advocates are currently calling for a global ban on the development, production and use of fully autonomous 'killer robots'; that is, weapons that can make decisions about targeting on software instructions alone. But the implications of robots for the conventions of classic international humanitarian law are far from being resolved. Nightmarish though robotic killers might seem, they could be more skilled at distinguishing between military and civilian targets than the indiscriminate methods of bombardment that have been employed so devastatingly in wars of the past. Thus, while many commentators question whether it is moral to allow machines to make decisions about who should live and who should die, the efficiency, precision and reduced risk they offer suggest that militaries will continue to acquire them.[31]

AUTONOMOUS WARFARE AND THE AUSTRALIAN DEFENCE FORCE

Australia has already played a role in autonomous warfare, with the Joint Defence Facility at Pine Gap operating as a 'key node' in drone strikes inflicted by the US military in the War on Terror.[32] Given that interoperability with the US is a key priority of the ADF's operational planning, this is bound to expand. As the ADF sees it, autonomous weapons systems offer many advantages. Notably, they can maximise the performance of defence personnel, improve decision-making, protect defence personnel and increase their efficiency. To quote from the 2020 Australian Army, *Robotic & Autonomous Systems Strategy*:

> Advances in AI, big data and cloud computing, combined with the proliferation and miniaturisation of sensing technology, create a previously unattainable degree of situational understanding across the battlespace. AI-enabled decision-making tools can enhance overall clarity and respond significantly faster than humans. This speed, coupled with greater reliability and accuracy, can create periods of 'decision advantage' and enable commanders at all levels to make faster, more informed decisions underpinned by comprehensive analysis.[33]

The Royal Australian Navy, for its part, aims to leverage robotics, autonomous systems and AI to increase its ability to project force in the maritime approaches of Australia's near region. This will be in the context of joint operations with alliance partners.[34] Under the AUKUS agreement, the trilateral security partnership signed in 2021 by Australia, the UK and the US, Pillar 2 will offer a program of technical cooperation that will aim to 'establish a network of autonomous and crewed systems that act as a team across a maritime battlespace with an ability to detect, track, and kill a threat on the surface or underwater'.[35] Meanwhile, a glider drone developed by a Perth company, and fitted with European-developed software and AI, offers the Royal Australian Navy the possibility of wide-scale ocean surveillance in anti-submarine warfare, via the analysis of acoustic data at (it is claimed) up to 40 times the rate of human operators.[36] The Royal Australian Air Force, meanwhile, has acquired the AI-enabled Boeing MQ-28

Ghost Bat, a pilotless vehicle capable of flying alongside crewed aircraft for support as part of an integrated system (hence its nickname the 'loyal wingman').

More widely, defence commentators across the political spectrum have called for Australia to develop a sovereign drone capability.[37] In response to the war in Ukraine, the Australian Strategic Policy Institute think tank advocated that Australia should rush into the so-called cheap small drone revolution: establishing a research centre of excellence to counter small drones, and developing global leadership in first-person-view drone technology (that is, the method of drone operation where the pilot uses a video feed from the drone's onboard camera to see the drone's perspective, often through goggles or a monitor).[38]

Notably, official documents about future Australian strategy do not speak of fully automated warfare, but rather of a spectrum involving a mix of humans and machines. These new weapons will enhance human intervention rather than replace it. To date, the ADF has deployed remote autonomous systems in a semi-conventional manner, improving reconnaissance, intelligence gathering and surveillance. For example, drones have delivered video and still images in real time to ground troops using ground terminals. If targets have been identified in this way, soldiers have called in air strikes by, for example, an armed helicopter or a fixed wing strike aircraft (in Afghanistan these were supplied by coalition partners).[39] Here we are reminded of the role of the early aircraft of the First World War. Their function was to assist the artillery by locating the sites of German guns, but not delivering the payload themselves, a task left to humans.

As yet, none of the ADF services has used its drones to target individual enemies. While Australia has been involved in counterterrorism operations and has collaborated with its

AUKUS partners in these, there is no publicly available evidence that Australian agencies have used drones to conduct targeted killings of terrorists. For one thing, Australian intelligence agencies do not have the same operational licence as the CIA has. They are limited to collection, analysis and dissemination of information. Military and paramilitary activities are forbidden, and the use of armed drones by civilian agencies would require legislative changes.[40] However, it is almost certainly only a matter of time before Australia's autonomous systems move beyond reconnaissance and intelligence gathering and become 'weaponised'. In 2024 Australia purchased the Switchblade 300 precision loitering munition with the avowed aim of 'equipping ADF personnel with world-leading *lethality* and protection' (emphasis added).[41] Known as the kamikaze of killer drones, the Switchblade can loiter for some time above targets and destroy them, either manually or autonomously, without the need for soldiers to call in air support.

The ADF clearly values autonomous weapons systems, not just for their operational advantages, but for their potential to limit casualties and minimise costly conventional troop deployments. Following the Vietnam War, casualty aversion became a priority in downsized, professionalised, 'western' or liberal democratic militaries.[42] Australia was no exception, and the government followed a policy of deliberate casualty minimisation in Afghanistan and Iraq. Its aim was not only to protect ADF personnel but also to maintain the support of the electorate for Australia's intervention in long, remote and potentially controversial conflicts.[43] Casualty minimisation also recommends itself as a way of mitigating the problem the ADF faces in attracting recruits and retaining personnel after some years of service. This is a common issue in peacetime but has become especially difficult in the early 2020s, when potential recruits, with AI-related skills in engineering, programming, mathematics and statistics, are attracted to alternative, and more lucrative, employment in the private job market. Recruiting for the ADF has fallen below the levels needed to offset voluntary separations, most notably in the Army.[44] Remote automated systems thus have the value of their supposed life-preserving potential. In theory, at least, they might mitigate the risk that potential defence personnel could encounter should they choose to volunteer. As the Australian Army concluded in 2022:

> Human exposure to high-risk situations will be reduced in the future battlespace through increased range of operations enabled by uncrewed platforms, improved sensors and AI. This will be achieved by using RAS [remote automated systems] technology to conduct highly dangerous activities … such as in highly contested environments, or in the deep operational environment, removing the human from the immediate danger and increasing force protection.[45]

ADF advertising campaigns in recent times have emphasised emerging technology and career advancement, rather than risk, killing, injury or death. To quote the careers website of May 2025: the 'Artillery soldier' will 'use powerful weapon systems, cutting edge battle management systems and advanced surveillance equipment to identify, target and destroy threats on land, in the air or at sea'.[46] Furthermore, just as video games were shaped by military technologies and war games, today's defence recruitment strategies replicate the aesthetics and aspirational narratives of video games. Potential soldiers are promised they will find a career 'unlike any other job' over montages of personnel hunting targets from sophisticated remote surveillance rooms, inside submarines, in swooping helicopters, and on the ground with tracking devices and laser-scoped rifles.[47] There is little here that evokes the supreme value of the traditional warrior, dying for one's country on a physical battlefield.

THE ANZAC WARRIOR IN THE AGE OF AUTONOMOUS WARFARE

So, what are the implications of autonomous weaponry for the status of the Anzac warrior? There is no simple answer. It depends on a range of variables, the most notable being the kind of war Australia will fight in the future, the technological sophistication of their defence force, and the function that narratives of war serve within the wider political culture and society.

On the one hand, it can be argued that warrior myths of the past are under serious challenge because they place soldiers using autonomous weapons at a great distance from the enemy they are killing. Autonomous warriors operating remotely are not at risk of sacrificing their own lives. In some ways, this is simply an extension of the trajectory of Western warfare, increasingly fought at a distance since the end of the Second World War. In Vietnam, three-quarters of Australian personnel were deployed in support roles on bases, while in Afghanistan, most Australian personnel never operated in the field beyond the perimeter of a forward combat post – though this did not necessarily guarantee their physical safety. Autonomous warfare is the logical endpoint of this trajectory: those inflicting violence from the safety of a drone-operating room may not even be in the same country as their enemy target – in some cases, they can return to their home and family after a day's work.

Yet this argument needs qualification. Although the separation of the soldier from possible danger in autonomous warfare marks a break from wider understandings of what it means to be a warrior, personnel using autonomous systems might still display traditional Anzac qualities. These, admittedly, might be cognitive rather than physical. Courage, for example, might take the non-physical form of challenging a direct order or pushing back on an intelligence report. Here, courage is about soldiers pursuing their beliefs despite a hierarchical military structure in which they have been conditioned to submit to those above them, and the penalties for non-compliance are severe. Endurance, too, might take a different form from that of traditional physical and emotional exhaustion on the battlefield. Drone operators conduct surveillance in a state of heightened vigilance for prolonged durations, fixated on screens across different time zones. This surveillance may extend from days to weeks.[48]

Furthermore, it has become clear over recent years that drone operators, even when operating remotely, are exposed to significant risks. They are not only placed under the stress of having to make fast and informed decisions, but they are exposed routinely to potentially traumatic graphic and vivid visual media. They stalk the territory for months ahead of time, getting to know the daily routines and banal life activities of their victims before they kill them. They witness remotely the destruction of homes and villages, torture and death, the recovery of bodies and the aftermath of strikes. In contrast to images projected in recruitment materials, this exposure to 'screen trauma' (repeated, real-time and highly distressing visual imagery) means that most drone operators do not see their work as a game.[49] Instead, they are confronted with an intimacy-in-distance that is unique to their labour.[50] Rather than distance and screen-saturated work producing emotional or ethical disengagement, it generates moral engagement.[51] As Peter Asaro writes, 'human subjectivity and agency [are] transformed in using the technology in ways that are more than mere reactions to the technology'.[52]

Given the burdens of increased operational tempo, and the witnessing of killing in ways that are simultaneously distant and intimate, remote drone operators might be considered to have an elevated risk of 'moral injury'. The term was developed by psychiatrist Jonathan Shay in the mid-1990s to capture the sense among Vietnam veterans that their personal morality had been undermined by the violence they were required to perpetrate.[53] Today, 'moral injury' is used mainly by psychiatrists when 'trauma' or other terms in the psychology lexicon do not capture the source of a person's emotional problems.[54] It is the feeling that one has 'betrayed a deep-seated belief about how a good person should behave'.[55] According to political scientist Christian Enemark, drone operators are prone to moral injury when killing remotely: firstly, because their failure to assume physical risks themselves means they forfeit the moral permission to harm others. Secondly, they move constantly and rapidly between worlds of violence and peace, and between military and civilian identities. Drone operators, even while part of teams, often work in physical isolation, without the support of fellow soldiers to provide camaraderie and validate their decision-making. Finally, the powerful video cameras on drones can restore a targeted individual's humanity and thus increase the moral weight of perpetuating drone violence relative to other forms of killing at a distance.[56]

The increasing salience of moral injury that drone operators face is evident in popular culture dealing with war. In the 2010s, as public awareness of the role of drones in the War on Terror grew, morally conflicted drone operators were depicted as protagonists in films and in television programs, including *Good Kill* (2014), *Eye in the Sky* (2015) and *Drone* (2017).[57] A 2013 British play, *Grounded,* was turned into an opera by the same name. It depicts the central character, Jess, who controls Reaper drones from a trailer near Las Vegas, intentionally crashing her drone. She tracks her target to his home but cannot proceed with the attack when a girl rushes from the house, humanising the target and his family. A backup pilot proceeds with the attack and Jess is court-martialled and sent to jail.[58] In such media, then, autonomous warriors are understood to be sacrificing their souls, rather than their lives.

THE IMPLICATIONS FOR THE ADF AND ANZAC

The full implications of autonomous warfare for the Anzac legend are yet to be seen. At the time of writing, it seems clear that autonomous weapons will not replace Australian defence personnel but rather assume some – probably many – of the functions they have performed in the past. Humans will not be eliminated, but the roles they play will change, as will the skills they require. This has always been the case – the weapons and methods of war have constantly changed – but physical stamina will possibly matter less than competence in science and technology, and AI literacy.

It is hard to envisage the ADF being committed in the future to any conflict that approaches the horrendous attrition of the war in Ukraine. No current threat to national interests would justify this, and the Australian public would be unlikely to tolerate casualties on the levels of this long and bitter conflict. Yet, if such a strategic scenario seems improbable in the short- to medium-term future, Australian defence personnel might still be deployed on physical battlefields, where they have to contend with the counterattacks of an equally AI-enabled enemy. Australian soldiers might not just be the operators of drones but also the victims of them.

In this situation, Australian defence personnel might well manifest endurance and courage: not just of the kind already noted as being inherent in remote drone operations, but that of the traditional battlefield. The need for endurance might actually increase. As the Army's *Robotic & Autonomous Systems Strategy* says: 'In the future machines will accompany the soldier on their mission, offering the opportunity to unburden the soldier of equipment … This will reduce fatigue and *increase endurance*, sustaining soldier performance and enabling concentration on more critical tasks' (emphasis added).[59] The representation of the Afghanistan war in the Australian War Memorial attests to the continuing importance attached to the Anzac values of courage and endurance. The ADF employed drones in this conflict, but the memory enshrined in the paintings by the official war artist, Ben Quilty, is that of the wounded, traumatised soldier.

It is possible, too, that the soldiers of the future will be able to lay a claim to the mateship that has always been at the core of the Anzac myth. To be sure, remote drone operators will not experience the sense of shared hardship and comradeship of serving together, as did soldiers exposed to the dust, heat, cold and apprehension of death in the physical battlefield. The bond between soldiers might be stretched to breaking point if only some of them have to contend with the increased risks of drone warfare, while others work remotely behind a screen. Yet, there is nothing new in members of the defence forces being exposed to different levels of risk, and this seems not to have compromised claims to mateship in the past. Moreover, 'mateship' has a far longer history than Anzac in the Australian cultural imagination. As Russel Ward's classic text on the Australian legend showed, it dates back to 19th-century bushrangers, miners and even convicts.[60] It is hard, then, to envisage 'mateship' slipping from the Australian vernacular, especially as it relates to war.

Likewise, the trope of 'sacrifice' might well remain a powerful element in the Australian commemoration of war, given that the Anzac legend has proved able over the past century to accommodate new ways of understanding injury and war damage. Since the Vietnam War, soldiers have increasingly been positioned as victims, rather than derring-do warriors. The recognition of post-traumatic stress disorder in the 1980s, which shifted the emphasis from valorisation of soldiers' martial ability towards sympathy for their suffering, coincided with the resurgence of public support for Anzac. Drone operators beset by moral injury might thus be incorporated into future constructions of the Anzac legend. However, this might raise a further problem for the ADF. The emphasis on psychological suffering in contemporary retellings of Anzac is surely unappealing to potential recruits, and utterly at odds with recruitment campaigns that portray war as a high-tech game. While dissonance between propaganda and the reality of war is not new, dying for one's country in battle is rather more heroic than being permanently damaged by years of service behind a screen.

It needs to be stressed that, even if future defence personnel struggle to conform to stereotypes of the Anzac warrior, the legend itself might retain its prominence within the Australian political culture. From its origins, 'Anzac' has never been a narrative that has been factually accurate.[61] It has always been dissonant, to some degree, with the realities of the experience of war. The claim by the official historian and early advocate for the Anzac myth, Charles Bean, that the 1st AIF's exceptionalism owed something to its being drawn from an unusually classless society, is just one example.[62] Rather, the Anzac myth has proved so enduring because it has served the function that myths commonly do: it has enshrined and promoted values and behaviours in the past that are seen, by political elites at least, to serve a sociopolitical function in the present. 'Anzac' has also become so flexible that it now incorporates civilians such as police officers, civil defence forces and even sportsmen.[63] It affirms as superior citizens any individuals who compromise their own interests for the sake of the collective.

Thus, even as the conduct of war continues to change, the Anzac myth might continue to frame memories of war at the national level. If it does so, it will be because the elites who play a key role in its promulgation embed their commemoration of war in the mythologised past, not in the realities of contemporary conflicts. The speech made on Anzac Day 2023 by Prime Minister Anthony Albanese was telling. It acknowledged the changing nature of warfare since the Gallipoli landing in 1915, but Albanese went on to claim that the values fought for by the Anzacs over a century ago remain integral to Australian identity and must be cherished by contemporary Australians.

> We gather before the dawn because they did. Picture those first Anzacs. Far from home, huddled in their boats, waiting, wondering … In all [Gallipoli's] stories of valour and resilience, in its simple truth of Australians

looking out for each other no matter how bad things got, it has come to stand for something so much bigger in our collective heart ... While so much has changed in warfare since, the great character of Australians at war has not ... Australians have gone overseas for us. They have gone because there is so much to fight for. And what we have created as Australians, and nurtured over generations, is something we must never take for granted.[64]

Nothing here suggests that the myth of the Anzac warrior has yet been rendered anachronistic.

14

HOW ANZAC EVOLVED AND WHY IT ENDURES – FOR NOW

CAROLYN HOLBROOK

In preparing this chapter, I recalled a conversation with (the now late) Professor Stuart Macintyre. I had been reading Diarmaid MacCulloch's *A History of Christianity* (2009) and said to Stuart that I saw no *categorical* difference between Christianity and the Anzac mythology, but rather a difference of scale.[1] Both had their origins in a traumatic event around which a set of moral values coalesced, along with a community of adherents, whose cohesion was affirmed through the enactment of powerful rituals.

Stuart seemed sceptical of my comparison, but it is a line of thinking that I have followed with increasing interest since my doctoral research on the history of how Australians have remembered the First World War. My observation of debates about Anzac commemoration during the centenary years of the First World War crystallised my impression that much of the argument about the history of the war was in fact a cipher for contests that were fundamentally ideological. In this sense, the history of 'what actually happened' was far less important than deeper human impulses about values and the groups to which people with particular values belonged.[2] These same themes – of

254

morality and solidarity – were those, I had come to believe, which lay at the heart of Anzac's power in the past and even today.

I suspected that our efforts as historians to understand the appeal of Anzac were hampered by a conceptual or theoretical deficit. We sought to apply the conventions of historical analysis to a phenomenon that functioned in Australian society, not as a historical episode, but as a mythology. I use the term 'mythology' in the encompassing sense of a 'story that means something to a culture', that helps to explain its 'worldview, values, or origin – and persists because of its cultural significance, not its factual accuracy'.[3] In other words, the meaning of Anzac, like that of Marlow's tale in *Heart of Darkness*, was 'not inside like a kernel but outside, enveloping the tale which brought it out only as a glow brings out a haze'.[4] Like religion, Anzac functioned beyond anything rational, but was no less important for that. To focus on the kernel of historical events, and to ignore the meaning that radiated from that core, was to misunderstand the Anzac legend altogether.

If we are to understand why Australian involvement in the Gallipoli campaign in 1915 evolved into something so profound and enduring, historians need to better account for the behaviour of the basic unit of our analysis, the human animal.[5] Our deficit might be a shortcoming we share with the social sciences; the social anthropologist Harvey Whitehouse observed that 'it is a basic dogma for most social scientists that one can and should study social and cultural systems without considering human nature'.[6] Yet, explaining the behaviour of humans in social groups is vital to many of the phenomena with which historians grapple, including nationalism, racialism, sexism and other forms of discrimination, as well as social cohesion and democratic decay.

The title of this chapter echoes that of a book by the evolutionary psychologist Robin Dunbar, *How Religion Evolved and Why It Endures* (2022), and challenges us to adopt a more scientifically and sociologically informed means of understanding the Anzac legend.[7] In an argument that has resonance with the French sociologist Émile Durkheim's landmark book *The Elementary Forms of the Religious Life* (1912), Dunbar claims that the fundamental purpose of religion – from which I am extrapolating the Anzac legend – is group cohesion – from which I am extrapolating the nation-state.[8] Both Dunbar and Durkheim focus on the importance of group rituals in the process of social bonding, a phenomenon that has been the subject of sustained research by Harvey Whitehouse.[9]

The chapter suggests that insights from sociology, anthropology and evolutionary psychology illuminate the complex dynamic between state-driven and grassroots commemoration in a way that helps us escape the simplistic division between top-down imposition and bottom-up expressions. In so doing, it does not diminish the significance of state-driven efforts, but rather argues they are insufficient in explaining the endurance of the Anzac myth. Nor does it assert that the Anzac myth requires universal allegiance or explicit expressions of faith across the Australian community to retain its mythological power.

I am not the first to call for a more holistic approach to understanding Anzac. Recent examples include the work of Bianca Slocombe and Michael Kilmister, who have observed that the tools needed to understand Anzac's status as a quasi-religion – 'namely, the psychological metalanguage – have been missing from the conversation'. They have argued that 'Academic disciplines working in isolation will be unable to comprehensively account for this modern-day Australian piety'.[10] Steve Vizard's 2025 book,

Nation, Memory, Myth: Gallipoli and the Australian Imaginary, draws on sociological theory in its call for an understanding of the Gallipoli myth that acknowledges the distinction between national mythology and national history.[11]

ANZAC CULTURE WARS

My own study of how Australians have remembered the First World War, *Anzac: The Unauthorised Biography*, came out in 2014, just in time for the centenary of the Gallipoli landing in 2015 and the accompanying debates about Anzac commemoration.[12] As an ingénue in these public debates, trained during my recently completed doctoral studies to prize the weighing of detailed evidence and historiographical themes, I quickly became disillusioned. The public conversation seemed ultimately to be about ideology rather than history. Critics from the left, academics and other commentators, questioned the amount of government funding allocated for the centenary of the Gallipoli landing. (The funding *was* extraordinary – more than any other country and almost more than all other nations combined, including the major combatant nations of 1914–18.)[13] These critics also condemned the commercialisation of Anzac, among the most blatant and notorious examples of which was the supermarket Woolworths' campaign, which asked people to upload images of their forebears to a picture generator, which added the slogan 'Fresh in our Memories' to the image.[14] With the public seeing this as a distasteful allusion to Woolworths' claim to be the 'Fresh Food People', the company was forced to withdraw the campaign.[15]

Alternatively, commentators on the right, publishing in outlets such as *Quadrant* magazine and the Murdoch-owned

Australian and *Daily Telegraph* newspapers, defended the centenary commemoration extravaganza and the amount of money being spent on it.[16] The retired academic Mervyn Bendle claimed that historian Marilyn Lake and the co-authors of the highly critical *What's Wrong with Anzac?* (2010) were 'operating like an academic Taliban, doing as much damage as possible to a unique and valuable tradition'; they were 'determined to destroy the Anzac centenary in the same way they had sabotaged the Bicentenary' in 1988.[17] Such conservatives scoffed at academics and other commentators who criticised a tradition they regarded as noble and sacred. To deride Anzac was not only to be un-Australian, but akin to being an apostate or a heretic. Much of this commentary revealed a cursory engagement with the subject matter of its criticism.[18] This was fundamentally an ideological exercise.

One of the clearest expositions of this conception of Anzac came five years after the centenary, from the former Coalition Education Minister Alan Tudge in 2020. His intervention was intended, I suspect, to activate the past to political advantage in the same way that John Howard had done during his prime ministership (1996–2007).[19] But Tudge was no John Howard. In a radio interview that was widely reported, he objected to the proposed new national history curriculum, in which a portion of Year 9 history dealing with the First World War would examine its commemoration, including 'different historical interpretations and contested debates about the nature and significance of the Anzac legend and the war'. The content would potentially include 'debating the difference between commemoration and celebration of war'.[20] Tudge countered that Anzac Day was not a contested idea apart from an absolute fringe element in our society … Instead of Anzac Day being presented as the most sacred of all days in Australia, where we stop, we reflect, we commemorate the hundred thousand people who have died for our freedoms … it's presented as a contested idea.[21]

The minister professed his concern that children would leave school with a hatred of their country rather than a love for it, making them less inclined to protect it, as 'a million Australians have through their military service'.[22]

The response to Tudge's comments from the academic community revealed the extent of the ideological divide about the purpose of history education. If Tudge believed its primary purpose was to teach young people to love their country so they would sacrifice their lives for it, education researcher Professor Susanne Gannon claimed:

> Choosing to present Anzac Day as 'sacred' and monolithic reveals an allegiance to simplistic ideas of the past, erasure of the experiences and histories of many in our communities, and a complete misunderstanding of historical consciousness and historical thinking that are foundational to the discipline of history.[23]

Another education expert, Associate Professor Sue Nicols, urged 'Minister Tudge to spend some time speaking with children and youth to learn what it means to be a globally connected, multilingual citizen of Australia'.[24] The controversy illustrated that attitudes to Anzac education and the Anzac legend itself were powered by deeply held values that were attached to and defined by the social groups with which their advocates identified – 'what actually happened' in the First World War was a long way down the list of priorities.[25]

Observing these debates about the meaning of Anzac commemoration, I found myself revisiting the wisdom of Ken Inglis's 70-year-old declaration that Anzac bore elements of a 'civic religion'.[26] Inglis was originally a historian of religion; after writing his doctoral thesis at Oxford about churches and the working classes in Victorian England, he returned to Australia driven by a desire to understand 'what had happened in the twentieth century to religiosity, faith, the sense of the sacred'.[27] Mindful that churches were not as full as they once were, Inglis began to think about Anzac Day as a quasi-religious event: 'The more I learned of it and thought about it, the more its ceremonies, monuments and rhetoric seemed to me to constitute in some respects a civic religion'.[28] Despite his ideological sympathy to the cause of his Marxist colleagues, Inglis believed throughout his career that their rationalist-materialist arguments were insufficient in explaining the complexity of human behaviour.

If Inglis's declining health (he died in 2017) had not precluded his capacity to comment on the 2015 Anzac centenary, he might have interpreted the intensity with which people prosecuted their arguments as evidence of an *emotional* as well as an intellectual engagement. Seeking to unsettle their attachment to the Anzac legend, critics pointed out inaccuracies in the recounting of the history of the First World War by Anzac boosters. They countered jingoistic distortions with empirical evidence: Australians comprised only 5 per cent of the total forces at Gallipoli; the Australian general John Monash was not an 'outsider' as claimed by the journalist-author Roland Perry, and he did not 'w[i]n the war'.[29] In 2015 came the revelation that Ottoman commander

Ataturk's famous reassurance to Australian mothers of the Gallipoli dead that their sons were 'now lying in our bosom and are in peace' was a later invention.[30] When this scoop went mostly unnoticed, it was apparent that attempts to counter attachment to the Anzac mythology with empirical evidence misconceived the nature of peoples' attachment to it. Questioning its accuracy was akin to pointing out to the Catholic faithful that bread cannot be transformed into flesh, nor wine into blood; or to a Donald Trump devotee that the 2020 election was not stolen. To better understand the power of Anzac, we need to accept that there is a category difference between history and myth, and resist the conflation of historical truth with 'symbolic, psychological and sacred truth'.[31] To summarily dismiss a national myth on the grounds that it is historically inaccurate is, in the words of Vizard, 'to dismiss human nature'.[32]

EXPLAINING ANZAC'S RESURGENCE

For many decades after the publication of Charles Bean's 12-volume *Official History* (1921–42), academic historians largely eschewed the subject. When Bill Gammage arrived at the Australian National University in 1961 as an 18-year-old, the subject of the Great War was neither taught nor researched by academic staff. Anybody who professed an interest in studying war was likely to be perceived as militaristic, he later recalled.[33] Gammage persevered and eventually published *The Broken Years* in 1974, based on his examination of First World War soldiers' letters and diaries. Around the same time as Gammage was pioneering a new social historiography of the war, Ken Inglis (1960) was exploring the nature of First World War memory and Anzac commemoration, while Lloyd Robson (1970) used enlistment records to counter the commonly held view that the 1st AIF (Australian Imperial Force) hailed predominantly from rural backgrounds.[34]

Much of the historiography of the last four decades has sought, like Robson's study of *The First AIF*, to pinpoint the construction of the Anzac legend by social elites and to challenge its factual foundations.[35] A burst of Anzac scholarship in the 2000s was prompted by the increasing political sponsorship of Anzac commemoration, beginning during the Hawke government in the 1980s. The rise of the politician as 'commemorator-in-chief' corresponded with increased crowds at Anzac Day services and the battlefield tourism phenomenon.[36] Many of those who travelled to Gallipoli and other battlefields to observe Anzac Day were veterans and their families. Others were young backpackers, whose visits transpired in an atmosphere of green- and gold-tinted reverie and sentimentality.[37]

The resurgence of Anzac sent historians looking for explanations, which they often found in the actions of government and social elites. Among the most influential publications to emphasise the hand of the state in Anzac commemoration was *What's Wrong with Anzac?*, published in 2010.[38] The book claimed that Australian history is overly weighted towards military themes at the expense of subjects such as the dispossession of Indigenous Australians (which ought to be considered a war in the same way as overseas wars), and late-19th-century and early 20th-century achievements in social welfare and industrial arbitration. *What's Wrong with Anzac?* argued that the government determined this emphasis, principally through increased funding to the Department of Veterans' Affairs for educational materials that served to indoctrinate in young Australians a militaristic and politically conservative view of the past. Most disturbingly, the authors argued, the obsession with Anzac was used by politicians to justify Australian military incursions in Iraq and Afghanistan. Implicit in this argument was the belief that nationalism is a constructed phenomenon, an instrument of state propagandising.

Academic historians' emphasis on the role of the state in Anzac commemoration is partly a product of their values, which tend to be progressive, if not radical, and suspicious of state-sponsored nationalism, particularly if it has a military flavour. It is also a product of reliance on the archive – the state leaves a paper trail, unlike the tens of thousands of 'ordinary' people who feel an attachment to the Anzac legend. But while an emphasis on top-down indoctrination explains much about the ubiquity of Anzac in contemporary Australia, it only gets us so far – people, especially those living in liberal democratic societies, are not empty vessels whose ingestion of state propaganda dictates their beliefs and behaviours. Indeed, such top-down arguments run the risk of denying ordinary people the agency we are otherwise often keen to impute to them. The limits of any government's capacity to determine public sentiment were demonstrated during the 2023 referendum campaign to establish an Indigenous Voice to Parliament in the Constitution.[39] A similar argument can be mounted for the 36 failed referendum campaigns that preceded the Voice.

Furthermore, arguments such as that made in *What's Wrong with Anzac?* ignore the substantial role of non-state agents in promulgating the Anzac legend. In *Broken Nation* (2013), Joan Beaumont applied the Italian Marxist Antonio Gramsci's concept of 'hegemony' to account for the pervasiveness of Anzac mythology. In seeking to explain fascist rule in interwar Italy, Gramsci argued that rulers secure the consent of the masses via the diffusion and popularisation of their world views through cultural, intellectual, educational, religious, media and other institutions.[40] By the Second World War, Beaumont claimed, 'the Anzac myth had become hegemonic in the sense that it seemed natural even to those who were not part of the elites that created it'.[41] As the centenary showed, media, business and community groups, and sporting organisations continue to actively participate in promoting the Anzac legend. These institutions and actors choose to support Anzac commemoration because they are harnessing a sentiment that is already afoot in the community, often for commercial benefit.

We can see how hegemonic efforts to remould the Anzac legend in the shape of contemporary political needs have failed. Paul Keating was unable during his prime ministership (1991–96) to reorient Anzac commemoration away from Gallipoli and towards Kokoda and the Pacific War of 1941–45. Keating's anti-imperialist vision for Australia's war heritage was bolstered by the Republican movement of the 1990s and coincided with the 'Australia Remembers' campaign of Second World War commemoration, and the emerging battlefield tourism industry in South-East Asia and the Pacific. His effort was buttressed by a range of hegemonic forces. Yet, Keating was unable to break the covenant between the Anzac faithful and their 'holy land' on the Dardanelles peninsula. As Vizard observes in *Nation, Myth, Memory*, the 'continual reactualising of a national myth through the agency of powerful institutional actors may be a necessary condition for the embedding of a national myth, but it is never sufficient'.[42]

Bruce Scates sought to understand the nature of popular attachment to the Anzac legend in his 2006 book, *Return to Gallipoli*. Using evidence from over 700 surveys with so-called 'pilgrims', Scates explored the 'hunger for meaning' and 'craving for ritual' that propelled thousands of Australians, many of whom were young backpackers, to visit the battlefields of the First World War.[43] Mark McKenna and Stuart Ward accused Scates of sentimentality and alleged that he had failed to consider adequately the extent to which 'pilgrims' had been manipulated or brainwashed; their emotional responses, McKenna and Ward argued, had 'less and less to do with "history" and more and more to do with the commerce and politics of nationalism in John Howard's Australia'.[44] McKenna and Ward lamented that Scates' focus on emotion, on 'the pain of grief and loss', obviated against 'historical understanding', by which they presumably meant understanding of why Australians travelled to historic battlefields.[45] But neither Scates' exploration of the emotional engagement at the heart of Australians' attachment to Anzac – absent of insights into the deeper human impulses behind such behaviour – nor McKenna and Ward's discounting of subjective experience, pierced the mystery of why nationalist myths, such as Anzac, can endure for decades and even centuries.[46]

THINKING MORE BROADLY ABOUT NATIONALISM

Like the scholarship on Anzac, the historiography of nationalism, to which debates about Anzac must inevitably turn, has tended to favour explanations that emphasise the role of the state. This is not surprising. Western explanations have been offered most influentially by men whose values and conceptions of human nature were shaped by the Great Depression and the Second World War, particularly the rise of Nazism and the perpetration of the Holocaust. The Austrian-British historian Eric Hobsbawm, for instance, had witnessed the rise of Nazism directly as a young Jew who lived briefly in Berlin in the 1930s, before moving as a 15-year-old to Britain in 1933.[47] Hobsbawm was a lifelong Marxist, who conceived nationalism in materialist terms, as an ideological instrument of industrialisation. Two other of the most influential scholars of nationalism, Benedict Anderson and Ernest Gellner, also emphasised the relationship between nationalism and modernity.[48] Anderson coined the enduring phrase 'imagined communities' to signify the arbitrariness of the nation as a category of social organisation, and the extent to which it reflected the demands of modernity rather than being an organic expression of communal identity.

While nationalism was identified as the 'culprit' that facilitated mass participation in many of the atrocities of the 20th century, historians were less inclined, and perhaps less equipped theoretically and methodologically, to probe the psychological processes by which it propelled people to commit violence, endure great suffering and deprivation, and even to die in its name. Sociologists, anthropologists and other social scientists have sought to explain how the nation, conceived as an 'emotional system', earned the devotion of the masses.[49] Many of these scholars have been influenced by the ideas of sociologist Émile Durkheim. Though Durkheim had little to say about nationalism itself, his intellectual interest in social solidarity – inspired by his childhood experience in German-occupied Alsace during the 1870s and by France's rapid industrialisation – has provided fertile intellectual ground for thinking about nationalism.

In *The Elementary Forms of the Religious Life*, published in 1912, Durkheim studied religion in small-group societies. Much of his ethnographic research concerned Indigenous Australians. While the shortcomings of Durkheim's characterisations of traditional Indigenous societies have been revealed by subsequent research, his insights about religion remain pertinent.[50] In traditional societies, Durkheim argued, the totem symbolised 'both the sacred energy and the identity of the clan group'.[51] Its fundamental purpose was to represent the superiority of the group and its moral rule over the individual.[52] While small-group religions lacked the entrenched institutional and power structures of religions in larger societies, Durkheim's crucial point was that the fundamental *social* function of religion remained constant across societies of all sizes and time periods. He famously wrote that 'the idea of society is the soul of religion'.[53] Whatever the object or subject of worship, the essence of the sacred ideal is the set of beliefs and rules that are necessary to maintain a cohesive social group. The sifting of the sacred from the profane provides the set of moral values and behaviours that define the boundaries of the social group.[54] To fail to prescribe to, or to transgress against, these sacred values is to be excised from the social group.

Crucial to maintaining adherence to the shared values that facilitate group cohesion is the performance of ritual activities. Durkheim claimed that 'society cannot make its influence felt unless it is in action, and it is not in action unless individuals who compose it are assembled together and act in common'.[55] In other words, the social-bonding benefits of religion are an *embodied* phenomenon. They are highly contingent on group members being gathered physically and engaged in prosocial communal activities. Durkheim described the feelings of excitement, goodwill and unity that these ritual occasions induce in human groups as 'collective effervescence'.

The anthropologist Harvey Whitehouse has probed deeply into the function of ritual using evidence derived from archaeology, history, social psychology and anthropology. Like Durkheim, Whitehouse concludes that ritual serves to 'generate group cohesion and loyalty and to promote cooperation'.[56] Whitehouse identifies two types of human ritual behaviours. The first is the intense, less commonly enacted modes that occur traditionally in small-scale societies and, in particular circumstances, in larger-scale societies. These so-called 'imagistic rituals' can lead to such intense bonds of attachment that he describes a fusion of individual identity with that of the group (an equivalent, perhaps, of Durkheim's 'collective effervescence' and Dunbar's endorphin-rich trance behaviour, described below).[57] These often painful and disturbing rituals create what Whitehouse calls an 'imagistic pathway' to group bonding, which revolves around 'mental images associated with past events that have a particularly haunting and meaningful quality'.[58] This intense form of social identification can inspire a willingness to sacrifice oneself for the group.

Whitehouse calls the second type of ritual behaviours 'doctrinal rituals'; these occur more frequently and less intensely, in larger-scale, post-Neolithic societies, and do not lead to the kind of fusion between individual and group identities that is seen in intense 'imagistic rituals'.[59] He argues that intermittent and highly intense, often painful, rituals are particularly effective at bonding small communities, and that more frequent and less intense doctrinal rituals foster cohesion in larger communities – among which I would include nations.

Considered alongside cutting-edge neuroscience and neuro-psychology, these sociological and anthropological findings offer even greater insight into how social groups function. The capacity to measure arousal levels via phenomena like blood pressure and heart-rate elevation has enabled researchers to quantify the group bonding effects that Durkheim observed.[60] The evolutionary psychologist Robin Dunbar's work on the evolution and longevity of religious practice verifies Durkheim's theory of the collective effervescence generated by religious rituals.

Dunbar has pioneered research into primate and human bonding and group behaviour. He is most famous for 'Dunbar's number' – the theory about humans' capacity for social relationships.[61] Across time and cultures, Dunbar has found a remarkably consistent phenomenon: humans tend to have about five intimate friends, about 15 at the next level of familiarity, 50 at the next level, and that we can maintain a maximum of 150 friends.

Dunbar's work has examined the role of religion in bonding social groups that stretch beyond our normal capacity for relationships. In line with a growing body of scholarship, he argues that the need to live in larger communities during the Neolithic period was driven by the desire for security, rather than by the development of agricultural technology as traditionally believed.[62] Larger groups afforded greater protection against raiders. This security-driven need to live in larger groups created a problem, according to Dunbar, that would no doubt sound familiar to scholars of nationalism like Eric Hobsbawm and Benedict Anderson: 'how to maintain the cohesion of social groups, and especially large social groups, in the face of the centrifugal forces created by the stresses of living in groups'.[63]

Whereas Anderson proposed that the technology of print communication along with the increased bureaucratic power of the state facilitated social cohesion, Dunbar argues that the production of endorphins allowed potentially acrimonious groups to cohabit. Endorphins are hormones that evolved as part of the human pain-management system. They create an opiate-like effect of calmness, a sense that all is well with the world. This induces a feeling of commitment and obligation towards those with whom one is interacting. Dunbar established in earlier research that the practice of grooming produces endorphins in primates, which solidifies their communities.[64] He argues that human social groups are too large for this time-consuming, one-on-one practice. Thus, humans have developed ways of triggering endorphins that do not require physical contact: laughter, singing, dancing, feasting, storytelling and, most effective of all, religious rituals. Dunbar identifies the evolutionary origins of ritual behaviour in joyful play, in the tradition of the sociologist of religion Robert Bellah, emphasising its role in producing feel-good hormones.[65]

Harvey Whitehouse, on the other hand, emphasises the conformity function of ritual, arguing that humans display the ability from a very young age to imitate ritualised behaviour as a means of being accepted by the social group.[66] Whatever the precise origins of human ritual behaviour and the mechanisms by which people are bonded, it serves to elevate and sacralise the values of the social group, as Durkheim identified in *The Elementary Forms of the Religious Life*.

Dunbar's crucial point, for our purposes, is that the effectiveness of religion does not derive simply from the imposition of doctrine from the institutional church (or equivalent), but from the *practice* of religion, from the rituals that produce endorphins and promote cohesion and compliance within groups.[67] This is evident from how institutional religions, such as Judaism, Christianity and Islam, appeared *after* humans settled in larger, agriculture-based communities, and developed from socially significant pre-existing practices that were then utilised by the emerging apparatus of the state.[68] Dunbar argues in his 2020 book, *How Religion Evolved and Why It Endures*:

There appears to be something about a specifically religious ideology that makes it possible for individuals to hang together as a community for much longer before frictions eventually lead to community fragmentation and demise. A religious ethos somehow seems to enable people to tolerate each other's foibles and irritating behaviour rather better than would otherwise be the case.[69]

The logic of Dunbar's claim, 'Rituals form the bedrock on which most, if not all, religions rest', can be extended to other powerful group mythologies, such as Anzac, which underpin the cohesion of the *national* group.[70]

RETHINKING ANZAC'S 'ANCHOR EVENT'

How specifically can these insights into human social behaviour help us to better understand the Anzac legend? First, they enable us to think more expansively about the event that lies at the heart of Anzac, the Gallipoli landing on 25 April 1915. Rather than explanations that look only at the ways in which 'powerful institutional actors' such as Charles Bean and the British journalist Ellis Ashmead Bartlett forged the Anzac legend, we can also consider how the campaign itself affected its participants and their loved ones, and how this, in turn, created the conditions for a nascent mythology.[71]

Whitehouse's concept of the imagistic ritual has clear application to soldiers fighting in war as it was conducted in the early 20th century.[72] Traumatic ordeals endured by small groups in which members are well known to each other, Whitehouse claims, cause transformative experiences, which sear 'themselves into the memories of participants ... triggering a process of exegetical reflection that lasts for years, sometimes for a whole lifetime'.[73] In other words, profound experiences such as battle not only bond humans extremely closely, but they trigger a long-lasting process of memory reflection and rumination – the 'imagistic pathway' in his terminology. Dunbar, for this part, would argue that painful rituals trigger the endorphin system, while others have posited the existence of a costly-signalling dynamic (whereby extreme sacrifice by group members facilitates deep social bonding) to account for the long-observed connection between group suffering and social cohesion.[74] Whatever the precise mechanism for attachment – the neuroscience is emerging – these insights about human psychology are crucial to understanding the true nature of the Anzac legend. This phenomenon by which social groups that endure traumatic experiences become deeply bonded also sheds scientific light on the much-vaunted camaraderie or 'mateship' among members of the 1st AIF.

Perspectives drawn from social science and evolutionary psychology also help us to understand how the harrowing experience at Gallipoli morphed into a national mythology. Steve Vizard has described how mythologies require an 'anchor event', whose impact, not just on a small group of people but on the collective memory of the social group, is traumatic.[75] The First World War certainly fits this bill, with 417 000 Australians enlisting from a population of fewer than five million, and around 330 000 of those enlistees serving overseas. More than 60 000 servicepeople were killed and around 155 000 listed officially as wounded.[76] Historians have written extensively about the weight of grief and the practices of mourning that an event of such devastating scale unleashed, as well as the experiences of the 'shattered Anzacs' who returned home, and the families who cared for them.[77] Rather than seeking to untangle top-down and bottom-up influences, this formulation allows us to see that they are engaged in a dynamic relationship; how it is the *combination* of a traumatic event with the circumstances of a social group that determines whether a particular event becomes mythologised.[78] The settler-colonial status of Australia and the pervasiveness of martial nationalism provided a context in which a traumatic event was transmuted into a story of the emergence of the Australian nation through the courage and sacrifice of its young men. The sacralisation of the anchor event or 'cultural trauma' at Gallipoli was advanced by what Vizard calls 'powerful carrier groups': most prominently, the official historian, Charles Bean; national, state and local governments; and the influential Returned and Services League.[79] The efforts of these powerful agents would have been ineffective, however, without the psychological circumstances created by the traumatic 'anchor event'.

RETHINKING THE ENDURING POWER OF ANZAC

While institutions and social elites play a key role in entrenching, invigorating and advancing mythic narratives, their actions are never sufficient to ensure longevity.[80] So how, then, has the Anzac legend endured for more than a century, particularly when many observers believed it was on its last legs in the 1980s?[81] In essence, it has harnessed the 'binding force and sacred power' of religion, including its customs and rituals, the latter infused with a distinctively Christian flavour.[82]

From the earliest commemorative occasions, the Anzacs were cloaked in the language of the sacred. Speaking in London on the first Anzac Day in 1916, which fell two days after Easter Sunday, Australian Prime Minister Billy Hughes extolled the soldiers as a balm for the self-interest and consumerism of everyday life: 'Into a world saturated by material things, which has elevated self into a deity, which has made wealth the standard of greatness, comes the sweet, purifying breath of self-sacrifice'.[83] The appropriating of Christian tropes and rituals in Anzac commemoration was so natural as to be almost instinctive.[84] As Joan Beaumont observed, Christianity 'provided a theology of atonement and redemption within which the deaths of so many young men could be given deeper meaning. Just as God's only son had died to save a sinful world, so the innocent of Australia were now sacrificing their lives for the sake of guilty mankind.'[85]

Anzac Day quickly became entrenched in the national calendar and was a public holiday in all states and territories by the late 1920s. Politicians routinely prepared statements and delivered speeches that deployed the heroic language of 'high diction', as described by Paul Fussell in *The Great War and Modern Memory*.[86] But it was the returned soldiers themselves who did much to shape the character of Anzac Day. The dawn service, that most moving of rituals, was followed later in the morning by the Anzac Day march. Drinking, socialising and gambling could be said to comprise other important elements of the Anzac Day ritual. The Returned and Services League (and its earlier incarnations) and battalion associations provided forums in which the Anzac 'group' could engage in its identity-defining behaviours, and where men might seek comfort as they contemplated the lingering memories and 'mental images', to use the language of Whitehouse, of their wartime experience.[87]

Historians have discerned the ways in which politicians succeeded the returned men as the 'commemorators-in-chief' of the Anzac legend, after a hiatus during the 1960s and 1970s when the unpopularity of Anzac deterred politicians from embracing that role.[88] Seeds of this trend can be found in Prime Minister Bob Hawke's trip to Gallipoli in 1990 with a group of elderly veterans to commemorate the 75th anniversary of the landing on 25 April

1915. Hawke later recalled the 'Gallipoli pilgrimage' – note the religious terminology – as 'one of the most moving experiences of my prime ministership'.[89] His fondest memory was of the camaraderie between the old diggers and young Australians, several thousand of whom had travelled to Türkiye (formerly Turkey) for the dawn service. As the old diggers took their places for the dawn service, 'the young people expressed their enthusiasm and they embraced this great generational gap, enthusing with one another. It was very, very moving', Hawke recalled.[90]

The camaraderie of the 1990 trip was replicated in the battlefield 'pilgrimages', which became popular soon after, and which Bruce Scates recorded in *Return to Gallipoli*. For descendants and groups of exuberant young backpackers, the shared ritual of Anzac commemoration at the site of the anchor event functioned as a powerful group-bonding experience. The fact that engagement of the 'pilgrims' with military history was cursory and easily manipulated, and that the battlefield pilgrimage phenomenon was created and exploited by travel companies, does not alter the fact that people were experiencing profound emotions, and that the Anzac legend was replenishing itself.[91]

The most powerful of Anzac rituals remains the dawn service, which requires some small degree of 'sacrifice' or 'cost' on the part of its participants in rising before dawn.[92] Research supports the intuition that environment is highly significant in inducing collective effervescence.[93] Dawn services are typically held at awe-inducing locations: the Shrine of Remembrance in Melbourne, the State War Memorial at Kings' Park in Perth, the Australian War Memorial in Canberra, or at local monuments in hundreds of country towns, inscribed with the names of local men. The sun emerges on the horizon, a minute of silent contemplation among the crowd is broken by the bugle playing the *Reveille* as the flags are slowly raised to the masthead and the ode to 'the fallen' is recited: 'They shall not grow old as we who are left grow old. Age shall not weary them, nor the years condemn. At the going down of the sun and in the morning, we will remember them.' Contemporary Australian rituals are rarely more moving and more conducive to the collective effervescence that facilitates social bonding.

Other Anzac Day rituals also facilitate social bonding and group cohesion. Harvey Whitehouse would characterise these as 'doctrinal rituals', because they lack the (often painful) intensity of more rarely performed imagistic rituals, but are effective in bonding larger social groups. In the context of Anzac commemoration, these rituals include the gunfire breakfast, wreath-laying ceremonies and the Anzac Day march, even the baking and consumption of Anzac biscuits. The former Coalition Opposition leader and director of the Australian War Memorial, Brendan Nelson, introduced a daily Last Post Ceremony in the Commemorative Courtyard. Each day, the story behind one of the names on the Roll of Honour is shared, a visitor is invited to lay a wreath, a minute's silence is observed, and the *Last Post* plays from the speakers. Government-sponsored school visits to the Australian War Memorial provide further opportunity to reinforce the moral values of the national social group. I suspect that Peter Weir's 1981 film *Gallipoli* – described by Bill Gammage as 'easily the most influential of all depictions of Australians at war' and still often watched – continues to be highly effective in perpetuating the sacred status of the Anzac story.[94] Its moving portrayal of the sacrifice of a young warrior is deeply allegorical and affecting, mirroring as it does the Christian story of sacrifice and redemption.

THE FUTURE OF ANZAC

The group bonding that is necessary for social cohabitation requires that people gather in forms that facilitate collective effervescence and hormone release. Benedict Anderson argued that print technologies played a vital role in the development of nationalism. Also important were the railways, churches and civic spaces that allowed people to gather physically. Much research remains to be done about the effects of digital communication on the human brain. Can it summon the necessary 'collective effervescence' to effectively bond groups in the way that embodied contact can? Robin Dunbar thinks not. Time will tell whether the fracturing effect of digital technology is due more to its capacity to narrowcast to millions of sub-national groups or its failure to produce collective effervescence via the physical gathering of groups of people. The COVID-19 pandemic illustrated the importance of the embodied aspect of Anzac commemoration – the driveway commemorations that Prime Minister Scott Morrison encouraged were a pale imitation of the communalism engendered by mass gatherings.[95]

The Anzac mythology has demonstrated substantial malleability over more than a century, in shedding its more overtly martial connotations and its imperial roots, and inviting women, gay and traumatised veterans into the fold.[96] In recent years, Indigenous veterans have been honoured in commemorative services, though this inclusion has inspired other demands that the violence between settlers and Indigenous peoples be officially recognised as war.[97] But can its appeal stretch to include significant portions of the population that have no ancestral connection to Britain and the nation's Anglo-Celtic and Christian heritage?

The answer depends not merely on the efforts of the state to inculcate people into what Graeme Davison called 'the habit of commemoration', but on the demotic or 'grassroots' connections by which Anzac initiation occurs.[98]

Rather than debating the role of top-down and bottom-up forces in explaining the enduring appeal of Anzac, applying knowledge about human social behaviour from other disciplines enables us to perceive that dynamic in a new way. When we look at Anzac through the lens of its quasi-religious status, bearing in mind the evolutionary role that religion plays in human societies, we begin to understand its 'sacred' status, its powerful rituals, its profession of moral values and, ultimately, its role as a vehicle for social cohesion.

Durkheim and Dunbar's insights about the purpose of religion and Whitehouse's work on rituals have application to all kinds of human beliefs and behaviours, whether they relate to sporting teams, political ideologies, religions, racialism, sexism or any other means by which we categorise ourselves socially and exclude those who do not conform to the values of the group. These insights can inform how we conceive and explain nationalism and the mythologies that support it; the same goes for religion and other belief systems that humans attach themselves to.

The perspectives of social science and evolutionary psychology do not detract from the fact that mythologies such as Anzac mandate codes of morality and discourage analytical thinking in the interests of group cooperation and social cohesion. Nor do they shield us from the capacity of bad-faith actors to coopt potent group myths for their own ends. But these insights do allow us to better understand the processes by which group mythologies emerge and are sustained. And they confirm that if Anzac did not exist to do the work of social bonding in the modern Australian nation-state, something, or someone, else would seek to take its place.

NOTES

CHAPTER 1 CHALLENGING ANZAC

1   Anthony Albanese, 'Anzac Day Commemorative Address Dawn Service 2023', 25 April 2023 <www.awm.gov.au/commemoration/speeches/commemoration/speeches/anzac-day-2023>.

2   The classic exposition by Bean can be found in his *The Story of Anzac*, vol. I of *The Official History of Australia in the War of 1914–1918* (Angus & Robertson, 1941, first published 1921), 3–7.

3   C. E. W. Bean, cited in K. S. Inglis, 'The Anzac Tradition' (1995), reproduced in John Lack, *Anzac Remembered: Selected Writings of K. S. Inglis* (University of Melbourne, 1998), 24.

4   T. W. Ashplant, Graham Dawson and Michael Roper, *The Politics of War Memory and Commemoration* (Routledge, 2000), 7.

5   For the evolution of Anzac, on which there is an extensive literature, the place to start is Carolyn Holbrook, *Anzac: The Unauthorised Biography* (NewSouth, 2014).

6   Joan Beaumont, 'Remembering the Heroes of Australia's Wars: From Heroic to Post-Heroic Memory', in Sibylle Scheipers (ed.), *Heroism and the Changing Character of War: Towards Post-Heroic Warfare?* (Palgrave Macmillan, 2014), 345.

7   'Aboriginal Service During the First World War', Australian War Memorial <www.awm.gov.au/about/our-work/projects/indigenous-service>.

8   C. E. W. Bean, 'Australia – the Australian', *Sydney Morning Herald*, 22 June 1907, 6; Bean, *The Story of Anzac*, 5.

9   K. S. Inglis, 'Anzac and the Australian Military Tradition' (1998), in Lack, *Anzac Remembered*, 135.

10   Christina Twomey, 'Trauma and the Reinvigoration of Anzac: An Argument', *History Australia* 10, no. 3 (2013): 85–108.

11   For the latest analysis of Anzac as sacred, see Steve Vizard, *Nation, Myth, Memory: Gallipoli and the Australian Imaginary* (Melbourne University Press, 2025).

12   'Anzac Day' (1964), 'The Anzac Tradition' (1965), 'Return to Gallipoli' (1966) and 'C. E. W. Bean, Australian Historian' (1970), all reproduced in Lack: *Anzac Remembered*, 13–17, 18–42, 43–62, 63–96. Another early contributor to the Anzac debate was Geoffrey Serle, 'The Digger Tradition and Australian Nationalism', *Meanjin Quarterly* 24, no. 2 (1965): 149–58.

13   L. L. Robson, 'The Origin and Character of the First A.I.F., 1914–18: Some Statistical Evidence', *Historical Studies* 15, no. 61 (1973): 737–49.

14   Jane Ross, *The Myth of the Digger: The Australian Soldier in the Two World Wars* (Hale & Iremonger, 1985). See further Joan Beaumont, *Australia's*

War 1914–18 (Allen & Unwin, 1995), 157–61; Alistair Thomson, *Stragglers and Shirkers: An Anzac Imperial Controversy* (University of London, 1991).

15   Bill Gammage, *The Broken Years: Australian Soldiers in the Great War* (ANU Press, 1974).

16   David Kent, '*The Anzac Book* and the Anzac Legend: C. E. W. Bean as Editor and Image-Maker', *Historical Studies* 21, no. 84 (1985): 376–90. Ellis Ashmead-Bartlett was the subject of a later biography: Fred and Elizabeth Brenchley, *Myth-Maker* (Wiley, 2005).

17   E. M. Andrews, *The Anzac Illusion: Anglo-Australian Relations during World War I* (Cambridge University Press, 1993), 57, 134–5.

18   Carmel Shute, 'Heroes and Heroines: Sexual Mythology in Australia', *Hecate* 1, no. 1 (1975): 6–22; Marilyn Lake, 'Mission Impossible: How Men Gave Birth to the Australian Nation – Nationalism, Gender and other Seminal Acts', *Gender & History* 4, no. 3 (1992): 305–22; Marilyn Lake and Joy Damousi (eds.), *Gender and War: Australians at War in the Twentieth Century* (Cambridge University Press, 1995).

19   Marilyn Lake, 'The Power of Anzac', in M. McKernan and M. Browne (eds.), *Australia: Two Centuries of War and Peace* (Australian War Memorial and Allen & Unwin, 1988), 194–222, quote at 221. The critique of the RSSILA (RSL) was taken up by Martin Crotty in, for example, 'The Veterans' Voice: The Returned Sailors' and Soldiers' Imperial League, 1916–19' in Ashley Ekins (ed.), *1918: Year of Victory* (Exisle, 2010), 226–43.

20   K. S. Inglis, 'The Substitute Religion', *Nation*, 23 April 1960, reprinted in Craig Wilcox (ed.), *Observing Australia 1959–1999: K. S. Inglis* (Melbourne University Press, 1999), 63–70.

21   K. S. Inglis, *Sacred Places: War Memorials in the Australian Landscape* (Miegunyah Press, 1998).

22   Inga Clendinnen, *The History Question: Who Owns the Past?*, *Quarterly Essay* 23, 2006; for Clendinnen's understanding of Anzac, see also Andrew Crook, 'It's War: Anzac Day Dissenters Create Bitter Split Between Historians', *Crikey*, 19 April 2010 <www.crikey.com.au/2010/04/19/its-war-anzac-day-dissenters-create-bitter-split-between-historians>; Bruce Scates, *Return to Gallipoli: Walking the Battlefields of the First World War* (Cambridge University Press, 2006).

23   Alistair Thomson, *Anzac Memories: Living with the Legend* (Oxford University Press, 1994).

24   See for example, Christina Twomey, *The Battle Within: POWS in Postwar Australia* (NewSouth, 2018); Chris Dixon, 'Redeeming the Warrior: Myth-Making and Australia's Vietnam Veterans', *Australian Journal of Politics & History* 60, no. 2 (2014): 214–28; Mia Martin Hobbs, '"We Went and Did an Anzac Job": Memory, Myth, and the Anzac Digger in Vietnam', *Australian Journal of Politics & History* 64, no. 3 (2018): 480–97; Mia Martin Hobbs, '"We, to Them, Are Their Heroes": Narratives of Rescue in White Australian Veterans' Memories of the Vietnamese', *Australian Journal of Politics & History* 71, no. 1 (2025): 496-519.

25 The literature is extensive but key works have been Stephen Garton,
    The Cost of War: Australians Return (Oxford University Press, 1996);
    Joy Damousi, *The Labour of Loss: Mourning, Memory and Wartime
    Bereavement* (Cambridge University Press, 1999); Joy Damousi, *Living
    with the Aftermath: Trauma, Nostalgia and Grief in Post-war Australia*
    (Cambridge University Press, 2001); Tanya Luckins, *The Gates of Memory:
    Australian People's Experiences and Memories of Loss in the Great
    War* (Curtin University Books, 2004); Marina Larsson, *Shattered Anzacs:
    Living with the Scars of War* (UNSW Press, 2009).

26 Twomey, 'Trauma and the Reinvigoration of Anzac'.

27 Joan Beaumont, 'Commemoration in Australia: A Memory Orgy?',
    Australian Journal of Political Science 50, no. 3 (2015): 536–44.

28 Robin Prior, *Gallipoli: The End of the Myth* (UNSW Press, 2009), xvi;
    Robin Prior, 'The Myths of Gallipoli' in Raelene Francis and Bruce Scates
    (eds.), *Beyond Gallipoli: New Perspectives on Anzac* (Monash University
    Publishing, 2016), 13–20.

29 Jenny Macleod and Gizem Tongo, 'Between Memory and History:
    Remembering Johnnies, Mehmets and the Armenians', in Francis and
    Scates (eds.), *Beyond Gallipoli*, 21–34. See also Vicken Babkenian and
    Peter Stanley, *Armenia, Australia & the Great War* (NewSouth, 2016).

30 Peter Stanley, *Bad Characters; Sex, Crime, Mutiny, Murder and the
    Australian Imperial Force* (Pier 9, 2010). For Ekins, see 'Fighting to
    Exhaustion: Morale, Discipline and Combat Effectiveness in the Armies
    of 1918', in Ekins (ed.), *1918*, 111–29.

31 Raden Dunbar, *The Secrets of the Anzacs: The Untold Story of Venereal
    Disease in the Australian Army, 1914–1919* (Scribe, 2014); and Ian
    Howie-Willis, *VD: The Australian Army's Experience* (Big Sky, 2020);
    Noah Riseman and Shirleene Robinson, *Pride in Defence: The Australian
    Military & LGBTI Service Since 1945* (Melbourne University Press, 2020).

32 'Our Objectives', *Honest History,* updated 26 June 2013 <honesthistory.
    net.au/wp/about-us/our-objectives/>.

33 David Stephens, '"Johnnies and Mehmets": Kemal Ataturk's "Quote"
    is an Anzac Confidence Trick', *Sydney Morning Herald,* 24 April 2017
    <www.smh.com.au/opinion/johnnies-and-mehmets-kemal-ataturks-
    quote-is-an-anzac-confidence-trick-20170423-gvqkrx.html>.

34 David Stephens, 'Total Australian Spending on World War I Centenary:
    An Aide Memoire for the Curious', *Honest History,* 19 February 2019
    <honesthistory.net.au/wp/stephens-david-total-australian-spending-on-
    world-war-i-centenary-an-aide-memoire-for-the-curious>.

35 James Brown, *Anzac's Long Shadow: The Cost of Our National Obsession*
    (Redback, 2014), 108.

36 See Brown, *Anzac's Long Shadow,* chapter 1; and Jo Hawkins, 'Anzac
    for Sale: Consumer Culture, Regulation and the Shaping of a Legend',
    Australian Historical Studies 46, no. 1 (2015): 7–26; Jo Hawkins,
    Consuming Anzac: The History of Australia's Most Popular Brand
    (UWAP, 2018).

37   Marilyn Lake, Henry Reynolds, Joy Damousi and Mark McKenna, *What's Wrong with Anzac? The Militarisation of Australian History* (NewSouth, 2010).

38   See further Peter Stanley, *Beyond the Broken Years: Australian Military History in 1000 Books* (NewSouth, 2024), 203–8.

39   For example, Riseman and Robinson, *Pride in Defence*; Noah Riseman and Richard Trembath, *Defending Country: Aboriginal and Torres Strait Islander Military Service Since 1945* (University of Queensland Press, 2016); Peter Rees, *Other Anzacs: The Extraordinary Story of Our World War I Nurses* (Allen & Unwin, 2009); Georgeina Whelan, 'We Are All Anzacs', *Time*, 18 April 2005 <time.com/archive/6672524/we-are-all-anzacs>.

40   Frank Lampart, at the Dedication Ceremony of the Aboriginal and Torres Strait Islander War Memorial, Adelaide, 10 November 2013, cited in Joan Beaumont, 'Commemoration', in Joan Beaumont and Alison Cadzow (eds.), *Serving Our Country: Indigenous Australians, War, Defence and Citizenship* (NewSouth, 2018), 324.

41   'Moving Rendition of *Last Post* Recorded with Didgeridoo for First Time', ABC Listen, 10 November 2023 <www.abc.net.au/listen/programs/kimberley-mornings/the-last-post/103092604>.

42   '"Neo-Nazis" boo Welcome to Country Address at Melbourne Anzac Day Dawn Service', ABC News <www.abc.net.au/news/2025-04-25/melbourne-anzac-day-welcome-to-country-hecklers/105215124>.

43   Csongor G. Oltvolgyi, Carla Meurk and Ed Heffernan, 'Suicide and suicidality in Australian Defence Force veterans: A systematic scoping review', *Australian & New Zealand Journal of Psychiatry* 58, no. 9 (2024): 760–74.

CHAPTER 2 THE FORGOTTEN ANZACS

1   The Gallipoli gallery at the Australian War Memorial cites Bean's ascription of these qualities to the Australian soldiers.

2   Stan Victor D'Altera, interviewed by Alistair Thomson, Australian Veterans of the Great War: Oral History Project, 1984. Transcript available in: Alistair Thomson, 'Forgotten Anzacs: Radical diggers challenge an Australian legend', Australian War Memorial, 7–22 <www.awm.gov.au/collection/C254876>.

3   Fred Farrall, interviewed by Alistair Thomson, Australian Veterans of the Great War: Oral History Project, 1984. Transcript available ibid.

4   Ern Morton, interviewed by Alistair Thomson, Australian Veterans of the Great War: Oral History Project, 1984. Transcript available ibid.

5   Sid Norris, interviewed by Alistair Thomson, Australian Veterans of the Great War: Oral History Project, 1984. Transcript available ibid.

6   Australian Veterans of the Great War: Oral History Project, Australian War Memorial, 1984. The wartime and postwar experiences of most working-class diggers were similar to those of the radical diggers in this book, but men like Fred Farrall developed a more radical understanding of their experiences.

7   Morton, 64.

8   D'Altera, 10–12.

9   Norris, 87.

10   The young C. E. W. Bean describes such life in his book *On the Wool Track* (Alston Rivers, 1920).

11   Morton, 65.

12   Farrall, 25.

13   John Keegan, *The Face of Battle* (Penguin, 1978, first published 1976), 48–9; Robert Graves, *Goodbye to All That* (Jonathan Cape, 1929), 236; Bill Gammage, *The Broken Years* (Penguin, 1975, first published 1974), 257.

14   Farrall, 29.

15   Paul Fussell's influential cultural history of *The Great War and Modern Memory* (Oxford University Press, 1975) concludes that the dominant British myth of the war is ironic. Other historians argue that this ironic memory coexists with a more patriotic story of gallant officers and loyal Tommies sticking out the war with true British character (unlike the mutinous French, Germans and Russians). The Anzac legend is not so unique. See Alun Howkins, 'The Monocled Mutineer', *New Socialist*, November 1980.

16   Morton, 67.

17   Farrall, 32.

18   Morton, 67.

19   Norris, 91.

20   'September 1915', in Kevin Fewster (ed.), *Gallipoli Correspondent: The Frontline Diary of C. E. W. Bean* (George Allen & Unwin, 1983), 156–9; C. E. W. Bean, *The Story of Anzac: Official History of Australia in the War of 1914–1918*, vol. 1 (University of Queensland Press, 1981, first published 1921), 571.

21   D'Altera, 12.

22   Norris, 90.

23   Currey O'Neil (ed.), *Bill Harney's War* (Currey O'Neil Press, 1980), 20.

24   Farrall, 33.

25   D'Altera, 12.

26   Farrall, 35.

27   John Keegan analyses this perverse psychology of fear in *The Face of Battle*, 45–52.

28   Farrall, 36.

29   Morton, 67.

30   Norris, 91.

31   D'Altera.

32   Norris, 88, 91.

33   C. E. W. Bean, *The AIF in France 1916: Official History of Australia in the War of 1914–1918*, vol. III (Angus & Robertson, 1929), 56–7.

34   Norris, 92.

35   William Allison and John Fairley, *The Monocled Mutineer* (Quartet Books, 1979), 66–104. The anti-authoritarian, 'wild colonial' image of the

diggers is still popular in Britain and was recently perpetuated in the BBC television series *The Monocled Mutineer*.

36   Farrall, 37–8.

37   D'Altera, 'War and Peace', *Smith's Weekly*, 1 August 1931.

38   '18 June 1915', in Fewster, *Gallipoli Correspondent*.

39   George Coppard, *With a Machine Gun to Cambrai: The Tale of a Tommy in Kitchener's Army, 1914–1918* (His Majesty's Stationery Office, 1969), 107.

40   Russel Ward, *The Australian Legend* (Oxford University Press, 1958); Marilyn Lake, 'The Power of Anzac', in Michael McKernan and Margaret Brown (eds.), *Australia: Two Centuries of War and Peace* (Australian War Memorial/Allen & Unwin, 1988).

41   Morton, 69.

42   Fussell, *The Great War and Modern Memory*, 82–90.

43   Morton, 75.

44   Fred Farrall and Sid Norris both mention this practice of 'fragging'. In other interviews, veterans Jack Flannery and E. L. Cuddeford from the western suburbs of Melbourne also describe fragging. Flannery recalls of the officers, 'Well, they don't last long if they're bad'. Australian Veterans of the Great War: Oral History Project, Jack Flannery, 22; E. L. Cuddeford, 12–13.

45   Lloyd Robson, 'The Origin and Character of the First AIF; 1914–1918: Some Statistical Evidence', *Historical Studies* 15, no. 61 (1973): 737–49.

46   Mike Roper, 'Memories of the Depression', *Melbourne Historical Journal* 13 (1981): 25.

47   O'Neil, *Bill Harney's War*, 25.

48   Farrall, 39.

49   Morton, 74.

50   D'Altera, 15.

51   Morton, 73.

52   Norris, 97.

53   The second half of the original chapter deals with returned servicemen's experiences in Australia after the war. Alistair Thomson, 'The forgotten Anzacs', no. MSS1180, Australian War Memorial <www.awm.gov.au/collection/C254876>.

54   For further elaboration of these experiences, see Alistair Thomson, *Anzac Memories: Living with the Legend* (Oxford University Press, 1994), 145.

CHAPTER 3 A MAN OF DISTINCTION?

1   Commonwealth War Graves Commission <www.cwgc.org/visit-us/find-cemeteries-memorials/cemetery-details/2600/esquelbecq-military-cemetery/>.

2   See, for example, Will Davies, *The Forgotten: The Chinese Labour Corps and the Chinese Anzacs in the Great War* (Wilkinson, 2020); Mark Dapin, *Jewish Anzacs: Jews in the Australian Military* (NewSouth, 2017); John Williams, *German Anzacs and the First World War* (UNSW Press, 2003); Elena Govor, *Russian Anzacs in Australian History* (UNSW Press,

2005); Joan Beaumont and Allison Cadzow (eds.), *Serving Our Country: Indigenous Australians, War, Defence and Citizenship* (NewSouth, 2018).

3   Permakoff, Nicholas, National Archives of Australia (NAA) B2455.

4   Karen Agutter, 'Foreign-Born Soldiers in the AIF: Australia's Multinational Fighting Force', in Kate Ariotti and James E. Bennett (eds.), *Australians and the First World War: Local-Global Connections and Contexts* (Palgrave Macmillan, 2017), 12; Govor, *Russian Anzacs*, 4, 6.

5   Govor, *Russian Anzacs*, 6.

6   'Russians in Australia May Enlist', *Age* (Melbourne), 15 October 1914, 8; 'Russians in Australia to Fight', *Register* (Adelaide), 31 December 1915, 4; 'Russians Must Enlist', *Advertiser* (Adelaide), 4 January 1916, 8.

7   'Russian Reservists Call to Colours', NAA MP16/1 1915/3/1674.

8   'Russians Must Enlist', *Sun* (Sydney), 22 February 1916, 6; 'All Russians Must Enlist', *Daily Herald* (Adelaide), 20 May 1916, 4.

9   Govor, *Russian Anzacs*, 75. Owing to an arrangement with the Russian imperial government, Russians could enlist in the AIF without becoming naturalised subjects. 'Russians May Be Enlisted Without Naturalisation', *Herald* (Melbourne), 24 February 1916, 10; 'Russians in the AIF', *Brisbane Courier*, 25 February 1916, 8.

10   Govor, *Russian Anzacs*, 75.

11   Ibid, 76.

12   Raymond Evans, *The Red Flag Riots: A Study of Intolerance* (University of Queensland Press, 1988), 32.

13   Govor, *Russian Anzacs*, 169.

14   Ibid, 169–70.

15   O.C. Darlinghurst Detention Barracks to O.C. Milson Island, 16 December 1916, Permakoff, Nicholas, NAA B2455.

16   Summary of Evidence in the Case of No. 7286 Private Nicholas Permakoff, 4th Aus Bn, NAA A471/1 8266.

17   Ibid.

18   *4th Battalion War Diary*, Australian War Memorial (AWM) 23/21/40.

19   Govor, *Russian Anzacs*, 166.

20   Ibid, 165, 171–3. Govor cites several cases of Russian soldiers being sent back to Australia 'on account of Russian nationality', including men with exemplary service records. One nurse of Russian origin was also terminated from the AIF due to suspicions she was 'an enemy national'.

21   Ibid, 184.

22   Proceedings of Court of Enquiry … 30th day of June 1918, Permakoff, Nicholas, NAA B2455.

23   Ibid.

24   Ibid.

25   Ibid.

26   'Report on accidental or self-inflicted injuries', Permakoff, Nicholas, NAA B2455.

27   Ibid.

28 British War Office, *Manual of Military Law* (His Majesty's Stationery Office, 1914), esp. 19–20.

29 British War Office, *Statistics of the Military Effort of the British Empire During the Great War, 1914–1920* (His Majesty's Stationery Office, 1922), esp. 648–9. Some historians have disputed the accuracy of these figures and have suggested that records are incomplete. Gerard Oram, for example, has claimed a figure of 361. See Gerard Oram, *Military Executions During World War I* (Palgrave Macmillan, 2002), 3–4.

30 Steven R. Welch, 'Military justice', in 1914–1918 Online: International Encyclopedia of the First World War <encyclopedia.1914-1918-online.net/article/military-justice/>.

31 *Defence Act*, 1903–09, section 98 <classic.austlii.edu.au/au/legis/cth/num_act/da190915190983/>.

32 C. E. W. Bean, *The Official History of Australia in the War of 1914–1918*, vol. V: *The A.I.F. in France during the Main German Offensive 1918* (University of Queensland Press, 1983, first published 1937), 26–32.

33 Present-day value of Permakoff's estate calculated using The Reserve Bank of Australia's online calculator <www.rba.gov.au/calculator/annualPreDecimal.html>.

34 Carol Rosenhein, *The Man Who Carried the Nation's Grief: James Malcolm Lean MBE and the Great War Letters* (Big Sky, 2016), 259.

35 Agutter, 'Foreign-Born Soldiers', 18–19.

36 Michael Challinger, *Anzacs in Arkhangel: The Untold Story of Australia and the Invasion of Russia, 1918–19* (Hardie Grant, 2010), 184–5.

37 K. S. Inglis and Jock Phillips, 'War Memorials in Australia and New Zealand: A Comparative Survey,' *Australian Historical Studies* 24, no. 96 (1991): 185–6; K. S. Inglis, *Sacred Places: War Memorials in the Australian Landscape* (Miegunyah Press, 1998), 184–5.

38 *The Constitution of the Returned Sailors' and Soldiers' Imperial League of Australia*, 5–6. National Library Australia (NLA) MS 6609/5/387a; *Soldier*, 4 no. 162, 1 August 1919, 30; Returned Sailors' and Soldiers' Imperial League of Australia, Verbatim report, Interviews, Minister of Defence, 1919, NLA MS6609/517; *Diggers' Gazette*, 1 no. 13, 15 May 1920, 30–1.

39 See Clem Lloyd and Jacqui Rees, *The Last Shilling: A History of Repatriation in Australia* (Melbourne University Press, 1994).

40 *After the Battle*, no. 45, 1984, 53.

41 *After the Battle*, no. 32, 1981, 28–42; Paul Johnson, *The Plot of Shame: US Military Executions in Europe During World War II* (Frontline, 2023), esp. 2–4, 220–3.

42 AWM Roll of Honour (Policy), AWM 746/001/002/01/B.

43 AWM Board of Management, 8 November 1955, AWM170 105715 1/75.

44 AWM Board of Management, 7 December 1954, AWM170 105715 1/74.

45 AWM Board of Management, 10 December 1956, AWM315 746/001/002 03. For an overview of the Roll of Honour and the deliberations over who should be included and who should not, see Michael McKernan,

Here Is Their Spirit: A History of the Australian War Memorial 1917–1990 (University of Queensland Press, 1991), 226–32.

46   AWM Board of Management, 10 December 1956.

47   Ibid.

48   Ibid.

49   Ibid.

50   AWM Roll of Honour (Policy).

51   AWM Board of Management, 28 October 1957, AWM170 105715 1/78; AWM Roll of Honour (Policy).

52   *Defence Act*, 1903–09, section 98 <classic.austlii.edu.au/au/legis/cth/num_act/da190915190983/>.

53   *The Great War 1914–1918: New Zealand Expeditionary Force – Roll of Honour* (Government Printer, 1924).

54   *Pardon for Soldiers of the Great War Act 2000*, Parliamentary Counsel Office <www.legislation.govt.nz/act/public/2000/0029/latest/DLM67152. html>.

55   Teresa Iacobelli, *Death and Deliverance: Canadian Courts Martial in the Great War* (UBC Press, 2013), 111–28.

56   Kieran McDaid, 'Execution of Irish soldiers Was Unjust, Says Report', *Irish Examiner*, 29 October 2004 <www.irishexaminer.com/news/arid-10058291. html>.

57   *Armed Forces Act 2006* <www.legislation.gov.uk/ukpga/2006/52/contents>. Importantly, the Act does not overturn the convictions of those who were executed.

58   Peter Stanley, *Bad Characters: Sex, Crime, Mutiny, Murder and the Australian Imperial Force* (Pier 9, 2010), 66–9.

CHAPTER 4 'THAT ABORTIVE ORGANISATION KNOWN AS THE IMPERIAL LEAGUE'

1   Cited in Carolyn Holbrook, *Anzac: The Unauthorised Biography* (NewSouth, 2014), 66.

2   Ibid, 117–19.

3   Martin Crotty, 'The Returned Sailors' and Soldiers' Imperial League of Australia 1916–46', in Martin Crotty and Marina Larrson (eds.), *Anzac Legacies: Australians and the Aftermath of War* (Australian Scholarly Publishing, 2010), 166.

4   Ibid, 166–77; Marilyn Lake, 'The Power of Anzac', in Michael McKernan and Margaret Brown (eds.), *Australia: Two Centuries of War and Peace* (Australian War Memorial and Allen & Unwin, 1988), 204–10.

5   See Joan Beaumont, *Australia's Great Depression* (Allen & Unwin, 2022), 203, 230–3.

6   Martin Crotty, 'The RSL and post-First World War Returned Soldier Violence in Australia', in Robert Mason (ed.), *Legacies of Violence: Rendering the Unspeakable Past in Modern Australia* (Berghahn Books Inc, 2016), 186.

7   'SS *Khyber*', BirtwistleWiki, October 2023 <www.birtwistlewiki.com.au/wiki/SS_Khyber>.

8   'The *Khyber* Incident', *West Australian,* 6 May 1919, 5.

9   For example: Bobbie Oliver, 'Disputes, Diggers and Disillusionment: Social and Industrial Unrest in Perth and Kalgoorlie, 1918–24', *Studies in Western Australian History,* 11 (1990): 19–28; Joan Beaumont, *Broken Nation. Australians in the Great War* (Allen & Unwin, 2013), 201, 237; Raymond Evans, *The Red Flag Riots: A Study of Intolerance* (University of Queensland Press, 1988); Raymond Evans, *Loyalty and Disloyalty: Social Conflict on the Queensland Homefront* (Allen & Unwin, 1987); Josephine Murray, 'The Kalgoorlie Woodline Strikes 1919–1920: A Study of Conflict Within the Working Class', *Studies in Western Australian History,* 5 (1982): 2–37; Crotty, 'The RSL and post-First World War Returned Soldier Violence in Australia', 185–98; Andrew Moore, *The Secret Army and the Premier. Conservative Paramilitary Organisations in New South Wales, 1930–32* (UNSW Press, 1989).

10   John Horne, 'Demobilizing the Mind: France and the Legacy of the Great War, 1919–1939', The George Rudé Society <h-france.net/rude/vol2/horne2>.

11   See Clem Lloyd and Jacqui Rees, *The Last Shilling: A History of Repatriation in Australia* (Melbourne University Press, 1994); Sue Summers, 'A Charity or a Right? Repatriation of Disabled Ex-Servicemen in Western Australia, Post-World War I', in Bobbie Oliver and Sue Summers, *Lest We Forget? Marginalised Aspects of Australia at War and Peace* (Black Swan Press, 2014), 15–52; Bobbie Oliver, *War and Peace in Western Australia: The Social and Political Impact of the Great War, 1914–1926* (UWA Press, 1996), 140–53.

12   'Edwin (Ted) Wilkie Corboy, 1896–1950', Parliament of Australia <www.aph.gov.au/About_Parliament/Parliamentary_departments/Parliamentary_Library/Members_who_served_in_First_World_War/Edwin_Wilkie_Corboy>.

13   Joseph Napoleon O'Neill, AIF Nominal Roll, Australian War Memorial, Accession No. AWM 8.

14   Joseph Napoleon O'Neill, Letter to the State ALP Secretary, Alex McCallum, 14 May 1919, Australian Labor Federation State Executive Correspondence Files (hereafter SE Correspondence Files), no. 82, State Archives of Western Australian (SLWA) Accession number 1688A.

15   A. Tyrrell Williams, Secretary, WA Branch of the RSSILA, 'Letters to the Editor', *West Australian,* 25 March 1918, 6; Edgar G. Bartlett, 'Letters to the Editor', *Northam Advertiser,* 29 June 1918, 3.

16   'Second Conference of RSA', *Tambellup Times,* 4 May 1918, 1; 'Returned Soldiers' Meeting', *West Australian,* 5 July 1918, 7; 'Soldiers' Meeting', *Collie Mail,* 15 June 1918, 3.

17   J. R. Duncan, 'A History of the Returned Services League in Western Australia', unpublished research essay, 1962, 62 ff., Anzac House, Perth; 'Verbatim report of the Adelaide Congress, 15/7/19', 31–4, RSL Papers, Series 3, Minutes, Anzac House, Perth. See also 'Returned Soldiers' Conference', *Western Mail* (Perth), 2 October 1919, 10.

18   'Diggers' Grievances. Procession to Parliament. Officers Not Wanted', *West Australian,* 6 January 1919, 4.

19   Ibid.

20   'Returned Soldiers' Affairs. A Too Vigorous Committee. Lively RSA Meeting. Heresy Committee's "Big Broom"', *West Australian*, 9 January 1919, 6.

21   'Returned Soldiers' Association, Perth, April 8', *Western Argus* (Kalgoorlie), 15 April 1919, 30; 'Returned Soldiers. The Trouble in the West', *Advertiser* (Adelaide), 10 April 1919, 9.

22   'Charges Against Returned Soldiers, Perth, April 17', *Register* (Adelaide), 18 April 1919, 5.

23   Joseph Napoleon O'Neill, Letter to Alex McCallum, 19 April 1919, SE Correspondence File, no. 82, SWLA, Accession number 1688A.

24   Alex McCallum, Letter to Joseph Napoleon O'Neill, 14 May 1919, in SE Correspondence File, no. 82, SWLA, Accession number 1688A; 'Position of Returned Soldiers: Disorderly Meeting', *West Australian*, 6 May 1919, 5.

25   The Returned Soldiers' and Sailors' Labor League of Queensland, *Soldiers and the Labor Movement* (Worker Press, 1919), 1–5.

26   Minutes of the State Executive of the ALP, 7 August 1919, SLWA, Accession no. 1573/A/2.

27   'Position of Returned Soldiers', 5.

28   Ibid. At this stage, the RSA was the numerically dominant organisation. The media usually refers to 'the RSA' in its accounts of soldiers' meetings, so I have assumed that these were RSA meetings except where the rival body, the RSSILWA, is specifically named.

29   'Report of a deputation from the State ALP re the Kalgoorlie and Boulder trouble', 18 November 1919, in Premier's Department File No 398/19, SLWA, Accession No. AN2/1, 1496.

30   See, for example, 'Goldfields Trouble. Soldiers and AWU Abortive Conference', *West Australian*, 24 November 1919, 7; 'Goldfields Riots. Police Court Prosecutions', *West Australian*, 28 November 1919, 7.

31   'The Gratuity. Cashing the Bonds. Government's Latest Proposals', *West Australian*, 26 November 1919, 6.

32   'The War Gratuity. Mass Meeting of Soldiers, State Executive Rebuked', *West Australian*, 24 November 1919, 7.

33   'The War Gratuity. Deputation to Senators', *West Australian*, 16 April 1920, 7; 'A "Diggers"' Telegram. Action by the RSA Executive. Messrs Maloney and O'Neill Expelled', *West Australian*, 10 December 1919, 6.

34   Joseph Napoleon O'Neill, Letter to Alex McCallum, 1 January 1920; McCallum to ALP District Councils, 28 January 1920, in SE Correspondence Files, no. 82, SWLA, Accession number 1688A.

35   Joseph Napoleon O'Neill, Letter to Alex McCallum, 9 April 1920, in SE Correspondence Files, no. 82, SWLA, Accession number 1688A.

36   Alex McCallum, APL State Secretary, Letter to Joseph Napoleon O'Neill, 21 April 1920; Joseph O'Neill to Alex McCallum, 9 May 1920; W. J. MacGilvray to Andrew Clementson, 13 May 1920, all in SE Correspondence File no. 82, SWLA, Accession number 1688A.

37   'Verbatim report of Central Council meeting', 3 June 1919, 23, RSL Papers, Series 10; 'Political Tit-Bits', *Westralian Worker*, 23 May 1919; 'Position of Returned Soldiers', 5.

38   'Verbatim report of Central Council meeting', 3 June 1919, 23, National Library of Australia, Accession No. 6609, RSL Papers, Series 10.

39   'Verbatim report of the Fifth Annual Federal Congress of the RSSILA, Perth', April 1920, National Library of Australia, Accession No. 6609, RSL Papers, Series 10.

40   Martin Crotty, '"What More Do You Want?": Billy Hughes and Gilbert Dyett in Late 1919', *History Australia* 16, no. 1 (2019): 52–71 <doi.org/10.1080/14490854.2018.1558069>.

41   Report of the Proceedings of the Fourth Annual Congress of then RSLWA Branch, 28 September 1920, 15, 48. RSL Papers, National Library of Australia, Accession No. 6609, Series 10. Cornell joined the conservative National coalition in 1917. Davy and Colebatch were members of the Western Australian Liberal Party. Wedd was a National Party candidate in several postwar state elections.

42   Murray, 'The Kalgoorlie Woodline Strikes', 22–37; Oliver, 'Disputes', 19–28; Oliver, *War and Peace in Western Australia*, chapters 4 and 5.

43   'The constitution of the Returned Sailors' and Soldiers' Imperial League of Australia, 1919' draft copy, 4, RSL Minutes of General Council and the Federal Executive, National Library of Australia, Accession No. 6609, RSL Papers, Box 82; 'Returned Sailors' and Soldiers' Imperial League of Australia Circular memo to branches, 9/5/18', 2–3, National Library of Australia, Accession No. 6609, RSL Papers, Box 95, File 'RSL Documents 10/5/1916–1919'.

44   Duncan, 'A History of the Returned Services League', 108.

45   'Verbatim report of the Fifth Annual Congress of the RSSILA', Perth, 1920. National Library of Australia, Accession No. 6609.

46   Sir William Birdwood to Sir Francis Newdegate, 29 March 1920, Sir Francis Newdegate Papers, National Library of Australia, Accession No. 1541.

47   'Charge of Stealing. O'Neill in Defence', *West Australian*, 16 April 1920, 7.

48   'Gratuity Bonds. A Disputed Receipt. Committee's Inquiry', *West Australian*, 8 December 1921, 10.

CHAPTER 5 FIGHTING ON THE WESTERN FRONT AND RETURNING HOME TO FIGHT AGAIN

1   'Aboriginal Service During the First World War', Australian War Memorial, 20 December 2019 <www.awm.gov.au/about/our-work/projects/indigenous-service>.

2   'Aboriginal Recruits', *Darling Downs Gazette*, 21 June 1917, 6.

3   Noah Riseman, 'Diversifying the Black Diggers' History', *Aboriginal History* 39 (2015): 137–42.

4   Noah Riseman and Richard Trembath, *Defending Country: Aboriginal and Torres Strait Islander Military Service since 1945* (University of Queensland Press, 2016), 7; James Arden and Richard King, cited in John

Maynard, 'The First World War', in Joan Beaumont and Allison Cadzow (eds.), *Serving Our Country: Indigenous Australians, War, Defence and Citizenship* (NewSouth, 2018), 78.

5   Jessica Horton, '"Willing to Fight to a Man": The First World War and Aboriginal Activism in the Western District of Victoria', *Aboriginal History* 39 (2015): 206.

6   'One of Our Indigenous Soldiers', *Milton Ulladulla Times*, 24 October 2014 <www.ulladullatimes.com.au/story/2639933/one-of-our-indigenous-soldiers/>.

7   R. Johnson, SERN 2660, NAA B2455.

8   Ernest Lacey, SERN 6085 N92079, NAA B2455.

9   A. G. Butler, *Official History of the Australian Army Medical Services, 1914–1918*, vol. III, *Special Problems and Services* (Australian War Memorial, 1943), 744.

10   Correspondence with Michael Bell, Australian War Memorial, 9 August 2024; Ernest Lacey, 6085 N92079, NAA B2455.

11   Louis Lacey, 6086, NAA B2455.

12   Claire Hunter, 'Remembering the Walker Brothers', Australian War Memorial, 4 July 2023 <www.awm.gov.au/articles/blog/edward-walker-and-the-first-world-war>.

13   Ibid.

14   Philippa Scarlett, 'Aboriginal Service in the First World War: Identity, Recognition and the Problem of Mateship', *Aboriginal History* 39 (2015): 170–1.

15   Lacey, 6086, NAA B2455.

16   Scarlett, 'Aboriginal Service in the First World War', 171.

17   Lacey, 6086, NAA B2455.

18   War diary, 17th Battalion, Australian War Memorial, RCDIG1005358 <www.awm.gov.au/collection/AWM4/23/34/34/>; M. C. Wenham, '"My Own Darling Laddie": In search of George Wenham: An Aboriginal ANZAC and the History of Denial' (PhD diss., University of Newcastle, 2015).

19   'Etaples 1917', Australian War Memorial, ART94211 <www.awm.gov.au/collection/C1264376>.

20   G. D. Mitchell, *Backs to the Wall* (Allen & Unwin, 2007, first published 1937), 118.

21   '13 Australian Infantry Battalion', Australian War Memorial <www.awm.gov.au/collection/U51453>.

22   Johnson, SERN 2600, NAA B2455.

23   Hunter, *Remembering the Walker Brothers*.

24   Sam Furphy, 'The Home Front in the First World War', in Beaumont and Cadzow (eds.), *Serving Our Country*, 109–10. See also Bruce Scates and Melanie Oppenheimer, *The Last Battle: Soldier Settlement in Australia 1916–1939* (Cambridge University Press, 2016), 60–5.

25   Andrea Gerrard and Kristyn Harman, 'Lives Twisted out of Shape! Tasmanian Aboriginal Soldiers and the Aftermath of the First World War', *Aboriginal History* 39 (2015): 190; Clem Lloyd and Jacqui Rees, *The Last*

Shilling: A History of Repatriation in Australia (Melbourne University Press, 1994), 107.

26 'Charge Against Publican', *Casino and Kyogle Courier and North Coast Advertiser*, 22 March 1919, 2.

27 'Maclean Police Court', *Daily Examiner* (Grafton), 24 February 1923, 2.

28 Ibid.

29 Ibid.

30 *Daily Examiner* (Grafton), 30 August 1918, 2.

31 Ibid.

32 Lacey, 6805, NAA B2455, 27.

33 Ibid.

34 'Boxers and Their Doings', *Arrow* (Sydney), 24 June 1921, 14.

35 Lacey, 6805, NAA B2455.

36 Scarlett, 'Aboriginal Service in the First World War', 172.

37 John Maynard, *Fight for Liberty and Freedom* (Aboriginal Studies Press, 2014), 40.

38 John Maynard, 'The Rise of the Modern Aboriginal Political Movement, 1924–39', in Beaumont and Cadzow (eds.), *Serving Our Country*, 118.

39 Maynard, *Fight for Liberty and Freedom*, 18–36; John Maynard, 'International Black Influence on Australian Aboriginal Activism', in K. Radcliffe, J. Scott and A. Werner (eds.), *Anywhere but Here: Black Intellectuals in the Atlantic World and Beyond* (University Press of Mississippi, 2014), 106; John Maynard, '"The Age of Unrest, the Age of Dissatisfaction": Marcus Garvey and the Rise of Aboriginal Political Protest 1920–1929', in R. J. Stephens and A. Ewing (eds.), *Global Garveyism* (University of Florida Press, 2019), 231.

40 'Federal Surveillance of Afro Americans (1917–25): The First World War, Red Scare and the Garvey Movement', Lamont Library, Harvard University, Index File A563.

41 F. Maynard, 1927a, Letter to the Premier, New South Wales Premier's Department, correspondence files, NSW State Archives, A27/915.

42 Anonymous letter, one of many cited in Philipa Scarlett, *Aboriginal and Torres Strait Islander Volunteers for the AIF: The Indigenous Response to World War One* (Indigenous Publishing, 2011), 40–5.

43 'Aborigine Congress: Self Determination Sought', *Daily Advertiser* (Wagga Wagga), 12 May 1925, 4.

44 'Australian Aboriginals Progressive Association', *Macleay Chronicle*, 19 August 1925, 3

45 Maynard, *Fight for Liberty and Freedom*, 72.

46 *Negro World*, 2 August 1924.

47 Ibid.

48 *The Voice of the North* (Newcastle, NSW), 11 January 1926.

49 *The Voice of the North* (Newcastle, NSW), 10 October 1927.

50 *The Voice of the North* (Newcastle, NSW), 10 November 1930.

51 Joan Beaumont and Tristan Moss, 'Australian Military Forces in the Second World War', in Beaumont and Cadzow (eds.), *Serving Our Country*, 152–3.

52   Ibid.

53   'Anzac Day Celebrations', *Daily Examiner* (Grafton), 29 April 1930, 2.

54   Maynard, *Fight for Liberty and Freedom*, 144.

55   *Abo Call*, April 1938, 2.

CHAPTER 6 BOLSHEVIK ANZAC

1   *Age (Melbourne)*, 16 September 1918, 4; Wills's Cigarettes War Incidents 2nd series, circa 1918, Papers of John and Roma Gilchrist, State Library of Western Australia (SLWA), ACC 3532A/1. The myth about Throssell's height probably stems from a misreading of a widely republished 1915 article (see below) about Throssell's conduct in battle. The article was based on an interview with Sergeant John MacMillan and claimed 'there is little less than seven feet of him', referring not to Throssell but to MacMillan (who himself was actually 6 feet 4 inches, according to his military record – MacMillan J. L., National Archives of Australia (NAA) BA255, 1965332.

2   *Truth* (Perth), 26 July 1919, 3.

3   'Captain Hugo Throssell, V.C. Declares Himself a Socialist', *Westralian Worker*, 25 July 1919, 4.

4   'His Eyes Are Opened', *Australian Communist*, 31 December 1920, 2.

5   Ibid.

6   Frank Bongiorno, *Dreamers and Schemers: A Political History of Australia* (La Trobe University Press, 2022), 59–62.

7   Ric Throssell, *My Father's Son* (William Heinemann, 1989), 17–18.

8   Frank Eric Throssell (1881–1917), known as Eric or Ric, namesake of Hugo's son, Ric Prichard Throssell (1922–99).

9   'On the Home Front: Australians and the 1914 Drought', in Georgina H. Endfield and Lucy Veale (eds.), *Cultural Histories, Memories and Extreme Weather: A Historical Geography Perspective* (Taylor & Francis, 2017), 34.

10   Hugo Vivian Hope Throssell, Military Record, NAA B2455, 1; Neville Browning and Ian Gill, *Gallipoli to Tripoli: History of the 10th Light Horse Regiment AIF: 1914–1919* (Hesperian Press, 2012), 15.

11   *Lieut Throssell VC: The Man I Want to Follow* (Colebatch & Co, c. 1915).

12   *Sunday Times*, 26 December 1915, 4.

13   Gallaher Great War Victoria Cross Heroes series no. 71, c. 1915, Past Time Postcards; Sniders and Abrahams Australian VCs and Officers, no date, Australian War Memorial (AWM), RC00752; Wills's Cigarettes War Incidents; 'Fighting Jim', c. 1915, Katharine Susannah Prichard Papers, National Library of Australia (NLA), MS6201/1/9.

14   *Northam Courier*, 5 May 1916, 3.

15   Katharine Susannah Prichard, *Child of the Hurricane: An Autobiography* (Angus & Robertson, 1963), 233.

16   'His Eyes Are Opened'.

17   Bongiorno, *Dreamers and Schemers*, 144.

18   Bobbie Oliver, '"For Only by the OBU Shall Workmen's Wrongs Be Righted". A Study of the One Big Union Movement in Western Australia, 1919 to 1922', *Papers in Labour History* 5 (1990): 2.

19   Prichard, *Child of the Hurricane*, 251.

20   "Engineering your own soul": Theory and Practice in Communist Biography and Autobiography & Communism: A Love Story (PhD diss., RMIT University, 2007), 110.

21   Bobbie Oliver, 'Fremantle's "Bloody Sunday"', in Charlie Fox, Bobbie Oliver and Lenore Layman (eds.), *Radical Perth, Militant Fremantle* (Black Swan Press, 2017), 35–42.

22   'His Eyes Are Opened'.

23   Ibid.

24   Prichard to Nettie Palmer, August 1919, Palmer Papers, NLA, MS1174/1/2206.

25   Jeff Rickertt, '"What is Good Enough for the Bolsheviks is Sure Good Enough for Me!": Founding the Communist Party of Australia, October 1920', *Queensland Journal of Labour History* 31 (19 March 2021): 29–32.

26   *Tribune*, 4 December 1963, 5.

27   *West Australian*, 17 June 1901, 4.

28   *West Australian*, 25 July 1917, 6.

29   *Westralian Worker*, 16 July 1920, 5.

30   Prichard to Nettie Palmer.

31   *Bunbury Herald*, 5 October 1918, 5.

32   *Westralian Worker*, 14 November 1919, 4.

33   Stuart Macintyre, *The Reds* (Allen & Unwin, 1998), 234.

34   Ibid, 27.

35   The initial security report on Throssell in November 1919 stated, 'he was struck on the head at Gallipoli and further he was a victim to Cerebro-spinal Meningitis, his mind perhaps having been affected'. Throssell, Katharine 1919–1940, ASIO file, NAA A6119, 27370, 127.

36   Throssell, *My Father's Son*, 81.

37   Ric Throssell, *Wild Weeds and Windflowers: The Life and Letters of Katharine Susannah Prichard* (Angus & Robertson, 1975), 62.

38   Prichard, *Child of the Hurricane*, 255.

39   *West Australian*, 12 May 1933, 1

40   *Workers' Weekly*, 2 June 1933, 1.

41   *West Australian*, 15 May 1933, 6.

42   Nathan Hobby, *The Red Witch: A Biography of Katharine Susannah Prichard* (Miegunyah Press, 2022), 231.

43   Prichard, *Child of the Hurricane*, 261.

44   *West Australian*, 20 November 1933, 7.

45   Throssell, Katharine 1919–1940, ASIO file, NAA A6119, 27370, 126.

46   Prichard to Ric Throssell, 9 December 1945, Ric Throssell Papers, NLA, MS8071.

47   *West Australian*, 21 November 1933, 14.

48   Throssell, *My Father's Son*, 74–75.

49 John Hamilton, *The Price of Valour: The Triumph and Tragedy of a Gallipoli Hero, Hugo Throssell, VC* (Pan Macmillan, 2012), 286, 288, 291.

50 *Northam Advertiser*, 11 October 1924, 2; *Northam Advertiser*, 10 January 1925, 2.

51 *Northam Advertiser*, 29 April 1925, 3.

52 *Listening Post*, 18 September 1936, 28.

53 *Truth* (Perth), 26 July 1919, 3.

54 *Swan Express*, 29 April 1921, 5.

55 *Swan Express*, 16 November 1923, 5.

56 *Daily News*, 26 April 1932, 4.

57 *West Australian*, 26 April 1933, 10.

58 Prichard to Repatriation Commission, 28 January 1934, Hugo Throssell Repatriation Commission file, NAA PP645/1, M5273.

59 Prichard Papers, NLA, MS6201/1/12.

60 Hugo Throssell to RSL, 14 September 1933, Prichard Papers, MS6201/1/12.

61 Throssell, *My Father's Son*, 112–13, 118–19.

62 Hobby, *Red Witch*, 226, 246.

63 *Smith's Weekly*, 11 November 1933, 23.

64 Peter Stanley, 'A Hundred in a Million: Obsession with the Victoria Cross', *Griffith Review* 48 (2015): 268.

65 Joan Beaumont, 'Remembering the Resilient', in Carolyn Holbrook and Keir Reeves (eds.), *The Great War: Aftermath and Commemoration* (UNSW Press, 2019), 151.

66 Ibid.

67 *Westralian Worker*, 25 July 1919, 4.

CHAPTER 7 SOLDIER SUICIDE

1 Royal Commission into Defence and Veteran Suicide, *Final Report, Volume 1: Executive Summary, Recommendations and Fundamentals* (Commonwealth of Australia, 2024).

2 John C. Weaver, *Sorrows of a Century: Interpreting Suicide in New Zealand, 1900–2000* (McGill-Queen's University Press, 2014), 9.

3 Ibid, 295–7.

4 Ibid, 9.

5 Olive Anderson, *Suicide in Victorian and Edwardian England* (Clarendon Press, 1987), 3–4.

6 Patricia Jalland, *Australian Ways of Death: A Social and Cultural History, 1840–1918*, ACLS Humanities E-Book (Oxford University Press, 2002), 274.

7 Ibid.

8 Ibid.

9 Jalland, *Australian Ways of Death*, 274–5. George Simpson, 'Introduction', in Emile Durkheim and George Simpson (eds.), *On Suicide: A Study in Sociology* (Routledge, 2005, first published 1897), xiii–xxxvii.

10   Jalland, *Australian Ways of Death*, 275; Sir George Knibbs, 'Suicide in Australia: A Statistical Analysis of the Facts' (Commonwealth Bureau of Census and Statistics, 1912).

11   Jalland, *Australian Ways of Death*, 276; Knibbs, 'Suicide in Australia'.

12   John C. Weaver, *A Sadly Troubled History: The Meanings of Suicide in the Modern Age* (McGill-Queen's University Press, 2009), 62–4.

13   Weaver, *A Sadly Troubled History*, 62–3.

14   Joy Damousi, *Freud in the Antipodes: A Cultural History of Psychoanalysis in Australia* (UNSW Press, 2005); Michael Tyquin, *Madness and the Military: Australia's Experience of Shell Shock in the Great War*, reprint edition (Arden, 2020), 114–16.

15   Tyquin, *Madness and the Military*, 114.

16   Ibid, 107.

17   A. G. Butler, *The Official History of the Australian Army Medical Services in the War of 1914-1918*, Vols I–III (Australian War Memorial, 1938–43).

18   Graham Seal, *Inventing Anzac: The Digger and National Mythology* (University of Queensland Press, 2004), 1–35.

19   D. A. Kent, '*The Anzac Book* and the Anzac Legend: C. E. W. Bean as Editor and Image-Maker', *Historical Studies* 21, no. 84 (1985): 376–90.

20   Joan Beaumont, *Australia's Great Depression: How a Nation Shattered by the Great War Survived the Worst Economic Crisis It Has Ever Faced* (Allen & Unwin, 2022), 233.

21   Ibid, 231.

22   Joan Beaumont, 'The Returned Soldier as a Site of Memory: Employment Preference and War Pensions During the Great Depression in Australia,' *Australian Historical Studies* 52, no. 1 (January 2021): 8–26.

23   Kevin J. Fewster, 'Albert Jacka (1893–1932)', in *Australian Dictionary of Biography*, 18 vols (National Centre of Biography, Australian National University) <adb.anu.edu.au/biography/jacka-albert-6808>.

24   Alistair Thomson, *Anzac Memories: Living with the Legend* (Oxford University Press, 1994).

25   Tyquin, *Madness and the Military*, 157.

26   Edward Davis Millen, cited in Stephen Garton, *The Cost of War: Australians Return* (Oxford University Press, 1996), 81.

27   Clem J. Lloyd and Jacqui Rees, *The Last Shilling: A History of Repatriation in Australia* (Melbourne University Press, 1994), 19–41.

28   Marina Larsson, *Shattered ANZACs: Living with the Scars of War* (UNSW Press, 2009), 18.

29   Garton, *The Cost of War*, 99.

30   Beaumont, *Australia's Great Depression*, 233.

31   Tyquin, *Madness and the Military*, 105.

32   Weaver, *A Sadly Troubled History*, 130.

33   Tyquin, *Madness and the Military*, 101; Stephen Garton, *Medicine and Madness: A Social History of Insanity in New South Wales 1880-1940*, The Modern History Series (UNSW Press, 1988), 11–25.

34   Ibid, 137–8.

35   George Taylor, cited in Garton, *The Cost of War*, 28.

36   Simon Cooke, 'A "Dirty Little Secret"? The State, the Press, and Popular Knowledge of Suicide in Victoria, 1840s–1920s', *Australian Historical Studies* 31, no. 115 (1 October 2000): 318.

37   'Demented Husband', *Brisbane Telegraph*, 14 June 1926, p. 10.

38   'Work performed by Aboriginal Protectors', Queensland Police file Batch 400 M (1) 1903-1905, POL J17, Item ID 86483, Queensland State Archives.

39   David Molloy, SERN 2437, National Archives of Australia (NAA) B2455.

40   Queensland Coronial Archives held at Queensland State Archives, JUS/N706/20/264.

41   Molloy, NAA B2455.

42   David Molloy, Deposits and findings in coroners' inquests, Queensland State Archives (QSA), ITM349301, JUS/N706, 1920/264.

43   'Shooting Tragedy', *Cairns Post*, 13 March 1920.

44   David Molloy, ITM349301.

45   Thomas Beaumont, Deposits and findings in coroners' inquests, QSA, ITM349217, JUS/N621 1917/5.

46   Thomas Beaumont, SERN 1615, B2455, NAA B2455.

47   Ibid.

48   Beaumont, ITM349217.

49   Ibid.

50   Ibid.

51   'Returned Soldier Commits Suicide', *Morning Bulletin* (Rockhampton), 19 December 1916.

52   'Death of Thomas Beaumont,' *Morning Bulletin* (Rockhampton), 6 January 1917.

53   Victor George Wilkins, SERN 2335, NAA B2455.

54   Victor Wilkins, Deposits and findings in coroners' inquests, QSA, ITM349340, JUS/N835 1926/1237.

55   Ibid.

56   Ibid.

57   Ibid.

58   Ibid.

59   'Shearer Commits Suicide,' *Longreach Leader*, 10 December 1926.

60   'Inquiry at Longreach,' *Western Champion (Parkes, NSW)*, 25 December 1926.

61   Ibid.

62   Beaumont, *Australia's Great Depression*, 339.

63   Minutes from Dr J. F. Agnew, Repatriation Department, 14 April 1920, NAA A2489 1920/1739.

64   Larsson, *Shattered ANZACs*, 78.

65   The inclusion period for First World War is 4 August 1914 to 31 March 1921. See Roll of Honour, Australian War Memorial <www.awm.gov.au/commemoration/honour-rolls/roll-of-honour>.

66   Patrick Lindsay, *Shining a Light: Stories of Trauma & Tragedy, Hope &
        Healing* (Commonwealth of Australia, 2024).
67   Royal Commission into Defence and Veteran Suicide, *Final Report*.

CHAPTER 8 'ALIEN TO OUR SPLENDID TRADITION'

1   For national memory, see James V. Wertsch, 'National Memory and
        Where to Find It', in Brady Wagoner (ed.), *Handbook of Culture and
        Memory* (Oxford Academic, 2017), 259–62.
2   Another version attributed to Lord Haw-Haw is that they were 'rats who
        would be smoked out of their holes'.
3   A definitive account of the negotiations leading to the installation of
        the Rats of Tobruk memorial on Anzac Parade can be found in Nicole
        Townsend, '"It Is Vital that We Should Not Keep It to Ourselves": The Rats
        of Tobruk Association and the Siege of Tobruk in Australian Memory',
        Australian Journal of Politics and History, 2025 <doi.org/10.1111/
        ajph.70021>.
4   Caleb Taylor, 'Tom Pritchard, Australia's Last Rat of Tobruk, Dead at 102',
        7News, 6 August 2024 <7news.com.au/sunrise/tom-pritchard-australias-
        last-rat-of-tobruk-dead-at-102-c-15603580>.
5   'Sir Peter Cosgrove's Emotional Push to Remember the Rats'
        [sic] of Tobruk', 7News, YouTube, 2024 <www.youtube.com/
        watch?v=E8sOs0nNkSE>.
6   Michael Grady, 'The Battles of Tobruk, 1941–42', National
        Archives (London), 2022 <webarchive.nationalarchives.gov.uk/
        ukgwa/20250613153734/https:/blog.nationalarchives.gov.uk/the-battles-
        of-tobruk-1941-42-part-one>.
7   David Coombes, *Morshead: Hero of Tobruk and El Alamein* (Oxford
        University Press, 2001), 108.
8   'Tobruk Ferry Service', Wikipedia, March 2025.
9   *Truth* (Brisbane), 26 January 1941, 13.
10   '"Anzac" Hat Hoisted over Tobruk', *Goulburn Evening Post*, 24 January
        1941, 5.
11   'Heroes of Tobruk', *Sydney Morning Herald*, 2 August 1941, 10.
12   'The Tobruk Garrison', *Shepparton Advertiser*, 11 August 1941, 2.
13   'Indomitable Tobruk', *Guardian* (Perth), 22 August 1941, 4. This was only
        one of many papers that carried this letter.
14   'Song of Tobruk', *Kyabram Free Press and Rodney and Deakin Shire
        Advocate*, 5 August 1941, 3.
15   Department of Veterans' Affairs, 'Greece and Crete', 2020
        <www.dva.gov.au/recognition-and-commemoration/memorials/
        memorials-europe/greece-and-crete#:~:text=Australian%20losses%20
        were%20594%20dead%2C%201%2C001%20wounded%20and,the%20
        German%2C%20Italian%20and%20Bulgarian%20occupation%20of%20
        1941-44>.
16   Graham Freudenberg, *Churchill and Australia* (Pan Macmillan, 2008),
        294.

17   The account that follows draws on the official histories: Barton Maughan, *Tobruk and El Alamein*, vol. II, *Australia in the War of 1939–1945*, series 1 – Army (Australian War Memorial, 1966), 305–13, 351–3, 376–80, 397–9; and Paul Hasluck, *The Government and the People 1939–1941*, vol. 1, *Australia in the War of 1939–1945*, series 4 – Civil (Australian War Memorial, 1952), 616–24. See also more recent studies: John Hetherington, *Blamey: Controversial Soldier* (Australian War Memorial and Australian Government Publishing Service, 1973); David Horner, *Blamey: The Commander-in-Chief* (Allen & Unwin, 1998), 231–47; Freudenberg, *Churchill and Australia*, 290–305.

18   Freudenberg, *Churchill and Australia*, 295; Horner, *Blamey*, 231–2.

19   Coombes, *Morshead*, 120.

20   Ibid.

21   Maughan, *Tobruk and El Alamein*, 311.

22   Ibid, 290.

23   Coombes, *Morshead*, 117, 111.

24   Winston Churchill, *The Second World War*, vol. III, *The Grand Alliance* (Cassell, 1950), 368.

25   Freudenberg, *Churchill and Australia*, 292.

26   Horner, *Blamey*, 242.

27   Maughan, *Tobruk and El Alamein*, 377.

28   Freudenberg, *Churchill and Australia*, 300.

29   I. S. O. Playfair, *The Mediterranean and the Middle East*, vol. III (Her Majesty's Stationery Office, 1960), 25.

30   *The Rats of Tobruk*, Dockermania, YouTube, 1944 <https://www.youtube.com/watch?v=wf3UDRrH7NM>.

31   Chester Wilmot, *Tobruk 1941: Capture, Siege, Relief* (Penguin, 2009, first published 1944), 343, 353.

32   The following account draws on David Reynolds, 'Churchill's Memoirs and Australia's War: Imperial Defence and "Inexcusable Betrayal"', *War & Society* 24, no. 2 (2005): 35–52; and David Reynolds, *In Command of History: Churchill Fighting and Writing the Second World War* (Allen Lane, 2004), 245–6, 257–9.

33   Cited in Reynolds, 'Churchill's Memoirs', 35.

34   Ibid, 41–2.

35   Ibid, 43–4.

36   'Clear the Air on Tobruk', *Herald* (Melbourne), 17 February 1950, 4.

37   'Reply to Churchill on Tobruk', *Morning Bulletin* (Rockhampton), 23 February 1950, 8.

38   'Taint on Tobruk', *Sun News-Pictorial* (Melbourne), 17 February 1950, 16.

39   'A.I.F. in Tobruk "Wanted to Stay"', *Daily Telegraph* (Sydney), 18 February 1950, 4.

40   Reynolds, 'Churchill's Memoirs', 44.

41   Hasluck, *The Government and the People*, 624.

42   Playfair, *The Mediterranean and the Middle East*, 23–4.

43   Maughan, *Tobruk and El Alamein*, 383.

44   Gavin Long, *The Six Years War: A Concise History of Australia in the 1939–45 War* (Australian War Memorial and Australian Government Publishing Service, 1973), 98–9.

45   K. S. Inglis, *Sacred Places: War Memorials in the Australian Landscape* (Miegunyah Press, 1998), 376.

46   See 'Rockhampton Rats of Tobruk War Memorial' <http://www.anzacsquare.qld.gov.au/memorials/rockhampton-rats-tobruk-war-memorial>.

47   'Tobruk Memorial Pool' <www.monumentaustralia.org/themes/conflict/ww2/display/90973-tobruk-memorial-pool>.

48   '80th Anniversary of the Siege of Tobruk' <www.monumentaustralia.org/display/119680-80th-anniversary-of-the-siege-of-tobruk>.

49   L. R. Killeen, Secretary and Manager, NCDC, to Secretary, Prime Minister's Department, 5 July 1968, National Archives of Australia (NAA) A1340 82/775 pt 1.

50   J. G. Gorton to C. J. Hughes, federal president of the Rats of Tobruk Association, 14 December 1970, ibid. The negotiations of the late 1960s are detailed in Townsend, 'It Is Vital'.

51   Kevin R. Black, Secretary National Memorials Committee, to Secretary and Manager, NCDC, n.d., A1340 82/775 pt 1.

52   A. J. W. Powell, NCDC, to A. S. Blum, Secretary Department of the Capital Territory, n.d., ibid.

53   Cited in Townsend, 'It Is Vital'.

54   'War Stories: Rats of Tobruk', Australian War Memorial, YouTube, 19 May 2011 <www.youtube.com/watch?v=USvx4PwbtmA>.

55   'Siege of Tobruk', Australian War Memorial <www.awm.gov.au/articles/encyclopedia/tobruk>.

56   Ibid.

57   Peter FitzSimons, *Tobruk* (HarperCollins, 2009, first published 2006), 533–5, 552–5, 557–9.

58   Horner, *Blamey*, 243, 246.

59   Freudenberg, *Churchill and Australia*, 304–05.

60   'Remembering Australia's Rats of Tobruk as Final Member Dies', *The Project*, Network Ten, YouTube, 2024 <www.youtube.com/watch?v=5XgCpgbR_pY>.

61   Taylor, 'Tom Pritchard'.

62   'Last Remaining "Rat" of Tobruk Dies Aged 102', ABC News, 2024, YouTube <www.youtube.com/watch?v=TIkhZZlLX6s>.

63   See, for example, Les Carlyon, *Gallipoli* (Macmillan, 2001), 519–25; Robin Prior, *Gallipoli: The End of the Myth* (UNSW Press, 2009), 226–32.

64   The official historian Allan S. Walker concluded that '[in] general the standard of health in Tobruk had remained high … Undoubtedly the defenders of Tobruk were under tension, but psychological factors were more important than physical wear and tear', *Middle East and Far East*, vol. II, *Australia in the War of 1939–1945*, series 5 – Medical (Australian War Memorial, 1953), 210.

65   Hetherington, *Blamey*, 184.

66   Hasluck, *The Government and the People*, 622.

CHAPTER 9 THE INCONVENIENT ENTITY

1   J. R. McClelland, J. Fitch and W. Jonas, *The Report of the Royal Commission into British Nuclear Tests in Australia*, vols 1–2 (Australian Government Publishing Service, 1985).

2   Ibid, 31.

3   Australian Government Department of Veterans' Affairs, 'Support for Civilians and Participants in the British Nuclear Tests', 27 November 2024 <www.dva.gov.au/get-support/financial-support/income-support/support-civilians-and-participants-british-nuclear-tests>.

4   J. L. Symonds, *A History of British Atomic Tests in Australia* (Australian Government Publishing Service, 1985).

5   Lorna Arnold and Mark Smith, *Britain, Australia and the Bomb: The Nuclear Tests and Their Aftermath* (Palgrave Macmillan, 2006), 274.

6   Adriana Petryna, *Life Exposed: Biological Citizens after Chernobyl* (Princeton University Press, 2013), xx.

7   Ibid.

8   E. W. Titterton, 'Ban War, Rather than Atomic Weapons', *Advertiser* (Adelaide), 22 September 1952; 'Atom Bomb Explodes', *News* (Adelaide), October 3, 1952; 'Our Atom Age Has Arrived', *News* (Adelaide), 3 October 1952; 'Atom Bomb Test', *Canberra Times*, 4 October 1952; 'History Has Been Made at Monte Bello', *Sydney Morning Herald*, 4 October 1952; 'The Big Bomb's Away!', *Argus* (Melbourne), 4 October 1952; 'Behind the Blast', *Argus* (Melbourne), 4 October 1952; 'British Bomb Deadliest Yet', *Daily Telegraph* (Sydney), 4 October 1952.

9   'Atomic Test off W.A.', *Daily Telegraph* (Sydney), 15 May 1952; 'Atomic Test May Be in September', *Weekly Times* (Melbourne), 21 May 1952; 'Atomic Test Ships Sail', *Wellington Times* (New South Wales), 4 August 1952.

10   'Aust. Part in Big Atom Test', *Daily Telegraph* (Sydney), 1 August 1953; 'Continuous Airlift from Woomera to Atomic Test Site', *Canberra Times*, 18 August 1953; 'Picked Force Builds Desert Atomic Test Base', *Armidale Express*, 16 October 1953.

11   'A-Bomb Blast Sweeps Central Australian Desert for 5 Miles', *Canberra Times*, 16 October 1953.

12   Petar Djokovic, 'Operations Hurricane and Mosaic', *Semaphore*, no. 2 (2016).

13   Symonds, *A History of British Atomic Tests in Australia*, 67.

14   Statement by Vincent John Douglas, Royal Commission into British Nuclear Tests in Australia: Statements from Australian Witnesses A–D, 1984–1985, National Australian Archives (NAA) 416015, A6450 1, 419–26.

15   Ibid.

16   Djokovic, 'Operations Hurricane and Mosaic'.

17   Statement by Vincent John Douglas.

18 HMAS *Hawkesbury* Reports of Proceedings, October 1952, quoted in Djokovic, 'Operations Hurricane and Mosaic'.
19 Howard L. Rosenberg, *Atomic Soldiers: American Victims of Nuclear Experiments* (Beacon Press, 1980), 38–75.
20 Ibid, 38.
21 Statement by William Robert Bovill, Royal Commission into British Nuclear Tests in Australia: Statements from Australian Witnesses A–D, 1984–1985, NAA 416015, A6450 1, 11–14.
22 Ibid.
23 Statement by Allen Henry Clark, Royal Commission into British Nuclear Tests in Australia: Statements from Australian Witnesses A–D, 1984–1985, NAA 416015, A6450 1, 296–7.
24 Statement by John Noel Coolahan, Royal Commission into British Nuclear Tests in Australia: Statements from Australian Witnesses A–D, 1984–1985, NAA 416015, A6450 1, 334–7.
25 Statement by Roy Edward Cosgrove, Royal Commission into British Nuclear Tests in Australia: Statements from Australian Witnesses A–D, 1984–1985, NAA 416015, A6450 1, 16–26.
26 Ibid.
27 Statement by Reginald Robert Beaver, Royal Commission into British Nuclear Tests in Australia: Statements from Australian Witnesses A–D, 1984–1985, NAA 416015, A6450 1, 156–63.
28 Ibid.
29 Statement by Leslie Victor Beevers, Royal Commission into British Nuclear Tests in Australia: Statements from Australian Witnesses A–D, 1984–1985, NAA 416015, A6450 1, 165–70.
30 Ibid.
31 Statement by Vincent Cannon, Royal Commission into British Nuclear Tests in Australia: Statements from Australian Witnesses A–D, 1984–1985, NAA 416015, A6450 1, 273–9.
32 Ibid.
33 Statement by Lewis Gordon Angel, Royal Commission into British Nuclear Tests in Australia: Statements from Australian Witnesses A–D, 1984–1985, NAA 416015, A6450 1, 93–7.
34 Ibid.
35 No 82 (Bomber) Wing – Operation 'Totem' – Report, NAA 28/34/AIR, BP349/1.
36 Ibid.
37 Buffalo Trials – Indoctrinee Force Instruction No. 1, DEFE16/541, National Archives (United Kingdom).
38 Ibid.
39 Ibid.
40 Statement by John Raymond Broadbent, Royal Commission into British Nuclear Tests in Australia: Statements from Australian Witnesses A–D, 1984–1985, NAA 416015, A6450 1, 224–32.
41 Ibid.

42   Ibid.

43   Paul Malone, 'Troops Close to Atomic Site', *Canberra Times*, 24 May 1984.

44   See Glenn Mitchell, 'See an Atomic Blast and Spread the Word: Indoctrination at Ground Zero', in Jordan Goodman, Anthony McElligott and Lara Marks (eds.), *Useful Bodies: Humans in the Service of Medical Science in the Twentieth Century* (Johns Hopkins University Press, 2003).

45   Statement by John Raymond Broadbent.

46   Statement by Arthur Alfred Andrews, Royal Commission into British Nuclear Tests in Australia: Statements from Australian Witnesses A–D, 1984–1985, NAA 416015, A6450 1, 79–91.

47   Ibid.

48   Ibid.

49   Kyle Harvey, 'Pacific Concerns: Nuclear Weapons and the Peace Movement in Australia, 1960–1967', in Christian Philip Peterson, William M Knoblauch and Michael Loadenthal (eds.), *The Routledge History of World Peace Since 1750* (Routledge, 2018).

50   Australian Nuclear Veterans Association [New South Wales] <web.archive.org/web/20150412135658/http://anva.org.au>.

51   Ibid.

52   Ibid.

53   Ibid.

54   *Atom Veteran* 1, no. 6 (July 1982).

55   D. Corrigan, *Commissioner for Employees' Compensation Annual Report: 1983–84* (Australian Government Publishing Service, 1984), 4–5.

56   Statement by Stanley Gerald Rae, Royal Commission into British Nuclear Tests in Australia: Statements from Australian Witnesses A–D, 1984–1985, NAA 416015, A6450 1, 378–80.

57   Statement by Vincent John Douglas.

58   Statement by Roy Edward Cosgrove.

59   McClelland, Fitch and Jonas, *The Report of the Royal Commission into British Nuclear Tests in Australia: Conclusions and Recommendations*, 31.

60   Peter Yeend and Amanda Biggs, *Australian Participants in the British Nuclear Tests (Treatment) Bill 2006* (Department of Parliamentary Services, 2006).

61   Ibid, 12.

62   Australian Nuclear Veterans Association.

63   Matt McDonald, 'Lest We Forget: The Politics of Memory and Australian Military Intervention', *International Political Sociology* 4, no. 3 (2010): 290–2.

64   Ibid.

65   Clem Lloyd and Jacqui Rees, *The Last Shilling: A History of Repatriation in Australia* (Melbourne University Press, 1994), 17.

66   McDonald, 'Lest We Forget'.

67   Cited in Philip Payton, *'Repat': A Concise History of Repatriation in Australia* (Australian Government Department of Veterans' Affairs, 2018), vii.

68   Statement by Roy Edward Cosgrove.
69   Statement by Francis William Beitzel, *Royal Commission into British Nuclear Tests in Australia: Statements from Australian Witnesses A–D, 1984–1985*, NAA 416015, A6450 1, 172–5.
70   Ibid.
71   Australian Government Department of Veterans' Affairs, 'Support for Civilians and Participants in the British Nuclear Tests'.
72   Ibid.
73   Clinton Fernandes, *Subimperial Power: Australia in the International Arena* (Melbourne University Press, 2022).
74   Ibid.

CHAPTER 10 'NO MORE SILENCE ABOUT SEXUAL VIOLENCE'

1   *Sydney Morning Herald*, 26 April 1977, 1.
2   *Sydney Morning Herald*, 17 February 1977, 6.
3   Christina Twomey, 'Trauma and the Reinvigoration of Anzac: An Argument', *History Australia* 10, no. 3 (2013): 85–108.
4   National Solicitor for RSL to Minister for Capital Territory, 11 March 1981, Papers of RSL, NLA, MS6609, Box 665, Folder: 'Wimmin Against Rape'.
5   Jocelynne Scutt, *Anzac 1984: The Issues for and Against* (Community Research Action Centre, Monash University, 1984).
6   Mark McKenna, 'Anzac Day: How Did It Become Australia's National Day?', in Marilyn Lake, Henry Reynolds, Joy Damousi and Mark McKenna (eds.), *What's Wrong with Anzac? The Militarisation of Australian History* (UNSW Press, 2010) and Twomey, 'Trauma and the Reinvigoration of Anzac'.
7   Caitlin Reed Weisner, 'The War on Crime and the War on Rape: The LEAA and Philadelphia WOAR, 1974–1978', *Modern American History* 7, no. 1 (2024): 24–45.
8   *Sydney Morning Herald*, 30 October 1974, 2; *Age* (Melbourne), 3 December 1974, 2. On the establishment of rape crisis centres, see Marilyn Lake, *Getting Equal: The History of Australian Feminism* (Allen & Unwin, 1989), 260–1.
9   *Age* (Melbourne), 22 November 1974, 12. 'Biographies for Victorian Women's Liberation and Lesbian Feminist Archives Inc: Women Against Rape (WAR), University of Melbourne Archives, UMA ACE 200000221, Women Against Rape (WAR) [Hereafter WAR Archives], Box 1.
10   *Age* (Melbourne), 20 April 1977, 8.
11   *Age* (Melbourne), 9 September 1976, 12.
12   *Sydney Morning Herald*, 29 August 1977, 7.
13   *Tribune*, 13 April 1977, 11.
14   *Tribune*, 8 March 1978, 6.
15   Women Against Rape, *Women at W.A.R.* (Falling Wall Press, 1978). Women Against Rape, or W.A.R, was a grassroots multiracial women's group founded in London in 1976.

16   *War on Rape* (Women Against Rape Collective, 1977).

17   Susan Brownmiller, *Against Our Will: Men, Women and Rape* (OpenRoad Integrated Media, online edition, first published 1975), 20.

18   *Tribune*, 27 April 1977, 3.

19   *Tharunka*, 1 May 1978, 4.

20   Ibid.

21   *Canberra Times*, 26 April 1978, 31.

22   Ibid.

23   *Tharunka*, 28 May 1979, 14.

24   *Women's Liberation Newsletter*, May 1979, 5–6, in WAR Archives, Box 1.

25   *Sydney Morning Herald*, 21 February 1977, 6.

26   Ibid.

27   *Tharunka*, 28 May 1979, 14; *Courier Mail*, 26 April 1979; *Canberra Times*, 26 April 1979, 8.

28   Anna McCormack, Letter to Editor, *Tribune*, 9 May 1979, 10.

29   *Canberra Times*, 26 April 1980, 11.

30   *Canberra Times*, 4 September 1980, 8.

31   *Woroni*, 18 September 1980, 6.

32   *Canberra Times*, 4 September 1980, 8.

33   *Canberra Times*, 15 January 1981, 8.

34   Flyer: 'A Non Violent Womens March', c. 1981, Papers of W.E.L. (Australia), NLA MS 3683, Box 38: Series 14, Folder 33. 'Anzac Day March, 1981'.

35   Ibid.

36   Open letter from Canberra Anzac Day March Collective, n.d. c. 1981, Papers of W.E.L. (Australia), NLA MS 3683, Box 38: Series 14, Folder 33. 'Anzac Day March, 1981'.

37   Mrs Bev Cains, letter to Sir William Keys, President RSL, 15 April 1981, RSL Papers, NLS BS6609, Box 665, 'Wimmin Against Rape'.

38   Alf Clarke, President ACT RSL, letter to Members of the National Executive, 29 April 1981, RSL Papers, NLA BS6609, Box 665, 'Wimmin Against Rape'.

39   *Senate Hansard*, 28 April 1981, 1432.

40   Susanne Davies, 'Women, War and the Violence of History: An Australian Perspective', in Sandy Cook and Judith Bessant (eds.), *Women's Encounters with Violence: Australian Experiences* (Sage, 1997).

41   *Canberra Times*, 27 April 1981, 1; *Senate Hansard*, 28 April 1981, 1429.

42   *Age* (Melbourne), 27 April 1981, 5; *Sydney Morning Herald*, 25 April 1981, 4.

43   *Sydney Morning Herald*, 25 April 1981, 4.

44   Community Law Reform Committee of the Australian Capital Territory, *Report on Peaceful Assemblies*, ACTCLRC12, 1997, paras 16–18 on 'Anzac Day Protests' <www.austlii.edu.au/cgi-bin/viewdoc/au/other/lawreform/ACTCLRC/1997/12.html>.

45   *Age* (Melbourne), 27 April 1981, 5.

46   Robin Handley, 'The Public Assemblies Ordinance (ACT)', *Legal Service Bulletin*, 7, April 1982, 81–4.

47 *Wimmin News,* published by Canberra Women's Centre, vol. 5, May 1982, 2. Cited in Gail Radford, 'Women Against Rape in War', Canberra Museum and Gallery, 9 October 2019 <www.cmag.com.au/blog/women-against-rape-in-war#_ftn27>.

48 Community Law Reform Committee of the Australian Capital Territory, *Report on Peaceful Assemblies.*

49 Kate Harrison, 'What Did You Do in the War, Mummy?', *Legal Services Bulletin* 8, June 1983, 132.

50 *Sydney Morning Herald,* 23 April 1983, 2.

51 Harrison, 'What Did You Do in the War, Mummy?', 132.

52 *Sydney Morning Herald,* 20 April 1984, 2.

53 Erika Sabina, 'Rape: Our Window of Vulnerability: The Sydney Women Against Rape Collective', *Social Alternatives* 4, no. 3 (1984): 18.

54 *Sydney Morning Herald,* 23 April 1983, 2.

55 Chris Ronalds, 'Anzac Day and the Aftermath', *Legal Services Bulletin* 8, June 1983, 133; Harrison, 'What Did You Do in the War, Mummy?', 133.

56 *Sydney Morning Herald,* 24 April 1986.

57 Genevieve Lloyd, 'Selfhood, War and Masculinity', in Carole Pateman and Elizabeth Grosz (eds.), *Feminist Challenges: Social and Political Theory* (Allen & Unwin, 1986), 68–75. Lloyd informed the archetypal feminist analysis of Anzac, Marilyn Lake's 'Mission Impossible: How Men Gave Birth to the Australian Nation – Nationalism, Gender and other Seminal Acts', *Gender & History* 4, no. 3 (1992): 305–22.

58 *Sun,* 26 April 1984, 1; *Age* (Melbourne), 25 April 1984, 4; Adrian Howe, 'Anzac Mythology and the Feminist Challenge' (1983) reprinted in Marilyn Lake and Joy Damousi (eds.), *Gender and War: Australians at War in the Twentieth Century* (Cambridge University Press, 1985), 303–10.

59 *Herald,* 25 April 1985, 3; *Sydney Morning Herald,* 24 April 1986, 17.

60 *Sun,* 27 April 1987.

61 *Age* (Melbourne), 27 April 1987.

62 'I Wonder Why We Bothered', *Sun,* 26 April 1985; Les Tanner cartoon, *Age* (Melbourne), 25 April 1985, 11.

63 Ann Curthoys, '"Vietnam": Public Memory of an Anti-War Movement', in Kate Darian-Smith and Paula Hamilton (eds.), *Memory and History in Twentieth Century Australia* (Oxford University Press, 1994), 123–8.

64 Gammage's later reflection quoted in *Australian,* 21 April 1997, 9.

65 *Age* (Melbourne), 6 October 1978, 11; Patsy Adam-Smith, *The Anzacs* (Nelson, 1978).

66 Didier Fassin and Richard Rechtman, *The Empire of Trauma: An Inquiry into the Condition of Victimhood* (Princeton University Press, 2009), 77–96; Allan Young, *The Harmony of Illusions: Inventing Post Traumatic Stress Disorder* (Princeton University Press, 1995), chapter 3.

67 Susan Jeffords, *The Remasculinization of America: Gender and the Vietnam War* (Indiana University Press, 1989).

68 *Sun,* 26 April 1985, 3; *Adelaide Advertiser,* 26 April 1985, 3.

69   *Canberra Times*, 21 April 1985, 1.
70   *Age* (Melbourne), 27 April 1987, 19.
71   *Tharunka*, 28 May 1979, 14; *Tribune*, 29 April 1981, 3.
72   *Sydney Morning Herald*, 12 January 1987, 2.
73   Catriona Elder, '"I Spit on Your Stone": National Identity, Women Against Rape and the Cult of Anzac in Australia', in Maja Mikula (ed.), *Women, Activism and Social Change: Stretching Boundaries* (Taylor and Francis, 2005), 94–106: Howe, 'Anzac Mythology and the Feminist Challenge'; Davies, 'Women, War and the Violence of History'.
74   *Australian*, 23 April 2011.

CHAPTER 11 ANTI-WAR VETERAN ACTIVISM FROM VIETNAM TO THE WAR ON TERROR

1   Email correspondence with Gerry Binder, 1 March 2017.
2   Interview with Gerry Binder, 25 April 2024.
3   This pattern is also evident among the much larger cohort of anti-war American Vietnam veterans I interviewed; see Mia Martin Hobbs, *Return to Vietnam: An Oral History of American and Australian Veterans' Journeys* (Cambridge University Press, 2021).
4   Interview with Gerry Binder.
5   Interview with Rob de Kok, 28 March 2017.
6   Ibid.
7   Terry Burstall, cited in Mark Dapin, *The Penguin Book of Australian War Writing* (Penguin Group, 2011), 371.
8   Interview with Rob de Kok.
9   Burstall, cited in Dapin, *Penguin Book of Australian War Writing*, 376.
10   Terry Burstall, cited in Stuart Rintoul, *Ashes of Vietnam: Australian Voices* (William Heinemann, 1987), 50.
11   Interview with Gerry Binder.
12   Ibid.
13   Ibid.
14   Terry Burstall, *A Soldier Returns: A Long Tan Veteran Discovers the Other Side of Vietnam* (University of Queensland Press, 1990), 9–10.
15   Interview with Rob de Kok.
16   Burstall, *A Soldier Returns*, 10–11.
17   Interview with Rob de Kok.
18   Burstall, *A Soldier Returns*, 187.
19   John Murphy, review of *Ashes of Vietnam* in *Australian Historical Studies* 23, no. 93 (1989): 500; Terry Burstall, 'Policy Contradictions of the Australian Task Force Vietnam, 1966', *Vietnam Generation* 3, no. 2 (1991): 35–49.
20   For examples of the 'quagmire' narrative, see: Robert McNamara, *In Retrospect: The Tragedy and Lessons of Vietnam* (Knopf, 1996); John Murphy, *Harvest of Fear: A History of Australia's Vietnam War* (Allen & Unwin, 1993).
21   Burstall, *A Soldier Returns*, 10–11.

22   Senior curator at the Australian War Memorial, cited in Adam Lucas, 'Australia's Viet Nam War', in *VietNam Voices: Australians & The Vietnam War* (Casula Powerhouse Arts Centre, 2000), 18.

23   *Dog Tags: An International Collection of Painting, Poetry & Sculpture by Vietnam Veterans*, Australian War Memorial, 1992 <www.awm.gov.au/collection/C235420>.

24   For example, Ray Beattie, *Doomed in Advance*, created in 1976 and acquired in 1994, ART40885, Australian War Memorial <www.awm.gov.au/collection/C174664>; Dennis Tew, *Names from the Book of the Dead*, created in 1992 and acquired in 1993, ART90255, Australian War Memorial <www.awm.gov.au/collection/C285300>. Quote describing Australian veteran artists in Lucas, 'Australia's Viet Nam War', 20.

25   'Veterans Put Vietnam in a New Perspective', *Uniken*, 14 September 1990 <nla.gov.au/nla.obj-252714605/view?sectionId=nla.obj-255243782&partId=nla.obj-252716093#page/n4/mode/1up>.

26   Lex McAuley, *The Battle of Long Tan: The Legend of Anzac Upheld* (Hutchinson, 1986); Bill Hayden, 'Speech: Vietnam Veterans' Remembrance Day, Australian Vietnam Forces National Commemoration, Canberra', Governor-General of the Commonwealth of Australia, 18 August 1992 <www.gg.gov.au/about-governor-general/media/speech-vietnam-veterans-remembrance-day-australian-vietnam-forces-national-memorial-canberra>.

27   Terry Eichler, in Jan Dirk Mittmann, *Beyond Duc My*, VCA Film and Television Digital Archive Project, YouTube, 1999 <www.youtube.com/watch?v=gkbTJf-Hg3w>.

28   Kate McCulloch, 'The Representation of War in Museums', *Double Dialogues* 7 (2007) <doubledialogues.com/article/the-representation-of-war-in-museums>.

29   Kathleen James, 'The Lingering Effects of Vietnam: Veterans' Art from "Dog Tags" to "Nam Bang!"', *Art Monthly Australasia* 240 (June 2011).

30   Interview with Gerry Binder.

31   For example, Gary McKay, *Vietnam Fragments* (Allen & Unwin, 1992); Gregory Pemberton (ed.), *Vietnam Remembered* (Lifetime, 1993).

32   Bob Buick and Gary McKay, *All Guts and No Glory: The Story of a Long Tan Warrior* (Allen & Unwin, 2000), 113.

33   Burstall, *A Soldier Returns*, 190

34   Terry Burstall, 'Hero of Long Tan's "Mercy Killing" Upsets Comrades', *7.30 Report*, ABC News, 17 August 2000.

35   Bob Buick, 'Hero of Long Tan's "Mercy Killing" Upsets Comrades', *7.30 Report*, ABC News, 17 August 2000.

36   John Howard, 'United States of America: Terrorist Attacks', House of Representatives, Parliamentary Debates, Commonwealth of Australia, 17 September 2001; Matt McDonald, '"Lest We Forget": The Politics of Memory and Australian Military Intervention', *International Political Sociology* 4, no. 3 (2010): 296.

37   Interview with Gerry Binder.

38   'Anti-War Protests Continue for Fourth Day', ABC News, 23 March 2003 <www.abc.net.au/news/2003-03-23/anti-war-protests-continue-for-fourth-day/1822236>.

39   'About Us', Australian Veterans for Peace <ozpeacevets.blogspot.com/>.

40   Interview with Gerry Binder.

41   Timor Sea Justice Campaign <www.laohamutuk.org/OilWeb/Boundary/TSJC/web/campaign.htm>.

42   'Anti-War Veterans Speak Out', Freedom Socialist Party, Summer/Autumn 2009 <socialism.com/fsb-article/anti-war-veterans-speak-out/>.

43   Hamish Chitts, 'Iraq Veterans Against the War Tour Speech', *Conscientious Dissent*, 11 August 2007 <http://conscientiousdissent.blogspot.com/2007>

44   Interview with Gerry Binder.

45   Interview with Rob de Kok.

46   Rob de Kok, 'This (Shared) Life', *Weekend Australian*, 22 May 2010.

47   Rob de Kok, 'I Am a Vietnam Veteran Not Marching Today', 25 April 2010 <robdekok.com/downloads>.

48   de Kok, 'This (Shared) Life'.

49   Noel Turnbull, 'Some Reflections on Anzac Day and Military Service', Noel Turnbull, 24 April 2024 <https://noelturnbull.com/blog/some-reflections-on-anzac-day-and-military-service/>.

50   Interview with Les Vincent.

51   Interview with Graham Edwards, 18 December 2015.

52   Interview with Wal Cameron, 18 May 2016.

53   Interview with John Osko, 13 May 2025.

54   Conversation with serving member at the Australian War College, March 2025.

55   Interview with John Abernathy.

56   Interview with Brian Cleaver, 23 June 2016.

57   Ibid.

58   Jerry Lembcke, *The Spitting Image: Myth, Memory, and the Legacy of Vietnam* (NYU Press, 2000).

59   Mia Martin Hobbs, '"We Went and Did an Anzac Job": Memory, Myth, and the Anzac Digger in Vietnam', *Australian Journal of Politics & History* 64, no. 3 (2018): 480–97.

60   Thomas D. Beamish, Harvey Molotch and Richard Flacks, 'Who Supports the Troops? Vietnam, the Gulf War, and the Making of Collective Memory', *Social Problems* 42, no. 3 (August 1995): 344–60 <doi.org/10.2307/3096852>.

61   'Navy Deserter Faces Music in Band Hall', *Canberra Times*, 25 September 1990 <http://nla.gov.au/nla.news-article122313013>.

62   'Politics Has No Place in Shipboard Loyalties', *Canberra Times*, 10 September 1990 <http://nla.gov.au/nla.news-article122310044>.

63   'Support the Troops, PM Tells Protesters', *Sydney Morning Herald*, 21 March 2003 <www.smh.com.au/world/middle-east/support-the-troops-pm-tells-protesters-20030321-gdggqm.html>.

64 'Veterans Accuse Govt of Disregarding Anzac Spirit', ABC News, 18 April 2005 <www.abc.net.au/news/2005-04-18/veterans-accuse-govt-of-disregarding-anzac-spirit/1553494>.

65 'ADF Veterans: The Way Australia Goes to War Must Change', Australians for War Powers Reform <warpowersreform.org.au/adf-veterans-the-way-australia-goes-to-war-must-change/>.

66 Sue Wareham, email correspondence, 14 May 2024.

67 'Gulf War Veterans Hand Back Medals', *Sydney Morning Herald*, 20 March 2003 <www.smh.com.au/national/gulf-war-veterans-hand-back-medals-20030320-gdgglq.html>; 'Support the Troops'. See also, 'Gulf War Veterans Return Their Medals in protest', ABC News, 20 March 2003 <www.abc.net.au/news/2003-03-20/gulf-war-veterans-return-medals-in-protest/1819900>.

68 'Anti-War Vets Protest at Clinton Meeting', SBS News, 8 November 2010 <www.sbs.com.au/news/article/anti-war-vets-protest-at-clinton-meeting/21ishntul>.

69 For example, see Daniel Hurst, 'War Hero Finally Wins Longest Battle', *Brisbane Times*, 18 August 2011 <www.brisbanetimes.com.au/national/queensland/war-hero-finally-wins-longest-battle-20110817-1iy6b.html>; 'Ben Roberts-Smith, Australia's Most Highly Decorated Living Soldier', ABC Radio, 25 April 2017 <www.abc.net.au/listen/programs/melbourne-breakfast/ben-roberts-smith/8469842>.

70 Amanda Meade, 'SBS Sports Reporter Scott Mcintyre Sacked over "Despicable" Anzac Tweets', *Guardian Australia*, 26 April 2015 <www.theguardian.com/media/2015/apr/26/sbs-sports-reporter-scott-mcintyre-sacked-over-direspectful-anzac-tweets>; Marissa Calligeros, 'Yassmin Abdel-Magied Courts Controversy with Anzac Day Facebook Post', *Sydney Morning Herald*, 25 April 2017 <www.smh.com.au/national/yassmin-abdelmagied-courts-controversy-with-anzac-day-facebook-post-20170425-gvs7yp.html>.

71 'A Proud Veteran Will Not Join Anzac Parade', *SBS Mandarin*, 25 April 2018 <www.sbs.com.au/language/chinese/en/podcast-episode/a-proud-veteran-will-not-join-the-anzac-parade/uvxsa6hy8>.

72 'Politics Has No Place in Shipboard Loyalties'.

73 Hamish Chitts, 'Stand Fast Barracks Speak-Outs Roll On', *Direct Action*, October 2010; Rosanna Ryan, 'Media Outnumber Activists at War Rally', ABC News, 9 September 2010 <www.abc.net.au/news/2010-09-09/media-outnumber-activists-at-war-rally/2254788>.

74 Interview with Anonymous, 13 June 2016.

75 Interview with Gerry Binder.

76 Email correspondence with Gerry Binder.

77 Interview with Anonymous.

78 Interview with Rob de Kok.

79 Ibid.

80 Chitts, 'Stand Fast Barracks Speak-Outs Roll On'.

81 Interview with Gerry Binder.

82 Ibid.

83   Chip Henriss, 'Australian Army Veteran Opposes the war in Iraq and Afghanistan at Palm Sunday Rally', Takvera – John Englart, YouTube, 5 April 2009 <www.youtube.com/watch?v=5vlhJBkUrgY>.

84   'Navy Deserter Faces Music in Band Hall'; Interview with Gerry Binder.

85   Jeff Doyle, 'Dismembering the Anzac Legend: Australian Popular Culture and the Vietnam War', *Vietnam Generation* 3, no. 2 (1991): 118–19.

86   Martin Hobbs, '"We Went and Did an Anzac Job"', 486.

87   One exception is Hamish Chitts' article 'Australian Death Squads in Afghanistan', which still mostly focuses on the American Phoenix Program in Vietnam. Chitts, 'Australian Death Squads in Afghanistan', *Direct Action*, June 2009.

88   In the US, see Neela Banerjee, 'Few but Organized, Iraq Veterans Turn War Critics', *New York Times*, 23 January 2005 <www.nytimes. com/2005/01/23/us/few-but-organized-iraq-veterans-turn-war-critics. html>; 'Occupy Veterans' Movement Growing across US', ABC News (US), 31 October 2011 <abcnews.go.com/Politics/occupy-veterans-movement-growing/story?id=14848003>. In the UK, see Ben Griffin, 'We Will Not Fight for Queen and Country', Oxford Union debate, YouTube, April 2013 <www.youtube.com/watch?v=eccMTIcd3ww>; Matt Dathan, 'Veterans Throw Away Their War Medals in Disgust at British Air Strikes in Syria', *Independent*, 8 December 2015 <www. independent.co.uk/news/uk/politics/veterans-throw-away-their-war-medals-in-disgust-at-british-air-strikes-in-syria-a6765446.html>.

89   For example, Smedley Butler, Siegfried Sassoon and Wilfred Owen.

CHAPTER 12 CRIMES CLOAKED IN ANZAC

1   Author conversation with Samantha Crompvoets, 19 August 2025; Samantha Crompvoets, *Blood Lust, Trust & Blame* (Monash University Publishing, 2021), 17–19. Crompvoets explains that the Lindt Café siege in 2014 had prompted debate about the use of Special Forces in counterterrorism operations.

2   Jeffrey Sengelmann, 'Special Operations Futures Summit', 28–30 April 2015 <www.defence.gov.au/sites/default/files/2021-10/Special-Operations-Futures-Summit-28-30-Apr-15.pdf>.

3   Ibid.

4   Rashida Yosufzai, 'The Expert Whose Work Sparked the Afghan War Crimes Report Says the Alleged Conduct Is "Unbelievable"', SBS News, 19 November 2020 <www.sbs.com.au/news/article/the-expert-whose-work-sparked-the-afghan-war-crimes-report-says-the-alleged-conduct-is-unbelievable/3t6p6276b>.

5   Andrew Probyn, 'The Afghanistan War Crimes Report Is a Nasty but Necessary Reckoning of a Shameful Recent History', ABC News, 19 November 2020 <www.abc.net.au/news/2020-11-19/afghanistan-war-crime-report-necessary-reckoning-of-history/12899984>.

6   Mark Baker, 'Murder He Wrote', *Inside Story*, 2 June 2023 <insidestory. org.au/murder-he-wrote/>.

7   Andrew Tillet, 'Inside the Warrior Culture that Shamed Australia', *Australian Financial Review*, 21 November 2020 <www.afr.com/politics/federal/inside-the-warrior-culture-that-shamed-australia-20201120-p56gc9>.

8   Martin Crotty and Carolyn Holbrook, 'The Anzac Legend Has Blinded Australia to Its War Atrocities. It's Time for a Reckoning', *The Conversation*, 7 December 2020 <theconversation.com/the-anzac-legend-has-blinded-australia-to-its-war-atrocities-its-time-for-a-reckoning-151022>.

9   Tom Frame, *Veiled Valour: Australian Special Forces in Afghanistan and War Crimes Allegations* (NewSouth, 2022), 2–3; Maeve McGregor, 'How Ben Roberts-Smith Shattered the Anzac Myth', *Crikey*, 2 June 2023 <www.crikey.com.au/2023/06/02/ben-roberts-smith-war-crimes-anzac/>.

10   Chris Masters, *Flawed Hero: Truth, Lies, and War Crimes* (Allen & Unwin, 2023), 533.

11   Paul Brereton, *Inspector-General of the Australian Defence Force Afghanistan Inquiry Report: Questions of Unlawful Conduct Concerning the Special Operations Task Group in Afghanistan* (Commonwealth of Australia, 2020), 334.

12   'Dawn of the Legend: 25 April 1915', Australian War Memorial <www.awm.gov.au/visit/exhibitions/dawn>.

13   Brereton, *Afghanistan Inquiry Report*, 24.

14   Jamie McKinnell and Paige Cockburn, 'Witness Tells Ben Roberts-Smith Trial He Drank from Dead Man's Prosthetic Leg to "Bond" with Other Soldiers', ABC News, 8 February 2022 <www.abc.net.au/news/2022-02-08/sas-soldier-denies-throwing-ben-roberts-smith-under-bus-in-court/100812550>.

15   Masters, *Flawed Hero*, 91; Mark Willacy, *Rogue Forces: An Explosive Insiders' Account of Australian SAS War Crimes in Afghanistan* (Simon & Schuster, 2021), 231–2.

16   Nick McKenzie, Chris Masters and Joel Tozer, 'Buried Evidence and Threats: How Ben Roberts-Smith Tried to Cover up His Alleged Crimes', *Age* (Melbourne), 11 April 2021 <www.theage.com.au/national/buried-evidence-and-threats-how-ben-roberts-smith-tried-to-cover-up-his-alleged-crimes-20210408-p57hlr.html>.

17   Masters, *Flawed Hero*, 236.

18   Willacy, *Rogue Forces*, 250–3.

19   Masters, *Flawed Hero*, 123.

20   'Video – Inside the Fat Ladies Arms', ABC News, 24 August 2021 <www.abc.net.au/news/2021-08-24/the-fat-ladies-arms-sas-bar-in-afghanistan/13512072>.

21   McKinnell and Cockburn, 'Witness tells Ben Roberts-Smith Trial He Drank from Dead Man's Prosthetic Leg'.

22   Brereton, *Afghanistan Inquiry Report*, 446.

23   Samantha Crompvoets, 'Special Operations Command (SOCOMD) Culture and Interactions: Insights and Reflection', Department of Defence, January 2016, 3 <afghanistaninquiry.defence.gov.au/resources>.

24   Ibid, 5.

25   Brereton, *Afghanistan Inquiry Report*, 29.

26   Ibid, 447, 33.

27   Bradley Chapman, in Mark Willacy, 'Culture of Cover-Up', ABC News, 17 March 2020 <www.abc.net.au/news/2020-03-17/four-corners-sas-allegations-war-crimes/12028522>.

28   Willacy, *Rogue Forces*, 251–3, 181.

29   Ben Doherty, '"Hundreds" of Photos Exist of Australian Soldiers Drinking from Dead Afghan's Prosthetic Leg, Court Told', *Guardian Australia*, 3 June 2021 <www.theguardian.com/australia-news/2021/jun/02/hundreds-of-photos-exist-of-australian-soldiers-drinking-from-dead-afghans-prosthetic-leg-court-told>.

30   Dan Oakes and Jeremy Story Carter, 'Australian Special Forces Instagram Account Mocks War Crime Allegations, Calls to "Make Diggers Violent Again"', ABC News, 3 September 2020 <www.abc.net.au/news/2020-09-03/instagram-account-from-australian-special-forces-mocks-killings/12595062>.

31   Crompvoets, 'Special Operations Command (SOCOMD) Culture and Interactions: Insights and Reflection', 3.

32   Willacy, *Rogue Forces*, 201.

33   Ibid, 315.

34   Crompvoets, 'Special Operations Command (SOCOMD) Culture and Interactions: Insights and Reflection', 3.

35   Jeffrey Sengelman, in Frame, *Veiled Valour*, 202.

36   Masters, *Flawed Hero*, 96.

37   Frame, *Veiled Valour*, 200.

38   Masters, *Flawed Hero*, 96.

39   Author interview with former Defence analyst, 18 June 2025.

40   Frame, *Veiled Valour*, 9.

41   Major Jeffrey Sengelmann, 'Commanding in Adversity – Modernising Special Operations Command', Department of Defence, October 2015, 3 <www.defence.gov.au/sites/default/files/2021-10/Commanding-in-Adversity.pdf>.

42   Nick McKenzie, *Crossing the Line: The Inside Story of Murder, Lies and a Fallen Hero* (Hachette, 2023), 23; James Law, 'The Power of Ten: The Heroes Ben Roberts-Smith, VC, Looks up To', News.Com, 10 April 2015 <www.news.com.au/entertainment/tv/tv-shows/the-power-of-ten-the-heroes-ben-robertssmith-vc-looks-up-to/news-story/1e9c3b64bc9e282a16a6521652c44bf0>.

43   Nick McKenzie and Chris Masters, 'Abdul's Brother Went out to Buy Flour. He Never Came Home', *Sydney Morning Herald*, 8 June 2018 <www.smh.com.au/politics/federal/abdul-s-brother-went-out-to-buy-flour-he-never-came-home-20180607-p4zk38.html>.

44   Sean Cowan and Nick Taylor, 'WA Digger Awarded VC Medal', *West Australian*, 22 January 2011 <thewest.com.au/news/australia/wa-digger-awarded-vc-medal-ng-ya-183585>.

45   'Chain of Command Breaks When Esteem Outstrips Rank on the
      Battlefield', *Sydney Morning Herald*, 2 June 2023 <www.smh.com.au/
      politics/federal/chain-of-command-breaks-when-esteem-outstrips-rank-
      on-the-battlefield-20230602-p5dddl.html>; 'Victoria Cross Recipient
      Ben Roberts-Smith Leaving Army for Career in Business', ABC News,
      2 October 2013 <www.abc.net.au/news/2013-10-02/victoria-cross-
      recipient-ben-roberts-smith-to-leave-army/4992718>.

46   Masters, *Flawed Hero*, 45.

47   Susan Johnson, 'Ben Roberts-Smith Says Battlefield Skills Serve Him
      Well in the Boardroom', *Courier-Mail*, 14 April 2017
      <www.couriermail.com.au/news/queensland/ben-robertssmith-
      says-battlefield-skills-serve-him-well-in-the-boardroom/news-story/
      d6ebe57d93975626bf9dddd8f5e20f15>.

48   Amber Schultz, 'War Hero's Reputation Fought on the Media Frontline',
      Crikey, 12 November 2019 <www.crikey.com.au/2019/11/12/ben-roberts-
      smith-media-frontline/>.

49   Masters, *Flawed Hero*, 45.

50   Ibid, 41.

51   '300 – Official Trailer', Warner Bros, YouTube, 12 February 2012
      <www.youtube.com/watch?v=UrIbxk7idYA>.

52   Nick McKenzie and Chris Masters, 'SAS Soldier Accused of
      Killing Innocent Villager', *Sydney Morning Herald*, 8 June 2021
      <www.smh.com.au/politics/federal/sas-soldier-accused-of-killing-
      innocent-villager-20180531-p4zinw.html>; Lauren Ferri, 'One Thing
      Ben Roberts-Smith Said Linked Him to War Crimes Allegation
      Articles', News.com.au, 2 June 2023 <www.news.com.au/technology/
      innovation/military/one-thing-ben-roberts-smith-said-linked-him-to-
      war-crime-allegation-articles/news-story/6f2387e53911c1bc9d58e197669
      a6cbc>.

53   Masters, *Flawed Hero*, 46.

54   Carolyn Holbrook, 'Adaptable Anzac: Past, Present and Future', in
      David Stephens and Alison Broinowski (eds.) *The Honest History Book*
      (NewSouth, 2017), 54–7.

55   Brereton, *Afghanistan Inquiry Report*, 31; David Wroe and Deborah Snow,
      'Afghans Captive to Murky ADF Protocols', *Age* (Melbourne), 18 May
      2013, 4.

56   Crompvoets, 'Special Operations Command (SOCOMD) Culture
      and Interactions: Perceptions, Reputation, and Risk', 21. See for
      instance, 'Australia's secret war – Tour of duty', Network Ten, YouTube,
      28 November 2011 <www.youtube.com/watch?v=xZpL9LtyJZQ>.

57   Brereton, *Afghanistan Inquiry Report*, 446.

58   Ibid, 334.

59   Masters, *Flawed Hero*, 20.

60   Ibid, 22.

61   Willacy, *Rogue Forces*, 27, 15–16, 264.

62   Brereton, *Afghanistan Inquiry Report*, 334.

63   Dan Oakes and Rafael Epstein, 'Afghan Death Charges Thrown Out', *Age* (Melbourne), 20 May 2011 <www.theage.com.au/national/afghan-death-charges-thrown-out-20110520-1ewup.html>.

64   Frame, *Veiled Valour*, 22.

65   Crompvoets, 'Special Operations Command (SOCOMD) Culture and Interactions: Insights and Reflection', 3

66   Schultz, 'War Hero's Reputation Fought on the Media Frontline'.

67   Keith Payne, cited in Trent Dalton and Rory Callinan, 'No Front Line: An Explosive Account of Death in Afghanistan', *Australian*, 20 October 2017 <www.theaustralian.com.au/nation/inquirer/no-front-line-an-explosive-account-of-death-in-afghanistan/news-story/590ebb1d28e82892805fdf89 5e732f4f>.

68   Jennifer Oriel, 'Our Ignorant Broadcaster Is Guilty of Soft Treason', *Australian*, 23 October 2017, 12 <www.proquest.com/newspapers/our-ignorant-broadcaster-is-guilty-soft-treason/docview/1953729756/se-2>.

69   Masters, *Flawed Hero*, 20.

70   Ibid, 210.

71   Neil James, 'Special Forces Issues Have Deep Historical Roots', *The Strategist*, 22 October 2019 <www.aspistrategist.org.au/special-forces-issues-have-deep-historical-roots/>; Leigh Sales, 'Sir Peter Cosgrove Concerned Repeated Deployments Could Have Contributed to Alleged War Crimes in Afghanistan', ABC News, 27 October 2020 <www.abc.net.au/news/2020-10-27/peter-cosgrove-concerned-over-repeat-deployments/12807732>.

72   Ben Packham, 'SAS in Afghanistan: Pawns in a Deadly Game', *Australian*, 19 September 2020 <www.theaustralian.com.au/inquirer/sas-in-afghanistan-pawns-in-a-deadly-game/news-story/2f10b89fc3474d084f709 8111c33a3a0>.

73   'Nation's Moment of Truth on Alleged War Crimes', *Australian*, 13 November, 2020 <www.theaustralian.com.au/commentary/editorials/nations-moment-of-truth-on-alleged-war-crimes/news-story/0d224e1bc3 b199a4b7b040e3ddf5541d>.

74   Brendan Nelson, 'No National Interest in "Tearing down our Heroes"', SkyNews, 20 October 2018 <www.skynews.com.au/australia-news/no-national-interest-in-tearing-down-our-heroes-nelson/video/446879c6e4480310a6edb81de0b1431b>; Schultz, 'War Hero's Reputation'.

75   Dalton and Callinan, 'No Front Line'.

76   'Letters to the Editor', *Australian*, 23 October 2017, 12 <www.proquest.com/newspapers/letters-editor/docview/1953674068/se-2>; 'Letters', *Sydney Morning Herald*, 14 August 2018 <www.smh.com.au/national/nsw/population-growth-stunted-by-dry-and-unliveable-land-20180813-p4zx8l.html>.

77   McKenzie, *Crossing the Line*, 10.

78   Malcolm Quekett, 'RSL Digs in Behind WA War Hero Ben Roberts-Smith', *West Australian*, 14 August 2018 <thewest.com.au/news/conflict/rsl-digs-in-behind-wa-war-hero-ben-roberts-smith-ng-b88927101z>.

79   'Stop the Witch Hunt. Support the SASR and Ben Roberts-Smith',
      Change.org <www.change.org/p/scott-morrison-stop-the-witch-hunt-
      support-the-sasr-and-ben-roberts-smith>.

80   Facebook pages include 'We Stand with Ben Roberts-Smith VC MG'
      with 4100 members; 'ADF and SAS we support Ben Roberts-Smith VC
      MG' with 28 000 members; 'A Pardon for Ben Roberts-Smith', with
      16 000 members.

81   Cited in Shane Wright, 'SAS Inquiry: Gossip, Rumours Behind Army
      Chief Angus Campbell's Special Forces Inquiry', *West Australian*,
      26 October 2017 <thewest.com.au/news/australia/gossip-rumours-
      behind-army-chief-angus-campbells-special-forces-inquiry-ng-
      b88640172z>.

82   Alan Jones, '"This Is Disgusting Stuff!": Calls to Resolve Ben Roberts-
      Smith Accusations', 2GB, 24 September 2019 <www.2gb.com/this-is-
      disgusting-stuff-calls-to-resolve-ben-roberts-smith-accusations/>;
      Paul Maley, 'Ben Roberts-Smith Blasts Nine's "Abuse of Power"',
      Australian, 7 October 2019 <www.theaustralian.com.au/nation/
      ben-robertssmith-blasts-nines-abuse-of-power/news-story/3f7663
      694d01acb65c2f65d50824c20a>; Phoebe Wearne, 'Defence Leaders
      under Fire over Ben Roberts-Smith Allegations', *West Australian*,
      13 August 2018 <thewest.com.au/news/conflict/defence-leaders-under-
      fire-over-ben-roberts-smith-allegations-ng-b88925866z>; 'They're
      Calling Me a Murderer: War Hero Ben Roberts-Smith', *Australian*,
      16 December 2019 <www.theaustralian.com.au/nation/defence/
      theyre-calling-me-a-murderer-war-hero-ben-robertssmith/news-story/
      d890d1268897a0c646774c3f02d37964>.

83   Aaron Patrick, 'The Defamation Trial of the Century', *Australian
      Financial Review*, 29 December 2020 <www.afr.com/companies/media-
      and-marketing/the-defamation-trial-of-the-century-20201202-p56jw2>.

84   Roberts-Smith, cited in Masters, *Flawed Hero*, 250–4.

85   Kieran Gair, 'War Hero Thought Life "Wasn't Worth It"', *Australian*,
      16 June 2021 <www.theaustralian.com.au/nation/defamation-trial-war-
      hero-ben-robertssmith-thought-life-wasnt-worth-it/news-story/5ef39594b
      70f613964009ad9f9515b69>.

86   Roberts-Smith, cited in Wearne, 'Defence Leaders under Fire'.

87   Gair, 'War Hero Thought Life "Wasn't Worth It"'.

88   'D-Day for Wounded Warrior but Will He Show for Defamation Ruling?',
      Daily Telegraph (Sydney), 31 May 2023.

89   Jackson Graham and David Estcourt, 'Five Things You Need to Know
      About the Ben Roberts-Smith Decision', *Sydney Morning Herald*, 1 June
      2023 <www.smh.com.au/national/five-things-you-need-to-know-about-
      the-ben-roberts-smith-decision-20230601-p5dd5u.html>.

90   'A Pardon for Ben Roberts-Smith', Change.org, August 2023
      <www.change.org/p/a-pardon-for-ben-roberts-smith>.

91   Danielle Le Messurier and Adelaide Lang, 'Gina Rinehart Slams
      "Gloating" Nine as She Backs Ben Roberts-Smith', *West Australian*,

18 May 2025 <thewest.com.au/news/court-justice/gina-rinehart-slams-gloating-nine-as-she-backs-ben-roberts-smith-c-18722831>; Sherri Markson, 'Nine Reporter Exposed over Allegations of "Unethical Behaviour" in Ben Roberts-Smith Trial', SkyNews, 24 March 2025 <www.skynews.com.au/opinion/sharri-markson/nine-reporter-exposed-over-allegations-of-unethical-behaviour-in-ben-robertssmith-trial/video/f9e2c7e64fd7736e2748b4e13ddade02>; Sarah Steger, 'Nine Paid $700,000 Hush Money to Silence BRS Witness', *West Australian*, 4 May 2025 <thewest.com.au/news/court-justice/nine-paid-700000-hush-money-to-silence-ben-roberts-smith-witness-c-18581625>.

92 Author conversation with Samantha Crompvoets.

93 Stephanie Borys, 'Police Confirm New Investigation Launched into Allegations Linked to Ben Roberts-Smith During Senate Hearing', ABC News, 14 April 2021 <www.abc.net.au/news/2021-04-14/police-confirm-new-investigation-launched-ben-roberts-smith/100069256>.

94 Mark Willacy, 'The Inquiry into Australian Soldiers in Afghanistan Is Finally Over. The Reckoning is About to Begin', ABC News, 18 November 2020 <www.abc.net.au/news/2020-11-18/igadf-inquiry-into-special-forces-in-afghanistan-is-over/12816626>.

95 Packham, 'SAS in Afghanistan: Pawns in a Deadly Game'.

96 '"They Are Not One of Us": SAS Soldiers Condemn War Crime Perpetrators', *Sydney Morning Herald*, 16 November 2020 <www.smh.com.au/national/they-are-not-one-of-us-sas-soldiers-condemn-war-crime-perpetrators-20201116-p56ezv.html>.

97 'Nation's Moment of Truth on Alleged War Crimes', *Australian*, 13 November 2020 <www.theaustralian.com.au/commentary/editorials/nations-moment-of-truth-on-alleged-war-crimes/news-story/0d224e1bc3b199a4b7b040e3ddf5541d>.

98 Willacy, *Rogue Forces*, 201.

99 Hastie, 'For Ex-SAS Soldier Andrew Hastie the Brereton Report Is Personal', *Australian*, 24 November 2020 <www.theaustralian.com.au/exclusives/for-exsas-soldier-andrew-hastie-the-brereton-report-is-personal/news-story/6653a1cd2c2145c568531b074dc7f045>.

100 Masters, *Flawed Hero*, 527.

101 McKenzie and Masters, 'Abdul's Brother Went out to Buy Flour'.

102 Packham, 'SAS in Afghanistan: Pawns in a Deadly Game'.

103 Ben Packham, 'Brereton War Crimes Report: Defence Urges Probe into 19 Soldiers over 39 Alleged Murders', *Australian*, 19 November 2020 <www.theaustralian.com.au/nation/defence/brereton-report-defence-recommends-probe-into-19-soldiers-over-39-alleged-murders/news-story/c8887317c84db3cde1ec1066c13a44ab>.

104 Audie Moldre, 'Cancel the Flag Folding Ceremony – Restore 2 Squadron SASR', *Wandering Warriors*, 7 September 2021, cited in Masters, *Flawed Hero*, 281.

105 'Defence Minister Peter Dutton Overturns Decision to Strip Veterans of Military Decorations', ABC News, 19 April 2021 <www.abc.net.au/

news/2021-04-19/defence-peter-dutton-overturn-decision-strip-veterans-decoration/100078026>; Andrew Greene, 'Move to Strip Afghanistan War Veterans of Military Decorations Possible Due to Changes Signed off by Federal Governments', ABC News, 25 November 2020 <www.abc.net.au/news/2020-11-25/anger-over-moves-to-strip-afghanistan-war-veteran-of-decorations/12917030>.

106   'Defence Minister Peter Dutton Overturns Decision to Strip Veterans of Military Decorations'.

107   Martin Hamilton-Smith, 'The Afghan Saga of Bravery, Allegations and Betrayal', *The Strategist*, 27 September 2024 <www.aspistrategist.org.au/the-afghan-saga-of-bravery-allegations-and-betrayal/>.

108   Crompvoets, *Blood Lust, Trust & Blame*, 21.

109   *Bravery and Betrayal*, Wandering Warriors, April 2025 <wanderingwarriors.org/bravery-betrayal-the-documentary/>.

110   Erin Molan, '"Right Thing to Do": New Documentary Sheds Light on Real SAS Experience', SkyNews, YouTube, 27 July 2024 <www.youtube.com/watch?v=QT5ix-ciYq0>.

111   Dr Vivienne Thom and Robert Cornall, 'Afghanistan Inquiry Implementation Oversight Panel: Final Report to the Deputy Prime Minister and Minister of Defence', 8 November 2023, 4, 107 <www.defence.gov.au/sites/default/files/2024-05/Afghanistan-Inquiry-Implementation-Oversight-Panel-Final-Report-to-the-Deputy-Prime-Minister-and-Minister-to-Defence-8-Nov-23.pdf>.

112   Masters, *Flawed Hero*, 282.

113   Crompvoets, *Blood Lust, Trust & Blame*, 16.

114   See Richard Travers, *Above the Mists of Ages: The Anzac Legend in Historical Practice* (Australian Scholarly Publishing, 2023), 100–4, 121–30.

115   Dave Phillips, 'Trump Clears Three Service Members in War Crimes Cases', 15 November 2019 <www.nytimes.com/2019/11/15/us/trump-pardons.html>; 'Marine A – Can There Be Justice and Mercy', NavyLookOut.Com, 30 October 2014 <www.navylookout.com/marine-a-can-there-be-justice-and-mercy/>.

CHAPTER 13 THE ANZAC WARRIOR IN THE AGE OF AUTONOMOUS WARFARE

1   For the evolution of the Anzac legend, see Carolyn Holbrook, *Anzac: The Unauthorised Biography* (NewSouth, 2014); and Joan Beaumont, 'Remembering the Heroes of Australia's Wars: From Heroic to Post-Heroic Memory', in Sibylle Scheipers (ed.) *Heroism and the Changing Character of War* (Palgrave Macmillan, 2014), 334–48.

2   Christina Twomey, 'Trauma and the Reinvigoration of Anzac: An Argument', *History Australia* 10, no. 3 (2013): 85–103.

3   *Herald Sun* (Melbourne), 25 April 2011, cited in Beaumont, 'Remembering the Heroes', 245.

4   Australian Army, *Robotic & Autonomous Systems Strategy v.2* (2022), 4 <researchcentre.army.gov.au/sites/default/files/Robotic%20and%20Autonomous%20Systems%20Strategy%20V2.0.pdf>.

5   Ibid, 4.

6   International Committee of the Red Cross, 'ICRC Position on Autonomous Weapon Systems', 2021 <www.icrc.org/en/document/icrc-position-autonomous-weapon-systems>.

7   Christiane Wilke, 'Seeing and Unmaking Civilians in Afghanistan: Visual Technologies and Contested Professional Visions', *Science, Technology, & Human Values*, 42, no. 6 (2017): 1031–60. See also Lucy Suchman, Karolina Follis and Jutta Weber, 'Tracking and Targeting: Sociotechnologies of (In)Security,' *Science, Technology, & Human Values*, 42, no. 6 (2017): 1031–60 <doi.org/10.1177/0162243917731524>.

8   On the risks of machine learning algorithms in war, see Bianca Baggiarini, 'Algorithmic War and the Dangers of In-visibility, Anonymity, and Fragmentation,' *Australian Journal of International Affairs*, 78, no. 2 (2024): 257–65 <doi.org/10.1080/10357718.2024.2333824>.

9   Sarah Kreps, 'What Is "The First Drone Age"?', in James Patton Rogers (ed.), *De Gruyter Handbook of Drone Warfare* (De Gruyter, 2024), 107–10.

10   Brian Glyn Williams, *Predators: The CIA's Drone War on al Qaeda* (University of Nebraska Press, 2013).

11   Harley Dennett, 'Air Force's SkyGuardian or Reaper Lethal Drone Cancelled to Pay for Project REDSPICE', *Canberra Times*, 1 April 2022 <www.canberratimes.com.au/story/7682864/morrison-govt-cancels-countrys-only-armed-drones-project>.

12   Peter Asaro, 'The Labor of Surveillance and Bureaucratized Killing: New subjectivities of military drone operators', *Social Semiotics*, 23, no. 2 (2013): 196–224.

13   James Patton Rogers, 'What is 'The Second Drone Age'?', in James Patton Rogers (ed.), *De Gruyter Handbook of Drone Warfare*, 237–42.

14   Yuval Abraham, '"A Mass Assassination Factory": Inside Israel's Calculated Bombing of Gaza', +972, 30 November 2023 <www.972mag.com/mass-assassination-factory-israel-calculated-bombing-gaza>; Bianca Baggiarini, 'Israel's AI Can Produce 100 Bombing Targets a Day in Gaza. Is this the Future of War?', *The Conversation*, 6 December 2023 <theconversation.com/israels-ai-can-produce-100-bombing-targets-a-day-in-gaza-is-this-the-future-of-war-219302>.

15   Rebecca Armitage, 'The Skies over Gaza Are Abuzz with Drones. Some Are Israeli, Some Are American, and Some Are Flying Bombs Made by Hamas', ABC News, 6 November 2023 <www.abc.net.au/news/2023-11-06/drones-flying-over-and-within-gaza/103067280>.

16   Tom O'Connor, 'Iran Positions "Suicide Drones" in Yemen as Red Sea Tensions Rise', *Newsweek*, 13 January 2021 <www.newsweek.com/iran-suicide-drones-yemen-red-sea-tensions-1561395>.

17   'North Korea's Kim Jong Un Oversees Tests of New AI-Equipped Suicide Drones', *Al Jazeera*, 27 March 2025 <www.aljazeera.com/news/2025/3/27/north-koreas-kim-jong-un-oversees-tests-of-new-ai-equipped-suicide-drones>.

18   T. Erskine and S. E. Miller, 'AI and the Decision to Go to War: Future Risks and Opportunities', *Australian Journal of International Affairs* 78, no. 2 (2024): 135–47.

19   For an Australian perspective on Ukraine, see Mick Ryan, *The War for Ukraine: Strategy and Adaptation Under Fire* (Naval Institute Press, 2024).

20   David Axe, 'Ukraine's Sea Baby Drone Boats Shoot Back Now', *Forbes*, 9 December 2024 <www.forbes.com/sites/davidaxe/2024/12/09/ukraines-sea-baby-drone-boats-shoot-back-now/>.

21   Kateryna Zakharchenko, 'Ukraine Unveils Killer MAGURA Sea Drones After Destroying 17 Russian Targets, Forcing Fleet Retreat', *Kyiv Post*, 15 May 2025 <www.kyivpost.com/post/52689>.

22   Yogita Limaye, 'The Terrifying New Weapon Changing the War in Ukraine', BBC News, 29 May 2025 <www.bbc.com/news/articles/ckgn47e5qyno>.

23   James Waterhouse, 'Ukraine War: Soldier Tells BBC of Front-Line "Hell"', BBC News, 4 December 2023 <www.bbc.com/news/world-europe-67565508>.

24   United Nations, 'Short-Range Drones: The Deadliest Threat to Civilians in Ukraine', UN News, 11 February 2025 <news.un.org/en/story/2025/02/1160016>.

25   Annika Burgess and Brianna Morris-Grant, 'Ukraine Could Face Waves of 2000 Drones as Russia Ramps up Mass Production', ABC News, 19 September 2025 <www.abc.net.au/news/2025-09-19/russia-record-drone-missile-mass-strikes-ukraine-conflict/105753634>.

26   Kateryna Stepanenko, 'Russian Force Generation and Technological Adaptations Update', Institute for the Study of War, 9 October 2025 <understandingwar.org/research/russia-ukraine/russian-force-generation-technological-adaptations-update-october-9-2025/#:~:text=October%209%2C%202025-,Key%20Takeaways,since%20at%20least%20August%202025>.

27   Rosa Brooks, *How Everything Became War and the Military Became Everything* (Simon & Shuster, 2016), 131–4.

28   Zachary Kallenborn, 'Was a Flying Killer Robot Used in Libya? Quite Possibly', *Bulletin of the Atomic Scientists*, 20 May 2021 <thebulletin.org/2021/05/was-a-flying-killer-robot-used-in-libya-quite-possibly>.

29   'Automated Apartheid', Amnesty International, 2 May 2023 <www.amnesty.org/en/documents/mde15/6701/2023/en>.

30   Sheera Frenkel and Natan Odenheimer, 'Israel's A.I. Experiments in Gaza War Raise Ethical Concerns,' *New York Times*, 25 April 2025 <www.nytimes.com/2025/04/25/technology/israel-gaza-ai.html>.

31   Brooks, *How Everything Became War*, 134–8.

32   Dylan Wench, 'Pine Gap Communications Facility Operations "Ethically Unacceptable", Professor Des Ball Says', ABC News, 13 August 2014 <www.abc.net.au/news/2014-08-13/pine-gap-us-drone-program-

ethically-unacceptable-analyst/5669336>; Peter Cronau, 'Pine Gap Plays Crucial Role in America's Wars, Leaked Documents Reveal', ABC News, 20 August 2017 <www.abc.net.au/news/2017-08-20/leaked-documents-reveal-pine-gaps-crucial-role-in-us-drone-war/8815472>.

33   Australian Army, *Robotic & Autonomous Systems Strategy*, 11.

34   For RAN thinking, see Royal Australian Navy, *RAS-AI Strategy 2040*, 2024 <www.navy.gov.au/sites/default/files/2024-02/RASAI-Strategy-2040.pdf>.

35   Malcom Davis, 'Taking Robots and AI to War at Sea', *The Strategist*, 24 January 2024 <www.aspistrategist.org.au/taking-robots-and-ai-to-war-at-sea>.

36   Andrew Greene, 'Australian-Made Underwater Glider Drones Equipped with Artificial Intelligence Could Soon Bolster UK Naval Surveillance', ABC News, 15 May 2025 <www.abc.net.au/news/2025-05-15/australian-underwater-ai-drones-could-bolster-uk-surveillance/105293204>.

37   Hugh White, *How to Defend Australia* (La Trobe University Press, 2019); Albert Palazzo, *The Big Fix: Rebuilding Australia's National Security* (Melbourne University Press, 2025).

38   Carl Rhodes, 'Australia Needs a Centre of Excellence to Counter Small Drones', *The Strategist*, 3 September 2024 <www.aspistrategist.org.au/australia-needs-a-centre-of-excellence-to-counter-small-drones/>; Michael Spencer and Keirin Joyce, 'How Drone Racing Promotes Battlefield FPV Capability', *The Strategist*, 23 January 2025 <www.aspistrategist.org.au/how-drone-racing-promotes-battlefield-fpv-capability>.

39   Ibid.

40   Andrew Davies, 'The ADF and Armed Drones', *The Strategist*, 6 February 2015 <www.aspi.org.au/strategist-posts/the-adf-and-armed-drones>.

41   Australian Government, 'Australian Government Announces Acquisition of Precision Loitering Munition', 8 July 2024, <www.minister.defence.gov.au/media-releases/2024-07-08/australian-government-announces-acquisition-precision-loitering-munition>.

42   See Sebastian Kaempf, *Saving Soldiers or Civilians? Casualty-Aversion versus Civilian Protection in Asymmetric Conflicts* (Cambridge University Press, 2018).

43   Australian Army Research Centre, 'No Casualties Please, We're Soldiers', *Australian Army Journal* 5, no. 3 <researchcentre.army.gov.au/library/australian-army-journal-aaj/volume-5-number-3/no-casualties-please-were-soldiers>.

44   For retention problems, see Parliament of Australia, 'Retention in the Australian Defence Force', 20 June 2023 <www.aph.gov.au/about_parliament/parliamentary_departments/parliamentary_library/research/flagpost/2023/june/adf-retention>; Melissa George, 'Retention in the Australian Defence Force', *Flagpost*, Parliament of Australia, 20 June 2023 <https://www.aph.gov.au/About_Parliament/Parliamentary_departments/Parliamentary_Library/Research/FlagPost/2023/June/ADF-Retention>.

45   Australian Army, *Robotic & Autonomous Systems Strategy*, 15.

46   'Artillery Soldier', ADF Careers <www.adfcareers.gov.au/jobs/army/artillery-soldier>.

47   Nina B. Huntemann and Matthew Thomas Payne, *Joystick Soldiers: The Politics of Play in Military Video Games* (Routledge, 2010), 3–10; Stella Maynard, 'Selfies and Submarines: The Social Media of Military Recruitment', *Society and Space*, 9 March 2020 <www.societyandspace.org/articles/selfies-and-submarines-the-social-media-of-military-recruitment>; 'Unlike Any Other Job', ADF Careers, YouTube, 29 July 2024<www.youtube.com/watch?v=nreNGzeeGoc&t=2s>.

48   R. K. Saini, M. S. V. K. Raju and A. Chail, 'Cry in the Sky: Psychological Impact on Drone Operators', *Industrial Psychiatry Journal* 30, Suppl. 1 (2021): S15–S19 <http://doi.org/10.4103/0972-6748.328782>.

49   Eliot Atkins and Evan R. Seamone, 'Remote Combat Exposure and Moral Injury from Drone Operations', in Justin T. McDaniel, Evan R. Seamone and Stephen N. Xenakis (eds.), *Preventing and Treating the Invisible Wounds of War* (Oxford University Press, 2023), 207–36.

50   Christian Enemark, *Moralities of Drone Violence* (Edinburgh University Press, 2023).

51   Hugh Gusterson, *Drone: Remote Control Warfare* (MIT Press, 2016). See also Christian Enemark, 'Drones, Risk, and Moral Injury', *Critical Military Studies* 5, no. 2 (2019), 150–67.

52   Asaro, 'The Labor of Surveillance and Bureaucratized Killing', 196–224.

53   Jonathan Shay, *Achilles in Vietnam: Combat Trauma and the Undoing of Character* (Atheneum, 1994).

54   Jinkerson, cited in Enemark, *Moralities of Drone Violence*, 156.

55   Enemark, 'Drones, Risk, and Moral Injury', 151.

56   Ibid, 152.

57   Elisabeth Bummiler, 'Video Shows US Killing of Reuters Employees', *New York Times*, 5 April 2010 <www.nytimes.com/2010/04/06/world/middleeast/06baghdad.html>; Andrew Niccol, *Good Kill* (Voltage Films, 2014); Gavin Hood, *Eye in the Sky* (Raindog Films, 2015); Jason Bourque, *Drone* (Look to the Sky, 2017).

58   Mike Silverman, '"Grounded", a New Opera about a Female Fighter Pilot Turned Drone Operator, Prepares to Take Off', Associated Press, 27 October 2023 <apnews.com/article/grounded-opera-debut-5f32a8b0f47deced93bdb28b353a1759>.

59   Australian Army, *Robotic & Autonomous Systems Strategy*, 9.

60   Russel Ward, *The Australian Legend* (Oxford University Press, 1983, first published 1958).

61   For one academic's attempt to challenge perceived 'truths' of Australian military history, see Craig Stockings (ed.), *Zombie Myths of Australian Military History* (UNSW Press, 2010).

62   See C. E. W. Bean, *The Story of Anzac*, vol. I, *The Official History of Australia in the War of 1914–1918* (Angus & Robertson, 1921), 5.

63   Beaumont, 'Remembering the Heroes', 344–6.

64   Anthony Albanese, 'Anzac Day Commemorative Address Dawn Service 2023', 25 April 2023 <www.awm.gov.au/commemoration/speeches/commemoration/speeches/anzac-day-2023>.

CHAPTER 14 HOW ANZAC EVOLVED AND WHY IT ENDURES - FOR NOW

1   Diarmaid MacCulloch, *A History of Christianity: The First Three Thousand Years* (Penguin, 2011).

2   This argument is central to the thesis of Steve Vizard in *Nation, Memory, Myth: Gallipoli and the Australian Imaginary* (Melbourne University Press 2025).

3   Robert A. Segal, *Myth: A Very Short Introduction* (Oxford University Press, 2004).

4   Joseph Conrad, *Heart of Darkness* 2nd edn (W.W. Norton & Company, 1971), 3.

5   Bianca Slocombe and Michael Kilmister make a similar argument in relation to understanding Anzac in 'Breaking Disciplinary Walls in the Examination of Anzac as Religion', *Human Arenas* 4 (2021): 239–56.

6   Harvey Whitehouse, *Inheritance: The Evolutionary Origins of the Modern World* (Penguin Random House, 2024), 6.

7   Robin Dunbar, *How Religion Evolved and Why it Endures* (Pelican, 2023). See also Slocombe and Kilmister, 'Breaking Disciplinary Walls', whose argument focuses on 'social, cognitive, and environmental mechanisms of devotion', 251.

8   Émile Durkheim, *The Elementary Forms of the Religious Life*, 2nd edn, translated from the French by Joseph Ward Swain (Allen & Unwin, 1976).

9   See <www.harveywhitehouse.com/articles/academic> for a list of academic journal articles, and other publications by Harvey Whitehouse, including *The Ritual Animal: Imitation and Cohesion in the Evolution of Social Complexity* (Oxford, 2021) and *Inheritance: The Evolutionary Origins of the Modern World* (Oxford, 2024).

10   Slocombe and Kilmister, 'Breaking Disciplinary Walls', 240.

11   Vizard, *Nation, Memory, Myth*. Vizard's book is centred around events at Gallipoli and the resulting mythology, 'the Gallipoli myth' or 'mythic Gallipoli', rather than the Anzac legend more broadly. He also ascribes distinctive meanings to myth and legend, see pp. 42–3. My focus is the Anzac legend, and I use 'myth', 'mythology' and 'legend' interchangeably.

12   Carolyn Holbrook, *Anzac: The Unauthorised Biography* (NewSouth, 2014).

13   David Stephens, 'Total Australian Spending on World War I Centenary: An Aide Memoire for the Curious', *Honest History*, 19 February 2019 <honesthistory.net.au/wp/stephens-david-total-australian-spending-on-world-war-i-centenary-an-aide-memoire-for-the-curious/>.

14   Jo Hawkins, *Consuming Anzac: The History of Australia's Most Powerful Brand* (UWA Publishing, 2018).

15   David Stephens, 'Rotten Fresh: Can It Get More Crass?', *Honest History*, 14 April 2015 <honesthistory.net.au/wp/rotten-fresh-can-it-get-more-crass/>.

16   For example, Mervyn F. Bendle, *Anzac and Its Enemies: The History War on Australia's National Identity* (Quadrant Books, 2015); Miranda Devine, 'Insulting Charge of History-Lite Brigade', *Sunday Telegraph* (Sydney), 18 April 2015 <www.dailytelegraph.com.au/news/opinion/miranda-devine-insulting-charge-of-historylite-brigade/news-story/53f9ea213fbdc92d737cf9901a931017>.

17   Mervyn F. Bendle, 'Anzac in Ashes', Quadrant Online, 1 April 2010 <quadrant.org.au/magazine/uncategorized/anzac-in-ashes/>.

18   For example, Devine, 'Insulting Charge of History-Lite Brigade'.

19   See Holbrook, *Anzac: The Unauthorised Biography*; and Carolyn Holbrook, '"Commemorators-in-Chief": Australian Politicians and the Anzac Legend', in Tom Frame (ed.), *Anzac Day: Then & Now* (NewSouth Publishing, 2014), 214–31.

20   'Review of the Australian Curriculum', Australian Curriculum, Assessment and Reporting Authority <www.acara.edu.au/curriculum/curriculum-review>.

21   Daniel Hurst, 'Alan Tudge Says He Doesn't Want Students to be Taught "Hatred" of Australia in Fiery Triple J Interview', *Guardian Australia*, 8 September 2021 <www.theguardian.com/australia-news/2021/sep/08/alan-tudge-says-he-doesnt-want-students-to-be-taught-hatred-of-australia-in-fiery-triple-j-interview>.

22   Ibid.

23   Ibid.

24   Ibid.

25   The social psychologist Jonathan Haidt argued in *The Righteous Mind: Why Good People are Divided by Politics and Religion* (Pantheon Books, 2012), that much of what passes for reasoned argument is based on moral intuitions, and that these moral intuitions are deeply held, 'sacred' values that have their foundations in the social cohesion of the group.

262   John Lack (ed.), *Anzac Remembered: Selected Writings of K. S. Inglis* (University of Melbourne, 1998), 3.

27   K. S. Inglis, *Churches and the Working Classes in Victorian England* (Routledge and Kegan Paul PLC, 1963); Craig Wilcox (ed.), *Observing Australia: 1959–1999, K. S. Inglis* (Melbourne University Press, 1999), 5.

28   Lack (ed.), *Anzac Remembered*, 3.

29   David Stephens, 'Rebooting Anzac for the Next Century', *Sydney Morning Herald*, 23 April 2015 <www.smh.com.au/opinion/rebooting-anzac-for-the-next-century-20150422-1mqjab.html>; Roland Perry, *John Monash: The Outsider Who Won a War* (Random House, 2014).

30   Paul Daley, 'Ataturk's "Johnnies and Mehmets" Words about the Anzacs are Shrouded in Doubt', *Guardian Australia* <www.theguardian.com/news/2015/apr/20/ataturks-johnnies-and-mehmets-words-about-the-anzacs-are-shrouded-in-doubt>.

31   Vizard, *Nation, Memory, Myth*, 77; for a discussion of myth versus history, see 200–4.

32   Ibid, 3.

33   Bill Gammage, speech at Australian Defence Force Academy (ADFA), Canberra, 19 April 2002, cited in Holbrook, *Anzac: The Unauthorised Biography*, 126–7.

34   K. S. Inglis, 'The Substitute Religion', *Nation*, 23 April 1960, reprinted in Craig Wilcox (ed.), *Observing Australia* 63–70; K. S. Inglis, 'The Anzac Tradition', *Meanjin Quarterly* 24, no. 1 (1965): 25–44; L. L. Robson, *The First AIF: A Study of Its Recruitment, 1914–1918* (Melbourne University Press, 1970).

35   For example, D. A. Kent, 'The Anzac Book and the Anzac legend: C. E. W. Bean as Editor and Image-Maker', *Historical Studies* 21, no. 84 (1985): 376–90; Kevin Fewster, 'Ellis Ashmead Bartlett and the Making of the Anzac Legend', *Journal of Australian Studies* 10 (1982): 17–30. See the opening chapter of this book for more examples.

36   Holbrook, 'Commemorators-in-Chief', 214–31.

37   Hawkins, *Consuming Anzac*.

38   Marilyn Lake, Henry Reynolds, Joy Damousi and Mark McKenna, *What's Wrong with Anzac? The Militarisation of Australian History* (NewSouth, 2010).

39   The Commonwealth spent $411 million on the Voice referendum. 'Cost of Elections and Referendums', AEC, updated 31 October 2024 <www.aec.gov.au/elections/federal_elections/cost-of-elections.htm>. Big business, philanthropy and influential personalities also lent their support overwhelmingly to the Yes side. 'Yes Campaign Groups Received More than Five Times as Much in Donations as No Side in Voice Referendum', *Guardian Australia*, 2 April 2024 <www.theguardian.com/australia-news/2024/apr/02/voice-referendum-australia-donations-yes-no-campaign-groups-funding>.

40   Joan Beaumont, *Broken Nation: Australians in the Great War* (Allen & Unwin, 2013), 552. On hegemony, see Antonio Gramsci, *Selections from the Prison Notebooks of Antonio Gramsci*, trans. Q. Hoare and G. Nowell-Smith (International Publishers, 1971).

41   Beaumont, *Broken Nation*, 552.

42   Vizard, *Nation, Memory, Myth*, 70.

43   Bruce Scates, *Return to Gallipoli: Walking the Battlefields of the Great War* (Cambridge University Press, 2006), xx.

44   Stuart Ward and Mark McKenna, '"It Was Really Moving, Mate": The Gallipoli Pilgrimage and Sentimental Nationalism in Australia', *Australian Historical Studies* 38, no. 129 (2008), 144.

45   Ibid.

46   See Anna Clark, 'The Place of Anzac in Australian Historical Consciousness', *Australian Historical Studies* 48, no. 1 (2017): 19–34, for detail of the potency of Anzac and thoughtful analysis of the complex personal reasons for its enduring popularity.

47   Richard J. Evans, *Eric Hobsbawm: A Life in History* (Abacus, 2019).

48   Benedict Anderson, *Imagined Communities: Reflections on the Origins and Spread of Nationalism* (Verso, 1983); Ernest Gellner, *Nations and Nationalism* (Cornell University Press, 1983).

49   Vizard, *Nation, Memory, Myth*, 3.

50   For example, Warren D. TenHouten, 'On Durkheim's Notions of Time
     and Mind in Australian Aboriginal Cosmology and Social Life', in
     Richard Altschuler (ed.), *The Living Legacy of Marx, Durkheim and
     Weber: Applications and Analyses of Classical Sociological Theory by
     Modern Social Scientists*, vol. 2 (Gordian Knot, 2000), 370–403.

51   Anthony Giddens, *Capitalism and Modern Social Theory: An Analysis of
     the Writings of Marx, Durkheim and Max Weber* (Cambridge University
     Press, 1971), 109.

52   Ibid.

53   Durkheim, *The Elementary Forms*, 149.

54   Giddens, *Capitalism and Modern Social Theory*, 107.

55   Durkheim, *The Elementary Forms*, 465.

56   Whitehouse, *The Ritual Animal: Imitation and Cohesion in the Evolution
     of Social Complexity* (Oxford, 2021) 46.

57   Dunbar, *How Religion Evolved*, 33–8.

58   Whitehouse, *Inheritance*, 86.

59   Whitehouse, *The Ritual Animal*, 82.

60   Dimitris Xygalatas, Ivana Konvalinka, Joseph Bulbulia and Andreas
     Roepstorff, 'Quantifying Collective Effervescence: Heart-Rate Dynamics
     at a Fire-Walking Ritual', *Communicative Integrative Biology* 4, no. 6
     (2011): 735–8.

61   Robin Dunbar, 'Coevolution of Neocortical Size, Group Size and
     Language in Humans', *Behavioral and Brain Sciences* 16, no. 4 (1993):
     681–735.

62   David Graeber and David Wengrow, *The Dawn of Everything: A New
     History of Humanity* (Picador, 2023).

63   Robin Dunbar, 'Religion, the Social Brain and the Mystical Stance',
     Archive for the Psychology of Religion 42, no. 1 (2020): 50; R. A. Hill
     and Robin Dunbar, 'Social Network Size in Humans', *Human Nature*
     14 (2003): 53–72.

64   Robin Dunbar, 'The Social Role of Touch in Humans and Primates:
     Behavioural Function and Neurobiological Mechanism', *Neuroscience and
     Behavioral Reviews* 34, no. 2 (2010): 260–8.

65   Robert Bellah, *Religion in Human Evolution* (Harvard University Press,
     Cam. MA, 2011). Whitehouse defines ritualised behaviour as that which is
     'opaque', in having no instrumental outcome.

66   Whitehouse, *The Ritual Animal*, 25–52.

67   Dunbar identifies three categories of ritual: low-effort, medium-effort and
     extreme, *How Religion Evolved*, 131.

68   P. Turchin, H. Whitehouse, J. Larson, E. Cioni, E. J. Reddish et al.,
     'Explaining the rise of moralizing religions: a test of competing
     hypotheses using the Seshat Databank', *Religion, Brain & Behavior* 13,
     no. 2 (2023): 167–94.

69   Dunbar, 'Religion, the Social Brain and the Mystical Stance', 52.

70   Dunbar, *How Religion Evolved*, 129.

71   Vizard, *Nation, Memory, Myth*, 70.

72   Harvey Whitehouse, 'Dying for the Group: Towards a General Theory of Extreme Self-Sacrifice', *Behavioural and Brain Sciences* 41 (2018): 41.

73   Whitehouse, *The Ritual Animal*, 82.

74   Dunbar, *How Religion Evolved*, 135–7.

75   Vizard, *Nation, Memory, Myth*, 48.

76   'Enlistment Statistics, First World War', Australian War Memorial <www.awm.gov.au/articles/encyclopedia/enlistment/ww1#total)>.

77   For example, Joy Damousi, *The Labour of Loss: Mourning, Memory and Wartime Bereavement in Australia* (Cambridge University Press, 1999); Bart Ziino, *A Distant Grief, Australians: War Graves and the Great War* (University of Western Australia Press, 2007); Marina Larsson, *Shattered Anzacs: Living with the Scars of War* (UNSW Press, 2009).

78   Vizard, *Nation, Memory, Myth*, 50.

79   Ibid, 8.

80   Ibid, 68.

81   See Graeme Davison, 'The Habit of Commemoration and the Revival of Anzac Day', *Australian Cultural History*, no. 22 (2003), 78.

82   Vizard, *Nation, Memory, Myth*, 189.

83   W. M. Hughes, 25 April 1916, cited in Hawkins, *Consuming Anzac*, 11.

84   For example, Canon David John Garland's design of Anzac Day services, J. A. Moses, 'The Nation's Secular Requiem', in Frame (ed.), *Anzac Day: Then & Now*, 54–65; John A. Moses and George F. Davis, *Anzac Day Origins: Canon DJ Garland and Trans-Tasman Commemoration* (Barton Books, 2013).

85   Beaumont, *Broken Nation*, 180; also see Vizard, *Nation, Memory, Myth*, 185–90; and Slocombe and Kilmister, 'Breaking Disciplinary Walls', 244–5.

86   Paul Fussell, *The Great War and Modern Memory* (Oxford University Press, 1975).

87   Whitehouse, *Inheritance*, 86.

88   See Holbrook, *Anzac: The Unauthorised Biography*; and Holbrook, 'Commemorators-in Chief'.

89   Author interview with Bob Hawke, Sydney, 21 May 2012.

90   Ibid.

91   Hawkins, *Consuming Anzac*.

92   For information about the history of the dawn service, see David Watt, 'Anzac Day Traditions and Rituals: A Quick Guide', Parliament of Australia, 31 March 2017 <www.aph.gov.au/About_Parliament/ Parliamentary_Departments/Parliamentary_Library/pubs/rp/rp1617/ Quick_Guides/TraditionsRituals>.

93   Lasse Suonperä Liebst, 'Exploring the Sources of Collective Effervescence: A Multilevel Study', *Sociological Science* 6 (2019), 27–42.

94   Daniel Reynaud, *Celluloid Anzacs: The Great War Through Australian Cinema* (Australian Scholarly Publishing, 2007), 184; Gammage, speech at ADFA.

95   Matilda Bosely, 'Australians Turn Out for Driveway Dawn Service to
      Mark Anzac Day in Time of Coronavirus', *Guardian Australia*, 25 April
      2020 <www.theguardian.com/news/2020/apr/25/australians-turn-out-for-
      driveway-dawn-service-to-mark-anzac-day-in-time-of-coronavirus>.
96   See Holbrook, *Anzac: The Unauthorised Biography*.
97   Bronte Charles, 'Anzac Day Sees Greater Acknowledgement of Indigenous
      Soldiers', SBS News, 25 April 2023 <www.sbs.com.au/nitv/article/anzac-
      day-sees-greater-acknowledgment-of-indigenous-soldiers/g408rt9nl>.
      See also Joan Beaumont, 'Commemoration', in Joan Beaumont and
      Allison Cadzow (eds.), *Serving Our Country: Indigenous Australians, War,
      Defence and Citizenship* (NewSouth, 2018), 324–45.
98   Davison, 'The Habit of Commemoration'.

CONTRIBUTORS

Kate Ariotti is a historian at the University of Queensland. Her research examines the social and cultural impacts of war in Australia. Kate's research has centred on the experiences of Australian prisoners of war in both world wars, and she is currently working on an Australian Research Council–funded history of the Australian war corpse. With Martin Crotty, she is researching the stories and experiences of the 115 Australian soldiers who were sentenced to death in the First World War.

Bianca Baggiarini is a political sociologist and lecturer at Deakin University. Her book, *Governing Military Sacrifice: Privatization, Drones, and the Future of War* (University of Toronto Press, forthcoming) analyses how drones and military privatisation together reveal the breakdown of the citizen-soldier archetype and its links to sacrificial cults and idioms. Baggiarini is a researcher on a Defence Strategic Policy grant (2024–2027), which examines the role and meaning of Robotic and Autonomous Systems in deterrence theory and practice, and has recent publications on machine learning algorithms and resort-to-force decision-making and the discourse of 'trusted autonomy'.

Max Billington is a PhD candidate (History) at Deakin University and a History Honours (First class) graduate from the University of Melbourne. Their thesis concerns the role of Australian military personnel in the British nuclear testing in Australia and the Australian government's use of warrior mythology and biopolitics to control the representation of and deny recognition to so-called 'nuclear servicemen' within the nation's military history. Max is the 2023 recipient of the Australian War Memorial's Summer Vacation Scholarship and the 2023 winner of the Royal Air Force Museum's Undergraduate Prize.

Karen Bird is a Chief Investigator on the Australian Research Council project, Historical and Contemporary Dimensions of Veteran Suicide: 1914–2023. As a historian she is interested in how we think we know and what informs our knowledge and understanding – especially the values we choose to live by. Her specific interests are in the ethics of war, and role of human differences (including race and religion) in the transaction of geopolitical affairs across human history. Karen is the Deputy Chair, National Advisory Committee for Open Arms – Veterans & Families Counselling and Board Member, Australian War Memorial.

Martin Crotty is a historian at the University of Queensland. Martin has published widely on Australian masculinity and militarism, Australian war memory and its implications, the Returned and Services League and veterans. He is the editor of *The Great Mistakes of Australian History* (UNSW Press, 2006), *Anzac Legacies: Australians and the Aftermath of War* (Australian Scholarly Publishing, 2010) and *The Politics of Veteran Benefits in the Twentieth-Century: A Comparative History* (Cornell, 2020). With Kate Ariotti, he is researching the stories and experiences of the 115 Australian soldiers who were sentenced to death in the First World War.

Nathan Hobby is a biographer who has worked extensively on the lives of the Throssell family. He is the author of a biography of Hugo Throssell's wife, Katharine Susannah Prichard, *The Red Witch* (Miegunyah Press, 2022), which won the 2023 WA Premier's Award for Book of the Year. He is also the author of the *Australian Dictionary of Biography* entry on Prichard and Throssell's son, Ric Throssell. An honorary research fellow at the University of Western Australia and a special collections librarian/archivist at Curtin University, he is currently working on a new biography of Australian prime minister John Curtin. He blogs at <nathanhobby.com>.

Margaret Hutchison is a lecturer in the School of Humanities and Social Sciences at UNSW Canberra. Her research examines the policies and practices of care for Australian veterans and the cultural legacies of war. Her current work focuses on the history of veteran suicide in Australia. She is the author of *Painting War: A History of Australia's First World War Art Scheme* (Cambridge University Press, 2018). She is also a co-editor of *Portraits of Remembrance: Painting, Memory and the First World War* (University of Alabama Press, 2020) and *Exiting War: The British Empire and the 1918–20 Moment* (Manchester University Press, 2022).

John Maynard is a Worimi Aboriginal man from the Port Stephens region of New South Wales and Emeritus Professor at the University of Newcastle. His publications have concentrated on the intersections of Aboriginal political and social history, and the history of Australian race relations. He is the author of several books, including *Aboriginal Stars of the Turf* (Aboriginal Studies Press, 2002), *Fight for Liberty and Freedom: The Origins of*

Australian Aboriginal Activism (Aboriginal Studies Press, 2007), *The Aboriginal Soccer Tribe* (Magabala Books, 2011), *Aborigines and the Sport of Kings* (Aboriginal Studies Press, 2013) and *Living with the Locals: Early Europeans' Experiences of Indigenous Life* (National Library of Australia, 2016).

Bobbie Oliver is an Honorary Research Fellow at the University of Western Australia and Director of the Centre for Western Australian History. She taught History at Curtin University from 1997 to 2018 and prior to that was a Research Officer at the Australian War Memorial in Canberra. She is the author of *War and Peace in Western Australia: The Social and Political Impact of the Great War, 1914–1926* (UWA Publishing, 1995) and *Hell No! We Won't Go! Resistance to Conscription in Postwar Australia* (Melbourne Interventions, 2022). Her most recent book is *Peacemongers: Australian Resistance to War and Military Conscription, 1885 to 1945* (Cambridge Scholars, 2024).

Alistair Thomson has published widely on war memory, myth, and oral history theory and practice. His research explores the ways in which life stories can illuminate the past and its meanings in the present lives of individuals and society. His book *Anzac Memories: Living with the Legend* (1994) was a landmark study on Australian war experience. Thomson is Emeritus Professor of History at Monash University and served as President of the International Oral History Association and of Oral History Australia.

Christina Twomey is Professor of History at Monash University. She has published widely on the social and cultural history of war in Australia. Her prize-winning books, *The Battle Within:*

POWs in Postwar Australia and *Australia's Forgotten Prisoners: Civilians Interned by the Japanese in World War Two*, examine the individual legacies of captivity, and the changing public place of prisoners and internees in commemorations of war. As part of this work, she published the influential article 'Trauma and the reinvigoration of Anzac', which first set her thinking about the role of feminist protestors at Anzac Day in the 1980s.

ACKNOWLEDGEMENTS

We are grateful for the enriching conversations with scholars of war and radicalism in Australia throughout the genesis of this project, including Charlie Fox, Effie Karageorgos, Peter Stanley, Douglas Newton and Thomas Richardson, as well as our wonderful contributors for their time, their generous feedback to one another at our workshop, and for collectively shaping this project. In particular, thanks to Martin Crotty for sharing his wealth of knowledge and expertise. For their thoughtful conversations and ongoing interest in the many streams of research that are 'challenging Anzac', our authors also thank Jonathan Richards, Michael Bell, Gerry Binder and Steve Vizard.

This project was conceived and based at Deakin University, and we appreciate the generous support of the Centre for Contemporary Histories at Deakin for facilitating our early research, funding our workshop and supporting the publication of this book. Our authors also acknowledge the support of the Australian Army History Unit, the Australian War Memorial, the University of Western Australia, the Faculty of Arts at Deakin University and the Australian Research Council for funding the research that informs this book.

Printed and bound by CPI Group (UK) Ltd, Croydon, CR0 4YY

27/04/2026

14869537-0001